Spanish

lonely planet

phrasebooks
and
Marta López

Spanish phrasebook
3rd edition – March 2008
First published – August 1997

Published by
Lonely Planet Publications Pty Ltd ABN 36 005 607 983
90 Maribyrnong St, Footscray, Victoria 3011, Australia

Lonely Planet Offices
Australia Locked Bag 1, Footscray, Victoria 3011
USA 150 Linden St, Oakland CA 94607
UK 2nd floor, 186 City Rd, London, EC1V 2NT

Cover illustration
Life in Park Güell by Yukiyoshi Kamimura

ISBN 978 1 74059 982 5

10 9 8 7 6 5 4 3 2

Printed through Colorcraft Ltd, Hong Kong
Printed in China

acknowledgments

Lonely Planet Language Products and editor Meg Worby would like to thank this cast of thousands for living *la vida loca* …

Publishing manager Jim 'Gaudí' Jenkin, whose great vision saw the series develop from the ground up

Project manager Fabrice 'Don Qixote' Rocher

Series designer Yukiyoshi 'Ibiza' Kamimura

Commissioning editors Karin 'Macarena' Vidstrup Monk and Karina 'Las Ketchup' Coates and acting senior editor Emma 'Carmen' Koch

New managing editor Annelies 'Flamenco' Mertens who offered grammar and general Spanish expertise and editor Ben 'Rumba' Handicott for leading the way

Editor Piers 'Matador' Kelly for a gallant effort in sourcing regional languages and cultural information and editor Francesca 'Spanish Fly' Coles for assistance with the index

Layout designer Sally 'Arriba!' Morgan for super speedy layout

Layout designers Sonya 'Carnaval' Brooke and Katie 'Catalan' Cason for putting in the finishing touches

Freelance designer Patrick *'Jamón Jamón'* Marris for the ace illustrations throughout

Cartographer Natasha 'Basque-ing' Velleley for the map, with finishing touches by *los amigos*, special projects managing cartographer Paul Piaia and map editor Wayne Murphy

Design manager Nina 'Tapas' Sturgess for coordinating layout checks

Freelance proofer Adrienne 'Castanets' Costanzo

Peter and Marta Gibney for careful proofing of the Spanish

Special thanks to contracted author Marta López, who also produced the Sustainable Travel section for this new edition. Marta thanks Graciela Recogzy, David García Campelo and Andrew Tsirigotis.

make the most of this phrasebook ...

Anyone can speak another language! It's all about confidence. Don't worry if you can't remember your school language lessons or if you've never learnt a language before. Even if you learn the very basics (on the inside covers of this book), your travel experience will be the better for it. You have nothing to lose and everything to gain when the locals hear you making an effort. Spanish, as well as Latin American, is spoken in over many countries in Latin America. Spanish is also very widely spoken in parts of the Pacific (ie the Philippines), and Africa (ie Morocco).

finding things in this book

For easy navigation, this book is in sections. The Tools chapters are the ones you'll thumb through time and again. The Practical section covers basic travel situations like catching transport and finding a bed. The Social section gives you conversational phrases, pick-up lines, the ability to express opinions – so you can get to know people. Food has a section all of its own: gourmets and vegetarians are covered and local dishes feature. Safe Travel equips you with health and police phrases, just in case. Remember the colours of each section and you'll find everything easily; or use the comprehensive Index. Otherwise, check the two-way traveller's Dictionary for the word you need.

being understood

Throughout this book you'll see coloured phrases on the right hand side of each page. They're phonetic guides to help you pronounce the language. You don't even need to look at the language itself, but you'll get used to the way we've represented particular sounds. The pronunciation chapter in Tools will explain more, but you can feel confident that if you read the coloured phrase slowly, you'll be understood.

communication tips

Body language, ways of doing things, sense of humour – all have a role to play in every culture. 'Local talk' boxes show you common ways of saying things, or everyday language to drop into conversation. 'Listen for ...' boxes supply the phrases you may hear. They start with the phonetic guide (because you'll hear it before you know what's being said) and then lead in to the language and the English translation.

spanish

United States
of America

Cuba

Dominican Republic
Puerto Rico

Mexico

Guatemala
El Salvador

Nicaragua

Honduras

Venezuela

Costa Rica
Panama

Colombia

Ecuador

Peru

Bolivia

Paraguay

Uruguay

Chile   Argentina

- ■ national language
- ■ widely understood
- ■ regional language

For more details, see the **introduction**.

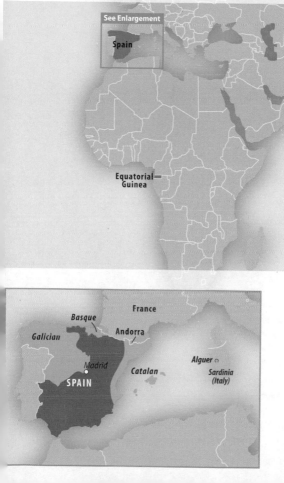

See Enlargement

Spain

Equatorial Guinea

Galician

Basque

France

Andorra

Madrid

SPAIN

Catalan

Alguer

Sardinia (Italy)

Spanish, or Castilian, as it's also called in Spain, is the most widely spoken of the Romance languages, the group of languages derived from Latin which includes French, Italian and Portuguese. Outside Spain, it's the language of most of Latin America and the West Indies and is also spoken in the Philippines and Guam, as well as in some areas of the African coast and in the US. Worldwide, there are more than 30 countries or territories where Spanish is spoken.

Spanish is derived from Vulgar Latin, which Roman soldiers and merchants brought to the Iberian Peninsula during the period of the Roman conquest (3rd to 1st century BC). By 19 BC Spain had become totally Romanised and Latin became the language of the peninsula in the four centuries that followed. Today's Castilian is spoken in the north, centre and south of Spain.

People are intensely proud of their language and generally expect visitors to know at least a little. English is less widely spoken in Spain than in many other European countries, especially outside the major cities.

This book gives you the practical words and phrases you need to get by, and the fun, spontaneous phrases that lead to a better experience of Spain and its people. Need more encouragement?

at a glance ...

language name: Spanish

name in language:
Español es·pa·*nyol*

language family: Romance

key country: Spain

approximate number of speakers:
over 390 million worldwide

close relatives: Latin American Spanish, Portuguese, Italian

donations to english: alligator, bonanza (lit: fair weather), canyon, guerilla, rodeo, ranch, stampede, tornado and many more familiar words ...

introduction

Remember, the contact you make through using Spanish will make your travels unique. Local knowledge, new relationships and a sense of satisfaction are on the tip of your tongue, so don't just stand there, say something!

> basque, catalan & galician

We also give you the basics of these languages because they are each considered official in Spain, even though Spanish, or Castilian, covers by far the largest territory.

Basque, a non-latin language, is spoken in parts of the north. Catalan is spoken in the east and Galician in the north-west. These last two are also Romance languages, so are closer in origin to Spanish.

If you're travelling widely in Spain, see the special section on these regional languages for some basic expressions, page 100.

> abbreviations used in this book

f	feminine
inf	informal
m	masculine
sg	singular
pl	plural
pol	polite

- Spanish pronunciation isn't hard, as many sounds are similar to sounds used in English.
- There are some easy rules to follow and once you learn them it's likely you'll be understood.
- The relationship between Spanish sounds and their spelling is straightforward and consistent.
- Like most languages, pronunciation can vary according to region. This book focuses on Castilian Spanish.

word stress

énfasis

- There is stress in Spanish, which means you emphasise one syllable over another. Rule of thumb: when a written word ends in *n*, *s* or a vowel, the stress falls on the second-last syllable. Otherwise, the final syllable is stressed.
- If you see an accent mark over a syllable, it cancels out these rules and you just stress that syllable instead.

vowel sounds

vocales

symbol	english equivalent	spanish example
a	alms	*agua*
e	red	*número*
ee	bee	*día*
o	go	*ojo*
oo	book	*gusto*
ai	aisle	*bailar*
ow	cow	*autobús*
oy	boy	*hoy*

pronunciation

consonant sounds

symbol	english equivalent	spanish example
b	big	*barco*
ch	chilli	*chica*
d	din	*dinero*
f	fun	*fiesta*
g	go	*gato*
k	kick	*cabeza/queso*
kh	loch	*jardín/gente*
l	loud	*lago*
ly	million	*llamada*
m	man	*mañana*
n	no	*nuevo*
ny	canyon	*señora*
p	pig	*padre*
r	run, but stronger and rolled	*ritmo/burro*
s	so	*semana*
t	tin	*tienda*
th	thin	*Barcelona/manzana*
v	soft 'b', somewhere between 'v' and 'b'	*abrir*
w	win	*guardia*
y	yes	*viaje*

There are some key things to remember about consonants in Spanish writing:

- the letter *c* is pronounced with a lisp, bar·the·*lo*·na (Barcelona), except when it comes before *a*, *o* and *u* or a consonant, when it's hard like *k* in 'king'.
- when ending a word, the letter *d* is also soft, like a th, or it's so slight it doesn't get pronounced at all.
- the Spanish letter *j* stands for a harsh and gutteral sound, so we use a kh symbol in our phonetic guides.
- try to roll your double *r*'s.
- the letter *q* is pronounced hard like a k.
- the letter *v* sounds more like a b, said with the lips pressed together.
- there are a few letters which don't appear in the English alphabet: *ch*, *ll* and *ñ*. You'll see these have their own entries in the spanish–english dictionary.

spanish alphabet					
a A	a	b B	be	c C	the
ch CH	che	d D	de	e E	e
f F	e·fe	g G	khe	h H	a·che
i I	ee	j J	kho·ta	k K	ka
l L	e·le	ll LL	e·lye	m M	e·me
n N	e·ne	ñ Ñ	e·nye	o O	o
p P	pe	q Q	koo	r R	e·re
s S	e·se	t T	te	u U	oo
v V	oo·ve	w W	oo·ve do·vle	x X	e·kees
y Y	ee·grye·ga	z Z	the·ta		

false friends

Beware of false friends – those words that sound like familiar English, but could land you in a bit of trouble if you use them unwittingly in Spanish. Here are some mistakes it's a little too easy to make:

el suburbio   el soo·*boor*·byo   **slum district**
  not 'suburb' which is *el barrio*, el *ba*·ryo

Estoy   es·*toy*   **I have a cold.**
constipado/a. m/f kons·tee·*pa*·do/a
  not 'I'm constipated' which is *estoy estreñido/a* m/f
  es·*toy* es·tre·*nyee*·do/a

Estoy   es·*toy*   **I'm pregnant.**
embarazada. em·ba·ra·*tha*·da
  not 'I'm embarassed' which is *estoy avergonzado/a* m/f
  es·*toy* a·ver·gon·*tha*·do/a

la injuria   la een·*khoo*·ree·a   **insult**
  not 'injury' which is *la herida*, la e·*ree*·da

largo/a m/f   *lar*·go/a   **long**
  not 'large' which is *grande*, *gran*·de

los parientes los pa·ree·*yen*·tes   **relatives**
  not 'parents' which is *los padres*, los *pa*·dres

sensible   sen·*thee*·ble   **sensitive**
  not 'sensible' which is *prudente*, proo·*den*·te

a–z phrasebuilder
construyendo frases

This chapter is designed to help you make your own sentences. It's arranged alphabetically for ease of navigation. If you can't find the exact phrase you need in this book, remember, there are no rules, only particular ways to say things! A little grammar, a few gestures, a couple of well-chosen words and you'll generally get the message across.

a/an & some

I'd like a ticket and a postcard.
> *Quisiera un billete y*   kee·*sye*·ra oon bee·*lye*·te ee
> *una postal.*   *oo*·na pos·*tal*
> (lit: I-would-like a ticket
> and a postcard)

Spanish has two words for 'a/an': *un* and *una*. The gender of the noun determines which one you use. *Un* and *una* have plural forms, *unos* and *unas*, meaning 'some'.

masculine	un sg	*un huevo* oon *hwe*·vo	an egg
	unos pl	*unos huevos* oo·nos *hwe*·vos	some eggs
feminine	una sg	*una casa* *oo*·na *ka*·sa	a house
	unas pl	*unas casas* oo·nas *ka*·sas	some houses

adjectives see describing things

articles see **a/an & some** and **the**

be

Spanish has two words for the English verb 'be': *ser* and *estar*.

use SER to express	examples	
permanent characteristics of persons/things	*Liz es muy guapa.* leez es mooy gwa·pa	Liz is very beautiful.
occupations or nationality	*Ana es de España.* a·na es de e·spa·nya	Ana is from Spain.
the time and location of events	*Son las tres.* son las tres	It's 3 o'clock.
possession	*De quién es esta mochila?* de kyen es es·ta mo·chee·la	Whose backpack is this?

use ESTAR to express	examples	
temporary characteristics of persons/things	*La comida está fría.* la ko·mee·da es·ta free·ya	The food is cold.
the time & location of persons/things	*Estamos en Madrid.* es·ta·mos en ma·dree	We are in Madrid.
the mood of a person	*Estoy contento.* es·toy kon·ten·to	I'm happy.

I	am	an anarchist	yo	soy	anarquisto
you sg inf	are	from Spain	tú	eres	de España
you sg pol	are	an artist	Usted	es	artista
he/she	is	an artist	él/ella m/f	es	artista
we	are	single	nosotros/as m/f	somos	solteros/as
you pl inf	are	kind	vosotros/as m/f	sois	simpáticos/as
you pl pol	are	students	Ustedes	son	estudiantes
they	are	students	ellos/as m/f	son	estudiantes

I	am	well	yo	estoy	bien
you sg inf	are	angry	tú	estás	enojado
you sg pol	are	drunk	Usted	está	borracho
he/she	is	drunk	él/ella m/f	está	borracho
we	are	happy	nosotros/as m/f	estamos	felices
you pl inf	are	on holiday	vosotros/as m/f	estáis	de vacaciones
you pl pol	are	learning	Ustedes	están	estudiando
they	are	learning	ellos/as m/f	están	estudiando

describing things

I'm looking for a comfortable hotel.
> *Estoy buscando un*   es·toy boos·kan·do oon
> *hotel cómodo.*   o·tel ko·mo·do
> (lit: I-am looking-for a
> hotel comfortable)

When using an adjective to describe a noun, you need to use a different ending depending on whether the noun is masculine or feminine, and singular or plural. Most adjectives have four forms which are easy to remember:

	singular	plural
masculine	*fantástico*	*fantásticos*
feminine	*fantástica*	*fantásticas*

un hotel fantástico	oon o·*tel* fan·*tas*·tee·ko	a fantastic hotel
una comida fantástica	oo·na ko·*mee*·da fan·*tas*·tee·ka	a fantastic meal
unos libros fantásticos	oo·nos *lee*·bros fan·*tas*·tee·kos	some fantastic books
unas tapas fantásticas	oo·nas *ta*·pas fan·*tas*·tee·kas	some fantastic tapas

Adjectives generally come after the noun in Spanish. However, 'adjectives' of quantity (such as 'much', 'a lot', 'little/few', 'too much') and adjectives expressing possession ('my' and 'your') always precede the noun.

muchos turistas	moo·chos too·rees·tas	many tourists
primera clase	pree·me·ra kla·se	first class
mi coche	mee ko·che	my car

gender

In Spanish, all nouns – words which denote a thing, person or idea – are either masculine or feminine.

The dictionary will tell you what gender a noun is, but here are some handy tips to help you determine gender:
- gender is masculine when talking about a man and feminine when talking about a woman
- words ending in -*o* are often masculine
- words ending in -*a* are often feminine
- words ending in -*d*, -*z* or -*ión* are usually feminine

See also **a/an & some**, **describing things**, **possession** and **the**.

have

I have two brothers.
Tengo dos hermanos.   *ten·go dos er·ma·nos*
(lit: I-have two brothers)

Possession can be indicated in various ways in Spanish. The easiest way is by using the verb *tener*, 'have'.

I	have	a ticket	yo	tengo	un billete
you sg inf	have	the key	tú	tienes	la llave
you sg pol	have	the key	Usted	tiene	la llave
he/she	has	aspirin	él/ella m/f	tiene	aspirinas
we	have	matches	nosotros/as m/f	tenemos	cerillas
you pl inf	have	tapas	vosotros/as m/f	tenéis	tapas
you pl pol	have	tapas	Ustedes	tienen	tapas
they	have	problems	ellos/as m/f	tienen	problemas

See also **my & your** and **somebody's**.

is & are see be

location see this & that

more than one

I'd like two tickets.
Quisiera dos billetes.   *kee·sye·ra dos bee·lye·tes*
(lit: I-would-like two tickets)

In general, if the word ends in a vowel, you add -s for a plural. If the noun ends in a consonant (or y), you add -es:

bed	cama	ka·ma	beds	camas	ka·mas
woman	mujer	moo·kher	women	mujeres	moo·khe·res

my & your

This is my daughter.
> Ésta es mi hija.   es·ta es mee ee·kha
> (lit: this is my daughter)

A common way of indicating possession is by using possessive adjectives before the noun they describe. As with any other adjective, they always agree with the noun in number (singular or plural) and gender (masculine or feminine).

	singular		plural	
	masculine	feminine	masculine	feminine
	gift	room	friends	glasses
my	mi regalo	mi habitación	mis amigos	mis gafas
your sg inf	tu regalo	tu habitación	tus amigos	tus gafas
your sg pol	su regalo	su habitación	sus amigos	sus gafas
his/her/its	su regalo	su habitación	sus amigos	sus gafas
our	nuestro regalo	nuestra habitación	nuestros amigos	nuestras gafas
your pl inf	vuestro regalo	vuestra habitación	vuestros amigos	vuestras gafas
your pl pol	su regalo	su habitación	sus amigos	sus gafas
their	su regalo	su habitación	sus amigos	sus gafas

See also **have** & **somebody's**.

negative

Just add the word *no* before the main verb of the sentence:

I'm not going to try the speciality.

No voy a probar   no voy a pro·*bar*
la especialidad.   la es·peth·ya·lee·*da*
(lit: not I-go to try
the speciality)

planning ahead

As in English, you can talk about your plans or future events by
using the verb *ir* (go) followed by the word *a* (to) and the infini-
tive of another verb, for example:

Tomorrow, I'm going to travel to Madrid.

Mañana, yo voy a viajar   ma·nya·na yo voy a vya·*jar*
a Madrid.   a ma·*dree*
(lit: tomorrow I go to travel
to Madrid)

I	am going	to call	yo	voy	a llamar
you sg inf	are going	to sleep	tú	vas	a dormir
you sg pol	are going	to dance	Usted	va	a bailar
he/she	is going	to drink	él/ella m/f	va	a beber
we	are going	to sing	nosotros/as m/f	vamos	a cantar
you pl inf	are going	to eat	vosotros/as m/f	vais	a comer
you pl pol	are going	to write	Ustedes	van	a escribir
they	are going	to learn	ellos/as m/f	van	a aprender

plural see more than one

pointing something out

To point something out, the easiest phrases to use are *es* (it is), *esto es* (this is) or *eso es* (that is).

Es una guía de Sevilla.	es *oo*·na *gee*·a de se·*vee*·lya	It's a guide to Seville.
Esto es mi pasaporte.	es·to es mee pa·sa·*por*·te	This is my passport.
Eso es gazpacho.	e·so es gath·*pa*·cho	That is gazpacho.

See also **this & that**.

possession see **have**, **my & your** and **somebody's**

questions

Is this the right stop?

¿Es esta la parada? (lit: is this the stop)	es es·ta la pa·ra·da

When asking a question, simply make a statement, but raise your intonation towards the end of the sentence, as you can do in English. The inverted question mark in written Spanish prompts you to do this.

question words		
Who?	*¿Quién?* sg *¿Quiénes?* pl	kyen *kye*·nes
Who is it?	*¿Quién es?*	kyen es
Who are those men?	*¿Quiénes son estos hombres?*	*kye*·nes son es·tos *om*·bres
What?	*¿Qué?*	ke
What are you saying?	*¿Qué está Usted diciendo?* pol	ke es·ta oo·*ste* dee·*thyen*·do

Which?	¿Cuál? sg ¿Cuáles? pl	kwal kwa·les
Which restaurant is the cheapest?	¿Cuál restaurante es el más barato?	kwal res·tow·ran·te es el mas ba·ra·to
Which local dishes do you recommend?	¿Cuáles platos típicos puedes recomendar?	kwa·les pla·tos tee·pee·kos pwe·des re·ko·men·dar
When?	¿Cuándo?	kwan·do
When does the next bus arrive?	¿Cuándo llega el próximo autobús?	kwan·do lye·ga el prok·see·mo ow·to·boos
Where?	¿Dónde?	don·de
Where can I buy tickets?	¿Dónde puedo comprar billetes?	don·de pwe·do kom·prar bee·lye·tes
How?	¿Cómo?	ko·mo
How do you say this in Spanish?	¿Cómo se dice ésto en español?	ko·mo se dee·the es·to en es·pa·nyol
How much?	¿Cuánto?	kwan·to
How much is it?	¿Cuánto cuesta?	kwan·to kwes·ta
How many?	¿Cuantos?	kwan·tos
For how many nights?	¿Por cuántas noches?	por kwan·tas no·ches
Why?	¿Por qué?	por ke
Why is the museum closed?	¿Por qué está cerrado el museo?	por ke es·ta the·ra·do el moo·se·o

some see a/an & some

somebody's

In Spanish, ownership is expressed through the word *de* (of).

That's my friend's backpack.

Esa es la mochila de
mi amigo.
(lit: that is the backpack of
my friend)

e·sa es la mo·*chee*·la de
mee a·*mee*·go

See also **have** and **my & your**.

this & that

There are three 'distance words' in Spanish, depending on whether something is close (this), away from you (that) or even further away in time or distance (that over there).

masculine	singular	plural
close	*éste* (this)	*éstos* (these)
away	*ése* (that)	*ésos* (those)
further away	*aquél* (that over there)	*aquéllos* (those over there)
feminine		
close	*ésta* (this)	*éstas* (these)
away	*ésa* (that)	*ésas* (those)
further away	*aquélla* (that over there)	*aquéllas* (those over there)

See also **pointing something out**.

the

The Spanish articles *el* and *la* both mean 'the'. Whether you use *el* or *la* depends on the gender of the thing, person or idea talked about, which in Spanish will always be either masculine or feminine. The gender is not really concerned with the sex of something, for example a fox is a masculine noun, even if it's female! There's no rule as to why, say, the sea is masculine but the beach is feminine.

When talking about plural things, people or ideas, you use *los* in stead of *el* and *las* instead of *la*.

	singular	plural
masculine	el	los
feminine	la	las

el coche	el *ko*·che	the car
los coches	los *ko*·ches	the cars
la tienda	la *tyen*·da	the shop
las tiendas	las *tyen*·das	the shops

See also **gender** and **a/an & some**.

word order

Sentences in Spanish have a basic word order of subject-verb-object, just as English does.

I study business.

Yo estudio comercio.　　　　yo es·*too*·dyo ko·*mer*·thyo
(lit: I study business)

However, Spanish often omits a subject pronoun: '*Estudio comercio*' is enough.

yes/no questions

It's not impolite to answer questions with a simple *sí* (yes) or *no* (no) in Spanish. There's no way to say 'Yes it is/does', or 'No, it isn't/doesn't'.

See also **questions**.

you

When talking to people familiar to you or younger than you, it's usual to use the informal form of you, *tú*, too, rather than the polite form, *Usted*, oo·ste.` The plural versions are we, *vosotros/vosotras*, vo·so·tros/vo·so·tras and (all of) you, *Ustedes*, oo·ste·des. Phrases in this book use the form of 'you' that is appropriate to the situation.

For more on polite language, see the box in **business**, page 77.

---

m (masculine) or f (feminine)?

In this book, masculine forms appear before the feminine forms. If you see a word ending in *-o/a*, it means the masculine form ends in *-o*, and the feminine form ends in *-a*, (that is, you replace the *-o* ending with the *-a* ending to make it feminine). The same goes for the endings *-os/as* (the plural endings). If you see an *(a)* between brackets on the end of a word, it means you have to add it in order to make that word feminine. In other cases we spell out the whole word.

There are two words for 'Spanish': *español* and *castellano*. *Español* is used in Spain, whereas *castellano* is more likely to be used by South Americans.

I speak a little Spanish.
　*Hablo un poco de
　español.*
　*ab·lo oon po·ko de
　es·pa·nyol*

Do you speak English?
　¿Habla inglés?
　ab·la een·gles

Does anyone speak English?
　*¿Hay alguien que hable
　inglés?*
　*ai al·gyen ke ab·le
　een·gles*

Do you understand?
　¿Me entiende?
　me en·tyen·de

I (don't) understand.
　(No) Entiendo.
　(no) een·tyen·do

How do you pronounce this word?
　*¿Cómo se pronuncia
　esta palabra?*
　*ko·mo se pro·noon·thya
　es·ta pa·lab·ra*

How do you write 'ciudad'?
　*¿Cómo se escribe
　'ciudad'?*
　*ko·mo se es·kree·be
　thee·oo·da*

What does ... mean?
　¿Qué significa ...?
　ke seeg·nee·fee·ka ...

Could you repeat that?
　¿Puedes repetir?
　pwe·des re·pe·teer

---

listen for ...

ko·mo	*¿Cómo?*	**Pardon?**
no	*No.*	**No.**
see	*Sí.*	**Yes.**

Could you please ...?	¿Puedes ... por favor?	pwe·des ... por fa·vor
speak more slowly	hablar más despacio	ab·lar mas des·pa·thyo
write it down	escribirlo	es·kree·beer·lo

dirty latin

Over the last 500 years, the Spanish spoken in Latin America has developed differently to the Spanish spoken in Europe. Variations in pronunciation, vocabulary and even grammar can lead to confusion or embarrassment. Here are two examples that could get you into trouble.

Quiero coger el autobús.
I want to catch the bus.
(Latin America: I want to bonk the bus.)

Hay un gran bicho en el baño.
There's a huge bug in the bathroom.
(Latin America: There's a big prick in the bathroom.)

cardinal numbers

los números cardinales

0	*cero*	*the*·ro
1	*uno*	oo·no
2	*dos*	dos
3	*tres*	tres
4	*cuatro*	*kwa*·tro
5	*cinco*	*theen*·ko
6	*seis*	seys
7	*siete*	*sye*·te
8	*ocho*	o·cho
9	*nueve*	*nwe*·ve
10	*diez*	dyeth
11	*once*	*on*·the
12	*doce*	*do*·the
13	*trece*	*tre*·the
14	*catorce*	ka·*tor*·the
15	*quince*	*keen*·the
16	*dieciséis*	dye·thee·*seys*
17	*diecisiete*	dye·thee·*sye*·te
18	*dieciocho*	dye·thee·*o*·cho
19	*diecinueve*	dye·thee·*nwe*·ve
20	*veinte*	*veyn*·te
21	*veintiuno*	veyn·tee·*oo*·no
22	*veintidós*	veyn·tee·*dos*
30	*treinta*	*treyn*·ta
40	*cuarenta*	kwa·*ren*·ta
50	*cincuenta*	theen·*kwen*·ta
60	*sesenta*	se·*sen*·ta
70	*setenta*	se·*ten*·ta
80	*ochenta*	o·*chen*·ta
90	*noventa*	no·*ven*·ta
100	*cien*	thyen

101	*ciento uno*	*thyen·to oo·no*
102	*ciento dos*	*thyen·to dos*
500	*quinientos*	*kee·nyen tos*
1,000	*mil*	mil
1,000,000	*un millón*	oon mee·*lyon*

ordinal numbers

los números ordinales

1st	*primero/a* m/f	pree·*me*·ro/a
2nd	*segundo/a* m/f	se·*goon*·do/a
3rd	*tercero/a* m/f	ter·*the*·ro/a
4th	*cuarto/a* m/f	*kwar*·to/a
5th	*quinto/a* m/f	*keen*·to/a

fractions

las fracciones

a quarter	*un cuarto*	oon *kwar*·to
a third	*un tercio*	oon *ter*·thyo
a half	*un medio*	oon *me*·dyo
three-quarters	*tres cuartos*	tres *kwar*·tos
all	*todo*	*to*·do
none	*nada*	*na*·da

amounts

las cantidades

a little	*un poquito*	oon po·*kee*·to
many	*muchos/as* m/f	*moo*·chos/as
some	*algunos/as* m/f	al·*goo*·nos/as
more	*más*	mas
less	*menos*	*me*·nos

telling the time

What time is it?	*¿Qué hora es?*	ke o·ra es
It's (one) o'clock.	*Es (la una).*	es (la oo·na)
It's (ten) o'clock.	*Son (las diez).*	son (las dyeth)
Quarter past one.	*Es la una y cuarto.*	es la oo·na ee kwar·to
Twenty past one.	*Es la una y veinte.*	es la oo·na ee veyn·te
Half past one.	*Es la una y media.*	es la oo·na ee me·dya
Twenty to one.	*Es la una menos veinte.*	es la oo·na me·nos veyn·te
Quarter to one.	*Es la una menos cuarto.*	es la oo·na me·nos kwar·to
It's early.	*Es temprano.*	es tem·pra·no
It's late.	*Es tarde.*	es tar·de
am	*de la mañana*	de la ma·nya·na
pm	*de la tarde*	de la tar·de

days of the week

Monday	*lunes*	loo·nes
Tuesday	*martes*	mar·tes
Wednesday	*miércoles*	myer·ko·les
Thursday	*jueves*	khwe·ves
Friday	*viernes*	vyer·nes
Saturday	*sábado*	sa·ba·do
Sunday	*domingo*	do·meen·go

the calendar

> months

January	enero	e·ne·ro
February	febrero	fe·bre·ro
March	marzo	mar·tho
April	abril	a·breel
May	mayo	ma·yo
June	junio	khoo·nyo
July	julio	khoo·lyo
August	agosto	a·gos·to
September	septiembre	sep·tyem·bre
October	octubre	ok·too·bre
November	noviembre	no·vyem·bre
December	diciembre	dee·thyem·bre

> seasons

summer	verano	ve·ra·no
autumn	otoño	o·to·nyo
winter	invierno	een·vyer·no
spring	primavera	pree·ma·ve·ra

dates

las fechas

What date?
¿Qué día?   ke *dee*·a

What date is it today?
¿Qué día es hoy?   ke *dee*·a es oy

It's (18 October).
Es (el dieciocho de   es (el dye·thee·o·cho de
octubre).   ok·too·bre)

present

now	*ahora*	a·o·ra
right now	*ahora mismo*	a·o·ra *mees*·mo
this ...		
afternoon	*esta tarde*	es·ta *tar*·de
month	*este mes*	es·te mes
morning	*esta mañana*	es·ta ma·*nya*·na
week	*esta semana*	es·ta se·*ma*·na
year	*este año*	es·te *a*·nyo
today	*hoy*	oy
tonight	*esta noche*	es·ta *no*·che

past

el pasado

... ago	*hace ...*	a·the ...
(three) days	*(tres) días*	(tres) *dee*·as
half an hour	*media hora*	*me*·dya *o*·ra
a while	*un rato*	un *ra*·to
(five) years	*(cinco) años*	(*theen*·ko) *a*·nyos
day before yesterday	*anteayer*	an·te·a·*yer*
last ...		
month	*el mes pasado*	el mes pa·*sa*·do
night	*anoche*	a·*no*·che
week	*la semana pasada*	la se·*ma*·na pa·*sa*·da
year	*el año pasado*	el *a*·nyo pa·*sa*·do
since (May)	*desde (mayo)*	*des*·de (*ma*·yo)
yesterday	*ayer*	a·*yer*
yesterday ...	*ayer por la ...*	a·*yer* por la ...
afternoon	*tarde*	*tar*·de
evening	*noche*	*no*·che
morning	*mañana*	ma·*nya*·na

future

in ...	dentro de ...	den·tro de ...
(six) days	(seis) días	(seys) dee·as
an hour	una hora	oo·na o·ra
(five) minutes	(cinco)	(theen·ko)
	minutos	mee·noo·tos
a month	un mes	oon mes
next ...	... que viene	... ke vye·ne
month	el mes	el mes
week	la semana	la se·ma·na
year	el año	el a·nyo
tomorrow	mañana	ma·nya·na
day after	pasado	pa·sa·do
tomorrow	mañana	ma·nya·na
tomorrow ...	mañana por la ...	ma·nya·na por la ...
afternoon	tarde	tar·de
evening	noche	no·che
morning	mañana	ma·nya·na
until (June)	hasta (junio)	as·ta (khoo·nyo)

during the day

afternoon	tarde f	tar·de
dawn	madrugada f	ma·droo·ga·da
day	día m	dee·a
evening	noche f	no·che
midday	mediodía m	me·dyo·dee·a
midnight	medianoche f	me·dya·no·che
morning	mañana f	ma·nya·na
night	noche f	no·che
sunrise	amanecer m	a·ma·ne·ther
sunset	puesta f del sol	pwes·ta del sol

Where's the nearest ATM?
¿Dónde está el cajero automático más cercano?
don·de es·ta el ka·khe·ro ow·to·ma·tee·ko mas ther·ka·no

Can I use my credit card to withdraw money?
¿Puedo usar mi tarjeta de crédito para sacar dinero?
pwe·do oo·sar mee tar·khe·ta de kre·dee·to pa·ra sa kar dee·ne·ro

What's the exchange rate?
¿Cuál es el tipo de cambio?
kwal es el tee·po de kam·byo

What's the charge for that?
¿Cuánto hay que pagar por eso?
kwan·to ai ke pa·gar por e·so

How much is this?
¿Cuánto cuesta esto?
kwan·to kwes·ta es·to

The price is too high.
Cuesta demasiado.
kwes·ta de·ma·sya·do

Can you lower the price?
¿Podría bajar un poco el precio?
po·dree·a ba·khar oon po·ko el pre·thyo

I'd like to change ...
  money
  a travellers cheque

Me gustaría cambiar ...
  dinero
  un cheque de viajero

me goos·ta·ree·a kam·byar ...
  dee·ne·ro
  oon che·ke de vya·khe·ro

Do you accept ...?   *¿Aceptan ...?*   a·*thep*·tan ...

   credit cards   *tarjetas de*   tar·*khe*·tas de
                  crédito   *kre*·dee·to

   debit cards   *tarjetas de*   tar·*khe*·tas de
                  débito   *de*·bee·to

   travellers   *cheques de*   *che*·kes de
    cheques   *viajero*   vya·*khe*·ro

Do I need to pay up front?
   ¿Necesito pagar por   ne·the·*see*·to pa·*gar* por
   adelantado?   a·de·lan·*ta*·do

Could I have a receipt please?
   ¿Podría darme un   po·*dree*·a *dar*·me oon
   recibo por favor?   re·*thee*·bo por fa·*vor*

I'd like my money back.
   Quisiera que me devuelva   kee·*sye*·ra ke me de·*vwel*·va
   el dinero.   el dee·*ne*·ro

getting around

desplazándose

What time does the ... leave?	¿A qué hora sale el ...?	a ke o·ra sa·le el ...
boat	barco	bar·ko
bus (city)	autobús	ow·to·boos
bus (intercity)	autocar	ow·to·kar
plane	avión	a·vyon
train	tren	tren
tram	tranvía	tran·vee·a

What time's the ... (bus)?	¿A qué hora es el ... (autobús)?	a ke o·ra es el ... (ow·to·boos)
first	primer	pree·mer
last	último	ool·tee·mo
next	próximo	prok·see·mo

I'd like a/an ... seat.	Quisiera un asiento ...	kee·sye·ra oon a·syen·to ...
aisle	de pasillo	de pa·see·lyo
non-smoking	de no fumadores	de no foo·ma·do·res
smoking	de fumadores	de foo·ma·do·res
window	junto a la ventana	khoon·to a la ven·ta·na

asking for an address

What's the/your address?

¿Cuál es la/su dirección?		kwal es la/soo dee·rek·thyon
avenue	avenida f	a·ve·nee·da
lane	callejón m	ka·lye·khon
street	calle f	ka·lye

Is there (a) ...?	¿Hay ...?	ai ...
air-conditioning	aire acon-dicionado	ai·re a·kon·dee·thyo·na·do
blanket	una manta	oo·na man·ta
toilet	servicios	ser·vee·thyos
video	vídeo	vee·de·o

The ... is delayed/cancelled.
El ... está retrasado/cancelado.
el ... es·ta re·tra·sa·do/kan·the·la·do

How long will it be delayed?
¿Cuánto tiempo se retrasará?
kwan·to tyem·po se re·tra·sa·ra

Is this seat free?
¿Está libre este asiento?
es·ta lee·bre es·te a·syen·to

That's my seat.
Ése es mi asiento.
e·se es mee a·syen·to

Can you tell me when we get to ...?
¿Me podría decir cuándo lleguemos a ...?
me po·dree·a de·theer kwan·do lye·ge·mos a ...

I want to get off here!
¡Quiero bajarme aquí!
kye·ro ba·khar·me a·kee

buying tickets

comprando billetes

Do I need to book?
¿Tengo que reservar?
ten·go ke re·ser·var

How much is it?
¿Cuánto cuesta?
kwan·to kwes·ta

Where can I buy a ticket?
¿Dónde puedo comprar un billete?
don·de pwe·do kom·prar oon bee·lye·te

It's full.
Está completo.
es·ta kom·ple·to

How long does the trip take?
¿Cuánto se tarda?
kwan·to se tar·da

Is it a direct route?
¿Es un viaje directo?
es oon vya·khe dee·rek·to

Can I get a stand-by ticket?
¿Puede ponerme en la lista de espera?
pwe·de po·ner·me en la lees·ta de es·pe·ra

I'd like to … my ticket.	*Me gustaría … mi billete.*	me goos·ta·ree·a … mee bee·lye·te
cancel	*cancelar*	kan·the·lar
change	*cambiar*	kam·byar
confirm	*confirmar*	kon·feer·mar

A one-way ticket to (Barcelona).
Un billete sencillo a (Barcelona).
oon bee·lye·te sen·thee·lyo a (bar·the·lo·na)

Two … tickets, please.	*Dos billetes …, por favor.*	dos bee·lye·tes … por fa·vor
child's	*infantil*	een·fan·teel
return	*de ida y vuelta*	de ee·da ee vwel·ta
student's	*de estudiante*	de es·too·dyan·te
1st-class	*de primera clase*	de pree·me·ra kla·se
2nd-class	*de segunda clase*	de se·goon·da kla·se

luggage

My luggage has been ...	Mis maletas han sido ...	mees ma·le·tas an see·do ...
damaged	dañadas	da·nya·das
lost	perdidas	per·dee·das
stolen	robadas	ro·ba·das

My luggage hasn't arrived.
Mis maletas se han perdido.
mees ma·le·tas se an per·dee·do

I'd like a luggage locker.
Quisiera un casillero de consigna.
kee·sye·ra oon ka·see·lye·ro de kon·seeg·na

Can I have some coins/tokens?
¿Me podía dar monedas/fichas?
me po·dee·a dar mo·ne·das/fee·chas

plane

When's the next flight to ...?
¿Cuándo sale el próximo vuelo para ...?
kwan·do sa·le el prok·see·mo vwe·lo pa·ra ...

What time do I have to check in?
¿A qué hora tengo que facturar mi equipaje?
a ke o·ra ten·go ke fak·too·rar mee e·kee·pa·khe

bus

Which city/intercity bus goes to ...?
   ¿Qué autobús/autocar   ke ow·to·*boos*/ow·to·*kar*
   va a ...?   va a ...

This/That one.
   Éste/Ése.   es·te/e·se

Bus number ...
   El autobús número ...   el ow·to·*boos* noo·me·ro ...

Please tell me when we get to ...
   ¿Puede avisarme   pwe·de a·vee·*sar*·me
   cuando lleguemos a ...?   kwan·do lye·ge·mos a ...

train

el tren

What station is this?
   ¿Cuál es esta estación?   kwal es es·ta es·ta·*thyon*

What's the next station?
   ¿Cuál es la próxima   kwal es la *prok*·see·ma
   estación?   es·ta·*thyon*

Does this train stop at (Madrid)?
   ¿Para el tren en (Madrid)?   pa·ra el tren en (ma·*dree*)

Do I need to change trains?
   ¿Tengo que cambiar de tren?   ten·go ke kam·*byar* de tren

Which carriage is ...?	*¿Cuál es el coche ...?*	kwal es el ko·che ...
1st class	*de primera clase*	de pree·*me*·ra kla·se
for (Madrid)	*para (Madrid)*	pa·ra (ma·*dree*)
for dining	*comedor*	ko·me·*dor*

boat

el barco

Are there life jackets?
¿Hay chalecos salvavidas? ai cha·*le*·kos sal·va·*vee*·das

What's the sea like today?
¿Cómo está el mar hoy? *ko*·mo es·*ta* el mar oy

I feel seasick.
Estoy mareado. es·*toy* ma·re·a·do

taxi

el taxi

I'd like a	Quisiera un	kee·*sye*·ra oon
taxi ...	taxi ...	*tak*·see ...
at (9am)	a (las nueve de la mañana)	a (las *nwe*·ve de la ma·*nya*·na)
now	ahora	a·o·ra
tomorrow	mañana	ma·*nya*·na

Is this taxi free?
¿Está libre este taxi? es·*ta lee*·bre es·te *tak*·see

Please put the meter on.
Por favor, ponga el taxímetro. por fa·*vor pon*·ga el tak·*see*·me·tro

How much is it to ...?
¿Cuánto cuesta ir a ...? *kwan*·to *kwes*·ta eer a ...

Please take me to (this address).
Por favor, lléveme a (esta dirección). por fa·*vor lye*·ve·me a (es·ta dee·rek·*thyon*)

I'm really late.
Voy con mucho retraso. voy kon *moo*·cho re·*tra*·so

How much is the final fare?
¿Cuánto es en total? *kwan*·to es en to·*tal*

Please ...	Por favor ...	por fa·vor ...
slow down	vaya más despacio	va·ya mas des·pa·thyo
wait here	espere aquí	es·pe·re a·kee

Stop ...!	¡Pare ...!	pa·re ...
at the corner	en la esquina	en la es·kee·na
here	aquí	a·kee

car & motorbike hire

Where can I hire a ...?
¿Dónde se puede alquilar ...?
don·de se pwe·de al·kee·lar ...

Does that include insurance/mileage?
¿Incluye el seguro/ kilometraje?
een·kloo·ye el se·goo·ro/ kee·lo·me·tra·khe

I'd like to hire a/an ...	Quisiera alquilar ...	kee·sye·ra al·kee·lar ...
4WD	un todoterreno	oon to·do·te·re·no
automatic car	un coche automático	oon ko·che ow·to·ma·tee·ko
manual car	un coche manual	oon ko·che ma·nwal
motorbike	una moto	oo·na mo·to

with ...	con ...	kon ...
air conditioning	aire acon- dicionado	ai·re a·kon- dee·thyo·na·do
a driver	chófer	cho·fer

How much for ... hire?	¿Cuánto cuesta el alquiler por ...?	kwan·to kwes·ta el al·kee·ler por ...
daily	día	dee·a
hourly	hora	o·ra
weekly	semana	se·ma·na

on the road

Is this the road to ...?
 ¿Se va a ... por esta se va a ... por es·ta
 carretera? ka·re·te·ra

Where's a petrol station?
 ¿Dónde hay una don·de ai oo·na
 gasolinera? ga·so·lee·ne·ra

What's the ... *¿Cuál es el límite* kwal es el lee·mee·te
speed limit? *de velocidad ...?* de ve·lo·thee·da ...
 city *en la ciudad* en la thyoo·da
 country *en el campo* en el kam·po

signs

Acceso	ak·the·so	**Entrance**
Aparcamiento	a·par·ka·myen·to	**Parking**
Ceda el Paso	the·da el pa·so	**Give Way**
Desvío	des·vee·o	**Detour**
Dirección Única	dee·rek·thyon oo·nee·ka	**One Way**
Frene	fre·ne	**Slow Down**
Peaje	pe·a·khe	**Toll**
Peligro	pe·lee·gro	**Danger**
Prohibido Aparcar	pro·ee·bee·do a·par·kar	**No Parking**
Prohibido el Paso	pro·ee·bee·do el pa·so	**No Entry**
Stop	es·top	**Stop**
Vía de Acceso	vee·a de ak·the·so	**Exit Freeway**

PRACTICAL

Please fill it up.
Por favor, lléneme el   por fa·*vor* lye·ne·me el
depósito.   de·*po*·see·to

I'd like (20) litres of …
Quiero (veinte)   *kye*·ro (*veyn*·te)
litros de …   lee·tros de …

petrol (gas)	*gasolina*	ga·so·*lee*·na
diesel	*diesel*	*dye*·sel
leaded (regular)	*gasolina normal*	ga·so·*lee*·na nor·*mal*
unleaded	*gasolina sin plomo*	ga·so·*lee*·na seen *plo*·mo

Please check the …	*Por favor, revise …*	por fa·*vor* re·*vee*·se …
oil	*el nivel del aceite*	el nee·*vel* del a·*they*·te
tyre pressure	*la presión de los neumáticos*	la pre·*syon* de los ne·oo·*ma*·tee·kos
water	*el nivel del agua*	*nee*·vel del a·gwa

petrol
gasolina f
ga·so·*lee*·na

windscreen
parabrisas m
pa·ra·*bree*·sas

battery
batería f
ba·ta·*ree*·a

engine
moteur m
mo·ter

headlight
faro m
fa·ro

tyre
rueda f
rwe·da

de ke *mar*·ka es
   ¿De qué marca es?   **What make/model is it?**

(How long) Can I park here?
   ¿(Por cuánto tiempo)   (por *kwan*·to *tyem*·po)
   Puedo aparcar aquí?   pwe·do a·par·*kar* a·kee

Where do I pay?
   ¿Dónde se paga?   *don*·de se *pa*·ga

problems

problemas

I need a mechanic.
   Necesito un/una   ne·the·*see*·to oon/*oo*·na
   mecánico/a. m/f   me·ka·*nee*·ko/a

The car has broken down (at ...).
   El coche se ha averiado   el *ko*·che se a a·ve·*rya*·do
   (en ...).   (en ...)

I had an accident.
   He tenido un   e te·*nee*·do oon
   accidente.   ak·thee·*den*·te

The motorbike won't start.
   No arranca la moto.   no a·*ran*·ka la *mo*·to

I have a flat tyre.
   Tengo un pinchazo.   *ten*·go oon peen·*cha*·tho

I've lost my car keys.
   He perdido las llaves   e per·*dee*·do las *lya*·ves
   de mi coche.   de mee *ko*·che

I've locked my keys inside.
   He cerrado con las llaves   e the·*ra*·do kon las *lya*·ves
   dentro.   *den*·tro

I've run out of petrol.
Me he quedado sin gasolina.
me e ke·*da*·do seen ga·so·*lee*·na

Can you fix it (today)?
¿Puede arreglarlo (hoy)?
pwe·de a·re·*glar*·lo (oy)

How long will it take?
¿Cuánto tardará?
kwan·to tar·da·*ra*

bicycle

la bicicleta

Where can I hire a bicycle?
¿Dónde se puede alquilar una bicicleta?
don·de se *pwe*·de al·kee·*lar* *oo*·na bee·thee·*kle*·ta

Where can I buy a (second-hand) bike?
¿Dónde se puede comprar una bicicleta (de segunda mano)?
don·de se *pwe*·de kom·*prar* *oo*·na bee·thee·*kle*·ta (de se·*goon*·da *ma*·no)

How much is it per ...?	*¿Cuánto cuesta por ...?*	*kwan*·to *kwes*·ta por ...
afternoon	una tarde	*oo*·na *tar*·de
day	un día	oon *dee*·a
hour	una hora	*oo*·na o·ra
morning	una mañana	*oo*·na ma·*nya*·na

I have a puncture.
Se me ha pinchado una rueda.
se me a peen·*cha*·do *oo*·na *rwe*·da

transport

47

local transport

el transporte local

People usually walk around cities and municipalities, but if you want to catch a bus, you could ask:

Are you waiting for more people?

¿Está esperando a	es·*ta* es·pe·*ran*·do a
más gente?	mas *khen*·te

Can you take us around the city please?

¿Nos puede llevar por	nos *pwe*·de lye·*var* por
la ciudad?	la thyoo·*da*

For phrases on disabled access, see **disabled travellers**, page 85.

For phrases on disabled access, see **disabled travellers**, page 85.

signs		
Aduana	a·*dwa*·na	**Customs**
Artículos Libres de Impuestos	ar·*tee*·koo·los *lee*·bres de eem·*pwes*·tos	**Duty-Free Goods**
Salida	sa·*lee*·da	**Exit/Way Out**
Control de Pasaporte	con·*trol* de pa·sa·*por*·te	**Passport Control**

passport control

control de pasaporte

soo ... por fa·*vor*	*Su ... por favor.*	**Your ... please.**
pa·sa·*por*·te	*pasaporte*	**passport**
vee·*sa*·do	*visado*	**visa**
es·*ta*	*¿Está*	**Are you**
vya·*khan*·do ...	*viajando ...?*	**travelling ...?**
en oon *groo*·po	*en un grupo*	**in a group**
kon oo·na	*con una*	**with a family**
fa·*mee*·lya	*familia*	
so·lo	*solo*	**on your own**

I'm here ...	*Estoy aquí ...*	es·*toy* a·*kee* ...
on business	*de negocios*	de ne·*go*·thyos
on holiday	*de vacaciones*	de va·ka·*thyo*·nes
in transit	*en tránsito*	en *tran*·see·to
I'm here for ...	*Estoy aquí por ...*	es·*toy* a·*kee* por ...
days	*días*	*dee*·as
months	*meses*	*me*·ses
weeks	*semanas*	se·*ma*·nas

customs

I have nothing to declare.
No tengo nada que
declarar.

no *ten*·go *na*·da ke
de·kla·*rar*

I have something to declare.
Quisiera declarar algo.

kee·*sye*·ra de·kla·*rar* al·go

I didn't know I had to declare it.
No sabía que tenía
que declararlo.

no sa·*bee*·a ke te·*nee*·a
ke de·kla·*rar*·lo

filling in forms

Apellido(s)	surname(s) – many Spanish use two surnames, their father's and their mother's
Domicilio	address (residence)
Exp. en	issued at
Fecha	date
Fecha di nacimiento	date of birth
Firma	signature
Lugar de nacimiento	place of birth
Nacionalidad	nationality
Nombre	given name
Pasaporte	passport
Profesión	occupation

accommodation

finding accommodation

buscando alojamiento

Where's a ...?	*¿Dónde hay ...?*	*don·de ai ...*
bed &	*una pensión*	*oo·na pen·syon*
breakfast	*con desayuno*	*kon de·sa·yoo·no*
camping ground	*terreno de*	*te·re·no de*
	cámping	*kam·peeng*
guesthouse	*una pensión*	*oo·na pen·syon*
hotel	*un hotel*	*oon o·tel*
youth hostel	*un albergue*	*oon al·ber·ge*
	juvenil	*khoo·ve·neel*
Can you	*¿Puede*	*pwe·de*
recommend	*recomendar*	*re·ko·men·dar*
somewhere ...?	*algún sitio ...?*	*al·goon see·tio ...*
cheap	*barato*	*ba·ra·to*
nice	*agradable*	*a·gra·da·ble*
luxurious	*de lujo*	*de loo·kho*
nearby	*cercano*	*ther·ka·no*
romantic	*romántico*	*ro·man·tee·ko*

What's the address?
  ¿Cuál es la dirección?   kwal es la dee·rek·thyon

For more on how to get there, see **directions**, page 61.

local talk		
dive	*tugurio* m	*too·goo·ryo*
rat-infested	*plagado de*	*pla·ga·do de*
	ratas	*ra·las*
top spot	*lugar* m *guay*	*loo·gar gwai*

booking ahead & checking in

haciendo una reserva & registrándose

I'd like to book a room, please.
Quisiera reservar una habitación.
kee·*sye*·ra re·ser·*var oo*·na a·bee·ta·*thyon*

I have a reservation.
He hecho una reserva.
e e·cho *oo*·na re·*ser*·va

My name's ...
Me llamo ...
me *lya*·mo ...

For (three) nights/weeks.
Por (tres) noches/ semanas.
por (tres) *no*·ches/ se·*ma*·nas

From (July 2) to (July 6).
Desde (el dos de julio) hasta (el seis de julio).
des·de (el dos de *khoo*·lyo) *as*·ta (el seys de *khoo*·lyo)

Do I need to pay upfront?
¿Necesito pagar por adelantado?
ne·the·*see*·to *pa*·gar por a·de·lan·*ta*·do

---

listen for ...

lo *syen*·to es·*ta* kom·*ple*·to
Lo siento, está completo. **I'm sorry, we're full.**

por *kwan*·tas *no*·ches
¿Por cuántas noches? **For how many nights?**

soo pa·sa·*por*·te por fa·*vor*
Su pasaporte, por favor. **Your passport, please.**

PRACTICAL

52

How much is it per ...?	¿Cuánto cuesta por ...?	kwan·to kwes·ta por ...
night	noche	no·che
person	persona	per·so·na
week	semana	se·ma·na
Can I pay by ...?	¿Puedo pagar con ...?	pwe·do pa·gar con ...
credit card	tarjeta de crédito	tar·khe·ta de kre·dee·to
travellers cheque	cheques de viajero	che·kes de vya·khe·ro

For other methods of payment, see **money**, page 35.

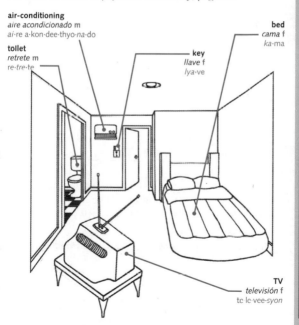

air-conditioning
aire acondicionado m
ai·re a·kon·dee·thyo·na·do

toilet
retrete m
re·tre·te

bed
cama f
ka·ma

key
llave f
lya·ve

TV
televisión f
te·le·vee·syon

Do you have a ... room?	¿Tiene una habitación ...?	tye·ne oo·na a·bee·ta·thyon ...
double	doble	do·ble
single	individual	een·dee·vee·dwal
twin	con dos camas	kon dos ka·mas

with/without (a) ...	con/sin ...	kon/seen ...
Can I see it?	¿Puedo verla?	pwe·do ver·la
It's fine. I'll take it.	Vale, la alquilo.	va·le la al·kee·lo

requests & queries

When/Where's breakfast served?
¿Cuándo/Dónde se sirve el desayuno?
kwan·do/don·de se seer·ve el de·sa·yoo·no

Please wake me at (seven).
Por favor, despiérteme a (las siete).
por fa·vor des·pyer·te·me a (las sye·te)

Can I get another ...?
¿Puede darme otro/a ...? m/f
pwe·de dar·me o·tro/a ...

Can I use the ...?	¿Puedo usar ...?	pwe·do oo·sar ...
kitchen	la cocina	la ko·thee·na
laundry	el lavadero	el la·va·de·ro
telephone	el teléfono	el te·le·fo·no

Is there a/an ...?	¿Hay ...?	ai ...
lift (elevator)	ascensor	as·then·sor
message board	tablón de anuncios	ta·blon de a·noon·thyos
safe	una caja fuerte	oo·na ka·kha fwer·te
swimming pool	piscina	pees·thee·na

Do you ... here?	*¿Aquí ...?*	a·*kee* ...
arrange tours	*organizan*	or·ga·*nee*·than
	recorridos	re·ko·*ree*·dos
change money	*cambian*	*kam*·byan
	dinero	dee·*ne*·ro

Can I leave a message for someone?
¿Puedo dejar un mensaje para alguien?
pwe·do de·*khar* oon men·*sa*·khe *pa*·ra al·gyen

Is there a message for me?
¿Tiene un mensaje para mí?
tye·ne oon men·*sa*·khe *pa*·ra mee

I'm locked out of my room.
Cerré la puerta y se me olvidaron las llaves dentro.
the·*re* la *pwer*·ta y se me ol·vee·*da*·ron las *lya*·ves *den*·tro

The (bathroom) door is locked.
La puerta (del baño) está cerrada.
la *pwer*·ta (del *ba*·nyo) es·*ta* the·*ra*·da

accommodation

55

complaints

It's too ...	Es demasiado ...	es de·ma·sya·do ...
cold	fría f	free·a
dark	oscura f	os·koo·ra
expensive	cara f	ka·ra
light	clara f	kla·ra
noisy	ruidosa f	rwee·do·sa
small	pequeña f	pe·ke·nya

The ... doesn't work.	No funciona ...	no foon·thyo·na ...
air-conditioning	el aire acondicionado	el ai·re a·kon·dee·thyo·na·do
fan	el ventilador	el ven·tee·la·dor
toilet	el retrete	el re·tre·te
window	la ventana	la ven·ta·na

This ... isn't clean.
Éste/Ésta ... no está limpio/a. m/f　　es·te/es·ta ... no es·ta leem·pyo/a

---

a knock at the door

Who is it?	¿Quién es?	kyen es
Just a moment.	Un momento.	oon mo·men·to
Come in.	Adelante.	a·de·lan·te

Can you come back later, please?
¿Puede volver más tarde, por favor?　　pwe·de vol·ver mas tar·de por fa·vor

checking out

What time is check out?
¿A qué hora hay que dejar — a ke o·ra ai ke de·khar
libre la habitación? — lee·bre la a·bee·ta·thyon

How much extra to stay until (6 o'clock)?
¿Cuánto más cuesta — kwan·to mas kwes·ta
quedarse hasta (las seis)? — ke·dar·se as·ta (las seys)

Can I have a late check out?
¿Puedo dejar la — pwe·do de·khar la
habitación más tarde? — a·bee·ta·thyon mas tar·de

Can I leave my bags here?
¿Puedo dejar las — pwe·do de·khar las
maletas aquí? — ma·le·tas a·kee

There's a mistake in the bill.
Hay un error en la cuenta. — ai oon e·ror en la kwen·ta

I'm leaving now.
Me voy ahora. — me voy a·o·ra

Can you call a taxi for me (for 11 o'clock)?
¿Me puede pedir un — me pwe·de pe·deer oon
taxi (para las once)? — tak·see (pa·ra las on·the)

Could I have ..., please?	*¿Me puede dar ..., por favor?*	me pwe·de dar ... por fa·vor
my deposit	mi depósito	mee de·po·see·to
my passport	mi pasaporte	mee pa·sa·por·te
my valuables	mis objetos de valor	mees ob·khe·tos de va·lor
I'll be back ...	*Volveré ...*	vol·ve·re ...
in (three) days	en (tres) días	en (tres) dee·as
on (Tuesday)	el (martes)	el (mar·tes)

I had a great stay, thank you.
He tenido una estancia
muy agradable, gracias.
e te·*nee*·do *oo*·na es·*tan*·thya
mooy a·gra·*da*·ble *gra*·thyas

You've been terrific.
Han sido estupendos.
an *see*·do es·too·*pen*·dos

I'll recommend it to my friends.
Se lo recomendaré a
mis amigos.
se lo re·ko·men·da·*re* a
mees a·*mee*·gos

camping

acampando

Where's the nearest ...?	¿Dónde está ...?	*don*·de es·*ta* ...
camp site	*el terreno de cámping más cercano*	el te·*re*·no de *kam*·peeng mas ther·*ka*·no
shop	*la tienda más cercana*	la *tyen*·da mas ther·*ka*·na
I'm looking for the nearest ...	*Estoy buscando ...*	es·*toy* boos·*kan*·do ...
showers	*las duchas más cercanas*	las *doo*·chas mas ther·*ka*·nas
toilet block	*los servicios más cercanos*	los ser·*vee*·thyos mas ther·*ka*·nos

Is it coin-operated?
¿Funciona con monedas?
foon·*thyo*·na kon mo·*ne*·das

Is the water drinkable?
¿Se puede beber el agua?
se *pwe*·de be·ber el *a*·gwa

Can I ...?	¿Se puede ...?	se *pwe*·de ...
camp here	*acampar aquí*	a·kam·*par* a·*kee*
park next to	*aparcar al lado*	a·par·*kar* al *la*·do
my tent	*de la tienda*	de la *tyen*·da

Do you have ...?	¿Tiene ...?	tye·ne ...
electricity	electricidad	e·lek·tree·thee·da
shower facilities	duchas	doo·chas
a site	un sitio	oon see·tyo
tents for hire	tiendas de	tyen·das de
	campaña para	kam·pa·nya pa·ra
	alquilar	al·kee·lar

How much is it per ...?	¿Cuánto vale por ...?	kwan·to va·le por ...
caravan	caravana	ka·ra·va·na
person	persona	per·so·na
tent	tienda	tyen·da
vehicle	vehículo	ve·ee·koo·lo

Whom do I ask to stay here?
¿Con quién tengo que hablar
para quedarme aquí?
kon kyen ten·go ke a·blar
pa·ra ke·dar·me a·kee

Could I borrow ...?
¿Me puede prestar ...?
me pwe·de pres·tar ...

For cooking utensils, see **self-catering**, page 155.

renting

alquilando

Do you have a/an ... for rent?	¿Tiene ... para alquilar?	tye·ne ... pa·ra al·kee·lar
apartment	un piso	oon pee·so
cabin	una cabaña	oo·na ka·ba·nya
house	una casa	oo·na ka·sa
room	una habitación	oo·na a·bee·ta·thyon
villa	un chalet	oon cha·le

furnished	amueblado/a m/f	a·mwe·bla·do/a
partly furnished	semi	se·mee
	amueblado/a m/f	a·mwe·bla·do/a
unfurnished	sin amueblar	seen a·mwe·blar

staying with locals

quedando con la gente de la zona

Can I stay at your place?
¿Me puedo quedar en
tu casa?
me pwe·do ke·dar en
too ka·sa

Can I help?
¿Puedo ayudar?
pwe·do a·yoo·dar

Can I use your telephone?
¿Puedo usar vuestra
teléfono?
pwe·do oo·sar vwe·stra
te·le·fo·no

Thanks for your hospitality.
Gracias por tu
hospitalidad.
gra·thyas por too
os·pee·ta·lee·da

I have my own ...	Tengo mi propio ...	ten·go mee pro·pyo ...
mattress	colchón	kol·chon
sleeping bag	saco de dormir	sa·ko de dor·meer

Can I ...?	¿Puedo ...?	pwe·do ...
bring anything	traer algo para	tra·er al·go pa·ra
for the meal	la comida	la ko·mee·da
do the dishes	lavar los platos	la·var los pla·tos
set/clear the table	poner/quitar	po·ner/kee·tar
	la mesa	la me·sa
take out the	sacar	sa·kar
rubbish	la basura	la ba·soo·ra

For compliments to the chef, see **food**, page 147.

signs

Caballeros	ka·ba·lye·ros	**Men**
Caliente	ka·lyen·te	**Hot**
Dirección Prohibida	dee·rek·thyon pro·hee·bee·da	**No Entry**
Frío	free·o	**Cold**
Señoras	se·nyo·ras	**Women**

Excuse me.
 Perdone. per·*do*·ne

Could you help me, please?
 ¿Perdone, puede per·*do*·ne *pwe*·de
 ayudarme por favor? a·yoo·*dar*·me por fa·*vor*

Where's ...?
 ¿Dónde está ...? *don*·de es·*ta* ...

I'm looking for ...
 Busco ... *boos*·ko ...

Which way is ...?
 ¿Por dónde se va a ...? por *don*·de se va a ...

How can I get there?
 ¿Cómo se puede ir? *ko*·mo se *pwe*·de eer

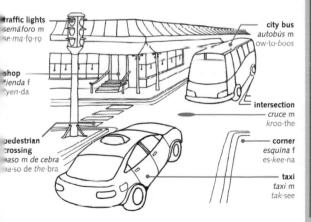

traffic lights
semáforo m
se·*ma*·fo·ro

shop
tienda f
tyen·da

pedestrian crossing
paso m *de cebra*
pa·so de *the*·bra

city bus
autobús m
ow·to·*boos*

intersection
cruce m
kroo·the

corner
esquina f
es·*kee*·na

taxi
taxi m
tak·see

How far is it?
> ¿A cuánta distancia
> está?

a kwan·ta dees·tan·thya
es·ta

Can you show me (on the map)?
> ¿Me lo puede indicar
> (en el mapa)?

me lo pwe·de een·dee·kar
(en el ma·pa)

It's ...	Está ...	es·ta ...
behind ...	detrás de ...	de·tras de ...
far away	lejos	le·khos
here	aquí	a·kee
in front of ...	enfrente de ...	en·fren·te de ...
left	por la izquierda	por la eeth·kyer·da
near	cerca	ther·ka
next to ...	al lado de ...	al la·do de ...
opposite ...	frente a ...	fren·te a ...
right	por la derecha	por la de·re·cha
straight ahead	todo recto	to·do rek·to
there	ahí	a·ee

Turn ...	Doble ...	do·ble ...
at the corner	en la esquina	en la es·kee·na
at the traffic lights	en el semáforo	en el se·ma·fo·ro
left/right	a la izquierda/ derecha	a la eeth·kyer·da/ de·re·cha

by bus	por autobús	por ow·to·boos
on foot	a pie	a pye
by taxi	por taxi	por tak·see
by train	por tren	por tren

It's ...	Está ...	es·ta ...
... metres	... metros	... me·tros
... kilometres	... kilómetros	... kee·lo·me·tros
... minutes	... minutos	... mee·noo·tos

For locations and compass directions, see the **dictionary**.

looking for ...

buscando ...

Where's ...?
¿Dónde está ...? — don·de es·ta ...

Where can I buy ...?
¿Dónde puedo comprar ...? — don·de pwe·do kom·prar ...

bank	*banco* m	*ban·ko*
camping store	*tienda* f *de provisiones de camping*	*tyen·da de pro·vee·syo·nes de kam·peeng*
supermarket	*supermercado* m	*soo·per·mer·ka·do*

For more on shops and how to get there, see **directions**, page 61 and the **dictionary**.

making a purchase

comprando algo

How much is this?
¿Cuánto cuesta esto? — kwan·to kwes·ta es·to

I'd like to buy ...
Quisiera comprar ... — kee·sye·ra kom·prar ...

I'm just looking.
Sólo estoy mirando. — so·lo es·toy mee·ran·do

Can I look at it?
¿Puedo verlo? — pwe·do ver·lo

Do you have any others?
¿Tiene otros? — tye·ne o·tros

Do you have something cheaper?
¿Tiene algo más barato? — tye·ne al·go mas ba·ra·to

Do you accept ...?	¿Aceptan ...?	a·*thep*·tan ...
credit cards	*tarjetas de crédito*	tar·*khe*·tas de kre·dee·to
debit cards	*tarjetas de débito*	tar·*khe*·tas de de·bee·to
travellers cheques	*cheques de viajero*	*che*·kes de vya·*khe*·ro
Could I have a ... please?	¿*Podría darme ... por favor?*	po·*dree*·a dar·me ... por fa·*vor*
bag	*una bolsa*	oo·na *bol*·sa
receipt	*un recibo*	oon re·*thee*·bo

Can you write down the price?
¿Puede escribir el precio?
pwe·de es·kree·*beer* el pre·thyo

Could I have it wrapped?
¿Me lo podría envolver?
me lo po·*dree*·a en·vol·ver

Does it have a guarantee?
¿Tiene garantía?
tye·ne ga·ran·*tee*·a

Can I have it sent overseas?
¿Pueden enviarlo por correo a otro país?
pwe·den en·vee·*ar*·lo por ko·*re*·o a o·tro pa·ees

Can you order it for me?
¿Me lo puede pedir?　　　　me lo *pwe*·de pe·*deer*

Can I pick it up later?
¿Puedo recogerlo más　　　*pwe*·do re·ko·*kher*·lo mas
tarde?　　　　　　　　　　*tar*·de

It's faulty.
Es defectuoso.　　　　　　es de·fek·too·o·so

I'd like ...,	*Quisiera ...,*	kee·*sye*·ra ...
please.	*por favor.*	por fa·*vor*
my change	*mi cambio*	mee *kam*·byo
my money back	*que me*	ke me
	devuelva	de·*vwel*·va
	el dinero	el dee·*ne*·ro
to return this	*devolver esto*	de·vol·*ver* es·to

local talk

bargain	*ganga* f	*gan*·ga
bargain hunter	*cazador* m *de ofertas*	ka·tha·*dor* de o·*fer*·tas
rip-off	*estafa* f	es·*ta*·fa
sale	*ventas* f pl	*ven*·tas
specials	*rebajas* f pl	re·*ba*·khas

bargaining

el regateo

That's too expensive.
Es muy caro.　　　　　　　es mooy *ka*·ro

Can you lower the price?
¿Podría bajar un　　　　　po·*dree*·a ba·*khar* oon
poco el precio?　　　　　　*po*·ko el *pre*·thyo

I'll give you ...
Te daré ...　　　　　　　　te da·*re* ...

clothes

Can I try it on?
¿Me lo puedo probar?   me lo *pwe*·do pro·*bar*

My size is ...
Uso la talla ...   *oo*·so la *ta*·lya ...

It doesn't fit.
No me queda bien.   no me *ke*·da byen

repairs

reparaciones

Can I have my	*¿Puede reparar mi*	pwe·de re·pa·*rar* mee
... repaired here?	*... aquí?*	... a·*kee*
backpack	*mochila*	mo·*chee*·la
camera	*cámara*	*ka*·ma·ra
When will my	*¿Cuándo estarán*	*kwan*·do es·ta·*ran*
... be ready?	*listos/as mis ...?* m/f	*lees*·tos/as mees ...
(sun)glasses	*gafas (de sol)* f	*ga*·fas (de sol)
shoes	*zapatos* m	tha·*pa*·tos

For more clothing items, see the **dictionary**.

darn holes		
buttons	*botónes* m pl	bo·*to*·nes
needle	*aguja* f	a·*goo*·kha
scissors	*tijeras* f pl	tee·*khe*·ras
thread	*hilo* m	*ee*·lo

hairdressing

I'd like (a) ...	Quisiera ...	kee·sye·ra ...
blow wave	un secado a mano	oon se·ka·do a ma·no
colour	un tinte de pelo	oon teen·te de pe·lo
haircut	un corte de pelo	oon kor·te de pe·lo
highlights	reflejos	re·fle·khos
my beard trimmed	que me recorte la barba	ke me re·kor·te la bar·ba
shave	que me afeite	ke me a·fey·te
trim	que me recorte el pelo	ke me re·kor·te el pe·lo

Don't cut it too short.
*No me lo corte
demasiado corto.*
no me lo kor·te
de·ma·sya·do kor·to

Shave it all off!
¡Aféitelo todo!
a·fey·te·lo to·do

Please use a new blade.
*Por favor, use una
cuchilla nueva.*
por fa·vor oo·se oo·na
koo·chee·lya nwe·va

worth a read

Spanish literature has a long history (dating from the 12th century), resulting in a thriving writing industry today. Look out for authors Ana María Matute, Jorge Luis Borges, Miguel de Unamuno, Carmen Martín Gaite, Juan Goytisolo, Miguel Delibes, Gabriel García Marquez and the 1989 Nobel Prize winner, Camilo José Cela.

books & reading

Is there a/an (English-language) ...?	¿Hay algún/ alguna ... en inglés? m/f	ai al·goon/ al·goo·na ... en een·gles
book by ...	libro m de ...	lee·bro de ...
bookshop	librería m	lee·bre·ree·a
entertainment guide	guía f del ocio	gee·a del o·thyo
section	sección f	sek·thyon

I (don't) like ...
(No) Me gusta/gustan ... sg/pl   (no) me goos·ta/goos·tan ...

Do you have Lonely Planet guidebooks?
¿Tiene libros de Lonely   tye·ne lee·bros de lon·lee
Planet?   pla·net

Do you have a better phrasebook than this?
¿Tiene algún libro de   tye·ne al·goon lee·bro de
frases mejor que éste?   fra·ses me·khor ke es·te

For more on books, see **interests**, page 109.

music

I heard a band called ...
Escuché a un grupo   es·koo·che a oon groo·po
que se llama ...   ke se lya·ma ...

I heard a singer called ...
Escuché a un/una   es·koo·che a oon/oo·na
cantante que se llama ... m/f   kan·tan·te ke se lya·ma ...

What's their best recording?
 ¿Cuál es su mejor disco?   kwal es soo me·*khor dees*·ko

Can I listen to this?
 ¿Puedo escuchar   pwe·do es·koo·*char*
 este … aquí?   es·te … a·*kee*

Is this a pirated copy?
 ¿Es copia pirata?   es ko·pya pee·*ra*·ta

I'd like (a) …   *Quisiera …*   kee·*sye*·ra …
 blank tape   *una cinta*   oo·na *theen*·ta
     virgen   veer·khen
 CD   *un cómpac*   oon *kom*·pak
 headphones   *unos*   oo·nos
     auriculares   ow·ree·koo·*la*·res

photography

I need a passport photo taken.
 Necesito fotos de   ne·the·see·to fo·tos de
 pasaporte.   pa·sa·*por*·te

How much is it to develop this film?
 ¿Cuánto cuesta revelar   kwan·to kwes·ta re·ve·*lar*
 este carrete?   es·te ka·*re*·te

Can you load my film?
 ¿Puede usted cargar   pwe·de oos·te kar·gar
 el carrete?   el ka·*re*·te

I'd like double copies.
 Quisiera dos copias.   kee·*sye*·ra dos *ko*·pyas

When will it be ready?
　¿Cuándo estará listo?　　　kwan·do es·ta·ra lees·to

I'm not happy with these photos.
　No estoy contento/a con　　no es·toy kon·ten·to/a kon
　estas fotos. m/f　　　　　es·tas fo·tos

I don't want to pay the full price.
　No quiero pagar el precio　no kye·ro pa·gar el pre·thyo
　íntegro.　　　　　　　　een·te·gro

Do you have slide film?
　¿Tiene diapositivas?　　　tye·ne dya·po·see·tee·vas

I need ... film for this camera.	*Necesito película ... para esta cámara.*	ne·the·see·to pe·lee·koo·la ... pa·ra es·ta ka·ma·ra
APS	*APS*	a pe e·se
B&W	*en blanco y negro*	en blan·ko y ne·gro
colour	*en color*	en ko·lor
(400) speed	*de sensibilidad (cuatrocientos)*	de sen·see·bee·lee·da (kwa·tro·thyen·tos)
batteries	*pilas* f pl	pee·las
camera	*cámara* f (fotográfica)	ka·ma·ra (fo·to·gra·fee·ka)
disposable camera	*cámara* f *desechable*	ka·ma·ra de·se·cha·ble
flash	*flash* f	flash
underwater camera	*cámara* f *submarina*	ka·ma·ra soob·ma·ree·na

post office

correos

I want to send a ...	*Quisiera enviar ...*	kee·sye·ra en·vee·ar ...
fax	*un fax*	oon faks
parcel	*un paquete*	oon pa·ke·te
postcard	*una postal*	oo·na pos·tal
I want to buy (an) ...	*Quisiera comprar ...*	kee·sye·ra kom·prar ...
aerogram	*un aerograma*	oon ae·ro·gra·ma
envelope	*un sobre*	oon so·bre
stamps	*sellos*	se·lyos
airmail	*por vía aérea*	por vee·a a·e·re·a
customs declaration	*declaración f de aduana*	de·kla·ra·thyon de a·dwa·na
domestic	*nacional*	na·thyo·nal
express mail	*correo m urgente*	ko·re·o oor·khen·te
fragile	*frágil*	fra·kheel
glue	*pegamento m*	pe·ga·men·to
international	*internacional*	een·ter·na·thyo·nal
mail box	*buzón m*	boo·thon
postcode	*código m postal*	ko·dee·go pos·tal
registered mail	*correo m certificado*	ko·re·o ther·tee·fee·ka·do
surface mail	*por vía terrestre*	por vee·a te·res·tre

Please send it by air/surface mail to ...
Por favor, mándelo por vía aérea/terrestre a ...
por fa·vor man·de·lo por vee·a a·e·re·a/te·res·tre a ...

It contains ...
Contiene ...
kon·tye·ne ...

Where's the poste restante section?

¿Dónde está la lista de correos? — *don*·de es·*ta* la *lees*·ta de ko·*re*·os

Is there any mail for me?

¿Hay alguna carta para mí? — ai al·*goo*·na *kar*·ta *pa*·ra mee

phone

el teléfono

What's your phone number?

¿Cuál es tu número de teléfono? — kwal es too *noo*·me·ro de te·*le*·fo·no

Where's the nearest public phone?

¿Dónde hay una cabina telefónica? — *don*·de ai *oo*·na ka·*bee*·na te·le·*fo*·nee·ka

I want to make a ... (to Singapore).	Quiero hacer ... (a Singapur).	*kye*·ro a·*ther* ... (a seen·ga·*poor*)
call	una llamada	*oo*·na lya·*ma*·da
reverse-charge/ collect call	una llamada a cobro revertido	*oo*·na lya·*ma*·da a *ko*·bro re·ver·*tee*·do
I want to ...	Quiero ...	*kye*·ro ...
buy a phone card	comprar una tarjeta telefónica	kom·*prar oo*·na tar·*khe*·ta te·le·*fo*·nee·ka
speak for (three) minutes	hablar por (tres) minutos	ab·*lar* por (tres) mee·*noo*·tos
How much does ... cost?	¿Cuánto cuesta ...?	*kwan*·to *kwes*·ta...
a (three)- minute call	una llamada de (tres) minutos	*oo*·na lya·*ma*·da de (tres) mee·*noo*·tos
each extra minute	cada minuto extra	*ka*·da mee·*noo*·to *ek*·stra

The number is ...
El número es ...   el *noo*·me·ro es ...

What's the area code for ...?
¿Cuál es el prefijo de   kwal es el pre·*fee*·kho de
la zona ...?   la *tho*·na ...

What's the country code for ...?
¿Cuál es el prefijo   kwal es el pre·*fee*·kho
del país ...?   del pa·*ees* ...

It's engaged.
Está comunicando.   es·*ta* ko·moo·nee·*kan*·do

I've been cut off.
Me han cortado   me an kor·*ta*·do
(la comunicación).   (la ko·moo·nee·ka·*thyon*)

The connection's bad.
Es mala conexión.   es *ma*·la ko·nek·*syon*

Hello. (making a call)   *Hola.*   o·la
Hello? (answering a call)   *¿Diga?*   *dee*·ga
Can I speak to ...?   *¿Está ...?*   es·*ta* ...
It's ...   *Soy ...*   soy ...

listen for ...

de *par*·te de kyen
¿De parte de quién?   **Who's calling?**

kon kyen kye·re a·*blar*
¿Con quién quiere   **Who do you want to**
hablar?   **speak to?**

lo *syen*·to pe·ro a·o·ra no es·*ta*
Lo siento, pero ahora   **I'm sorry, he's/she's**
no está.   **not here.**

lo *syen*·to tye·ne el *noo*·me·ro e·kee·vo·*ka*·do
Lo siento, tiene el   **Sorry, wrong number.**
numero equivocado.

oon mo·*men*·to   *Un momento.*   **One moment.**
see a·*kee* es·*ta*   *Sí, aquí está.*   **Yes, he's/she's here.**

Can I leave a message?
 ¿Puedo dejar un
 mensaje?

 pwe·do de·khar oon
 men·sa·khe

Please tell him/her I called.
 Sí, por favor, dile que he
 llamado.

 see por fa·vor dee·le ke e
 lya·ma·do

I'll call back later.
 Ya llamaré más tarde.

 ya lya·ma·re mas tar·de

mobile/cell phone

el teléfono móvil

I'd like a/an ...	Quisiera ...	kee·sye·ra ...
adaptor plug	un adaptador	oon a·dap·ta·dor
charger for	un cargador	oon kar·ga·dor
my phone	para mi teléfono	pa·ra mee te·le·fo·no
mobile/cell phone for hire	un móvil para alquilar	oon mo·veel pa·ra al·kee·lar
prepaid phone	una tarjeta prepagada	oo·na tar·khe·ta pre·pa·ga·da
SIM card for your network	una tarjeta SIM para su red	oo·na tar·khe·ta seem pa·ra soo red

What are the rates?
 ¿Cuál es la tarifa?

 kwal es la ta·ree·fa

(30c) per (30) seconds.
 (treinta centavos) por
 (treinta) segundos

 (treyn·ta then·ta·vos) por
 (treyn·ta) se·goon·dos

the internet

Where's the local Internet cafe?
¿Dónde hay un cibercafé   *don·de ai oon thee·ber·ka·fe*
cercano?   *ther·ka·no*

I'd like to ...	*Quisiera …*	*kee·sye·ra …*
check my email	*revisar mi*	re·vee·sar mee
	correo	ko·re·o
	electrónico	e·lek·tro·nee·ko
get Internet	*usar el*	oo·sar el
access	*Internet*	een·ter·net
use a printer	*usar una*	oo·sar oo·na
	impresora	eem·pre·so·ra
use a scanner	*usar un*	oo·sar oon
	escáner	es·ka·ner

How much	*¿Cuánto cuesta*	*kwan·to kwes·ta*
per ...?	*por …?*	*por …*
CD	*cómpact*	*kom·pakt*
hour	*hora*	*o·ra*
(five) minutes	*(cinco)*	*(theen·ko)*
	minutos	*mee·noo·tos*
page	*página*	*pa·khee·na*
Do you have ...?	*¿Tiene …?*	*tye·ne …*
Macs	*Apples*	a·pels
PCs	*PCs*	pe thes
a Zip drive	*unidad de Zip*	oo·nee·da de theep

How do I log on?
¿Cómo entro al sistema? ko·mo en·tro al sees·te·ma

It's crashed.
Se ha quedado colgado. se a ke·da·do kol·ga·do

I've finished.
He terminado. e ter·mee·na·do

a spangled web

Nowhere is the rise of 'Spanglish' (anglicised Spanish) more evident than on the Internet. New verbs such as *chatear*, *downloar*, *emailar*, *postear* and *surfear* are beginning to circulate freely in Hispanic cyberspace. In many cases, however, there are Spanish substitutes for common net-related terms. Here are just some of the officially-endorséd alternatives:

chat	*charlar*	char·lar
cyberspace	*ciberespacio*	see·ber·e·spa·thyo
download	*descargar*	des·kar·gar
homepage	*página Web inicial*	pa·jee·na web ee·nee·thyal
online	*en línea*	en lee·ne·a
search engine	*sistema de búsqueda*	sees·te·ma de boos·ke·da
surf	*correr tabla por la red*	ko·rer ta·bla por la re
username	*nombre de usuario*	nom·bre de oo·swa·ryo
website	*sitio Web*	see·tyo web

People usually shoot the breeze for a while before they get down to business.

I'm attending a ...	Asisto a ...	a·sees·to a ...
conference	un congreso	oon kon·gre·so
course	un curso	oon koor·so
meeting	una reunión	oo·na re·oo·nyon
trade fair	una feria de muestras	oo·na fe·rya de mwes·tras

I'm with ...	Estoy con ...	es·toy kon ...
my company	mi compañía	mee kom·pa·nyee·a
my colleagues	mis colegas	mees ko·le·gas
(two) others	otros (dos)	ot·ros (dos)

using your manners

If you're in a formal situation or you want to show respect to someone much older than yourself, you should use the polite form of address (see below). The best approach is to take the lead from how people address you and respond in the same way. It's always a good idea to use the polite form in business, and also with any service providers (be they kiosk attendants or doctors).

you sg	Usted	oo·ste
you pl	Ustedes	oo·ste·des

What's your name?

¿Cómo se llama	ko·mo se lya·ma
Usted? sg pol	oos·te

For more on polite forms, see **you** in the **a–z phrasebuilder**, page 26.

Where's the ...?   ¿Dónde está ...?   don·de es·ta ...
   business centre   el centro   el then·tro
         financiero   fee·nan·thye·ro
   conference   el congreso   el kon·gre·so

Where's the meeting?
   ¿Dónde es a reunión?   don·de es la re·oo·nyon

I'm alone.
   Estoy solo/a. m/f   es·toy so·lo/a

Let me introduce my colleague.
   ¿Puedo presentarle a mi   pwe·do pre·sen·tar·le a mee
   compañero/a? m/f   kom·pa·nye·ro/a

I'm staying at ..., room ...
   Me estoy alojando en ...,   me es·toy a·lo·khan·do en ...,
   la habitación ...   la a·bee·ta·thyon ...

I'm here for ... days/weeks.
   Estoy aquí por ... días/   es·toy a·kee por ... dee·as/
   semanas.   se·ma·nas

Here's my business card.
   Aquí tiene mi tarjeta   a·kee tye·ne mee tar·khe·ta
   de visita.   de vee·see·ta

I have an appointment with ...
   Tengo una cita con ...   ten·go oo·na thee·ta kon ...

That went very well.
   Eso fue muy bien.   e·so fwe mooy byen

Shall we go for a drink/meal?
   ¿Vamos a tomar/   va·mos a to·mar/
   comer algo?   ko·mer al·go

It's on me.
   Invito yo.   een·vee·to yo

bank

el banco

Where can I ...?	¿Dónde puedo ...?	don·de pwe·do ...
I'd like to ...	Me gustaría ...	me goos·ta·ree·a ...
cash a cheque	cambiar un cheque	kam·byar oon che·ke
change money	cambiar dinero	kam·byar dee·ne·ro
change a travellers cheque	cobrar un cheque de viajero	ko·brar oon che·ke de vee·a·khe·ro
get a cash advance	obtener un adelanto	ob·te·ner on a·de·lan·to
withdraw money	sacar dinero	sa·kar dee·ne·ro

What time does the bank open?
¿A qué hora abre el banco?　a ke o·ra a·bre el ban·ko

Can I arrange a transfer?
¿Puedo hacer una transferencia?　pwe·do ha·ther oo·na trans·fe·ren·thya

Where's the nearest foreign exchange office?
¿Dónde está la oficina de cambio más cercano?　don·de es·ta la o·fee·thee·na de kam·byo mas ther·ka·no

The ATM took my card.
El cajero automático se ha tragado mi tarjeta.　el ka·khe·ro ow·to·ma·tee·ko se a tra·ga·do mee tar·khe·ta

I've forgotten my PIN.
Me he olvidado del NPI.　me e ol·vee·da·do del e·ne pe ee

What's the charge for that?
¿Cuánto hay que pagar por eso?　kwan·to ai ke pa·gar por e·so

Can I have smaller notes?
¿Me lo puede dar en
billetes más pequeños?

me lo *pwe*·de dar en
bee·*lye*·tes mas pe·*ke*·nyos

Has my money arrived yet?
¿Ya ha llegado mi dinero?

ya a lye·*ga*·do mee dee·*ne*·ro

How long will it take to arrive?
¿Cuánto tiempo tardará
en llegar?

kwan·to *tyem*·po tar·da·*ra*
en lye·*gar*

What's the exchange rate?
¿Cuál es el tipo de cambio?

kwal es el *tee*·po de *kam*·byo

listen for ...

ai oon pro·*ble*·ma kon soo *kwen*·ta
*Hay un problema
con su cuenta.*

**There's a problem with
your account.**

no le *ke*·dan *fon*·dos
No le quedan fondos.

You have no funds left.

no po·*de*·mos a·*ther* e·so
No podemos hacer eso.

We can't do that.

por fa·*vor* *feer*·me a·*kee*
Por favor firme aquí.

Please sign here.

pwe·de es·kree·*beer*·lo
¿Puede escribirlo?

Could you write it down?

pwe·do ver soo ee·den·tee·fee·ka·*thyon*/
pa·sa·*por*·te por fa·*vor*
*¿Puedo ver su
identificación/
pasaporte, por favor?*

**Can I see some ID/your
passport, please?**

tye·ne oon des·koo·*byer*·to
Tiene un descubierto.

You're overdrawn.

en ...	En ...	In ...
(*kwa*·tro) *dee*·as	(cuatro) días	(four) working
la·bo·*ra*·bles	laborables	days
oo·na se·*ma*·na	una semana	one week

I'd like a/an ...	Quisiera ...	kee·sye·ra ...
audio set	un equipo audio	oon e·kee·po ow·dyo
catalogue	un catálogo	oon ka·ta·lo·go
guidebook in English	una guía turística en inglés	oo·na gee·a too·rees·tee·ka en een·gles
(local) map	un mapa (de la zona)	oon ma·pa (de la tho·na)

Do you have information on ... sights?	¿Tiene información sobre los lugares de interés ...?	tye·ne een·for·ma·thyon so·bre los loo·ga·res de een·te·res ...
cultural	cultural	kool·too·ral
local	local	lo·kal
religious	religioso	re·lee·khyo·so
unique	único	oo·nee·ko

Can we hire a guide?
¿Podemos alquilar un guía?
po·de·mos al·kee·lar oon gee·a

I'd like to see ...
Me gustaría ver ...
me goos·ta·ree·a ver ...

What's that?
¿Qué es eso?
ke es e·so

Who made it?
¿Quién lo hizo?
kyen lo ee·tho

How old is it?
¿De qué época es?   de ke e·po·ka es

Could you take a photograph of me?
¿Me puede hacer una foto?   me pwe·de a·ther oo·na fo·to

Can I take photographs (of you)?
¿(Le/Te) Puedo tomar   (le/te) pwe·do to·mar
fotos? pol/inf   fo·tos

I'll send you the photograph.
Le/Te mandaré la foto. pol/inf   le/te man·da·re la fo·to

getting in

la entrada

What time does it open/close?
¿A qué hora abren/cierran?   a ke o·ra ab·ren/thye·ran

What's the admission charge?
¿Cuánto cuesta la entrada?   kwan·to kwes·ta la en·tra·da

It costs ...
Cuesta ...   kwes·ta ...

Is there a discount for ...?	*¿Hay descuentos para ...?*	ai des·kwen·tos pa·ra ...
children	*niños*	nee·nyos
families	*familias*	fa·mee·lee·as
groups	*grupos*	groo·pos
pensioners	*pensionistas*	pen·syo·nees·tas
students	*estudiantes*	es·too·dyan·tes

signs

Abierto	a·byer·to	**Open**
Cerrado	the·ra·do	**Closed**

tours

Can you recommend a …?	¿Puede recomendar algún(a) …? m/f	pwe·de re·ko·men·dar al·goon/al·goo·na …
When's the next …?	¿Cuándo es el/la próximo/a …? m/f	kwan·do es el/la prok·see·mo/a …
boat-trip	paseo m en barca	pa·se·o en bar·ka
daytrip	excursión f de un día	eks·koor·syon de oon dee·a
excursion	excursión f	eks·koor·syon
tour	recorrido m	re·ko·ree·do

Do I need to take … with me?	¿Necesito llevar …?	ne·the·see·to lye·var …
Is … included?	¿Incluye …?	een·kloo·ye …
equipment	equipo	e·kee·po
food	comida	ko·mee·da
transport	transporte	trans·por·te

The guide will pay.
El guía va a pagar.   el gee·a va a pa·gar

The guide has paid.
El guía ha pagado.   el gee·a a pa·ga·do

How long is the tour?
¿Cuánto dura el recorrido?   kwan·to doo·ra el re·ko·ree·do

What time should I be back?
¿A qué hora tengo que volver?   a ke o·ra ten·go ke vol·ver

sightseeing

83

Be back here at ...
   Vuelva ...   *vwel·va ...*

I'm with them.
   Voy con ellos.   voy kon e·lyos

I've lost my group.
   He perdido a mi grupo.   e per·*dee*·do a mee *groo*·po

the royal lisp

According to a popular legend, one of the Spanish kings – some say Felipe IV, others Ferdinand I – had a slight speech impediment. Unable to pronounce the sound s properly, he lisped his way through conversation. In an epic act of flattery, the entire court, and eventually all of Spain, mimicked his lisp. This story provides a colourful explanation as to why Spaniards pronounce the word *cerveza* (beer) as ther·ve·tha, while Latin Americans continue to pronounce it ser·ve·sa.

It so happens, the story of the lisping king is a myth. After all, only the letters *c* and *z* are pronounced th (when they precede an *i* or an *e*), while the letter *s* remains the same as in English. The reason for this selectiveness is due to the way Spanish evolved from Latin and has nothing to do with lisping monarchs at all. In fact, when you hear someone say *gracias*, gra·thyas, they are no more lisping as when you say 'thank you' in English.

disabled travellers

I'm disabled.
   Soy minusválido/a. m/f   soy mee·noos·*va*·lee·do/a

What services do you have for disabled people?
   ¿Qué servicios tienen   ke ser·*vee*·thyos *tye*·nen
   para minusválidos/as? m/f   *pa*·ra mee·noos·va·lee·dos/as

Is there wheelchair access?
   ¿Hay acceso para la silla   ai ak·*the*·so *pa*·ra la *see*·lya
   de ruedas?   de *rwe*·das

Speak more loudly, please.
   Hable más alto, por favor.   *ab*·le mas *al*·to por fa·*vor*

I'm deaf.
   Soy sordo/a. m/f   soy *sor*·do/a

Are guide dogs permitted?
   ¿Se permite la entrada a   se per·*mee*·te la en·*tra*·da a
   los perros lazarillos?   los *pe*·ros la·tha·*ree*·lyos

Could you help me cross this street?
   ¿Me puede ayudar a   me *pwe*·de a·yoo·*dar* a
   cruzar la calle?   kroo·*thar* la *ka*·lye

I need assistance.
   Necesito asistencia.   ne·the·*see*·to a·sees·*ten*·thya

Braille library	*biblioteca* f *Braille*	bee·blee·o·*te*·ka *brai*·lye
disabled person	*persona* f *minusválida*	per·*so*·na mee·noos·va·*lee*·da
guide dog	*perro* m *lazarillo*	*pe*·ro la·tha·*ree*·lyo
wheelchair	*silla* f *de ruedas*	*see*·lya de *rwe*·das
ramp	*rampa* f	*ram*·pa
space	*espacio* m	es·*pa*·thyo

signs

Acceso para Sillas de Ruedas	ak·*the*·so *pa*·ra *thee*·lyas de ru·*e*·das	**Wheelchair Entrance**
Ascensor	as·then·*sor*	**Elevator/Lift**
Aseos para Minusválidos	a·*the*·os *pa*·ra mee·nus·va·lee·dos	**Disabled Toilets**
Carros de Minusválidos	*ka*·ros de mee·nus·va·lee·dos	**Disabled Trolleys (in major supermarkets)**

Is there a/an ...?	¿Hay ...?	ai ...
baby change room	una sala en la que cambiarle el pañal al bebé	oo·na sa·la en la ke kam·byar·le el pa·nyal al be·be
(English-speaking) babysitter	canguro (de habla inglésa)	kan·goo·ro (de ab·la een·gle·sa)
child-minding service	servicio de cuidado de niños	ser·vee·thyo de kwee·da·do de nee·nyos
children's menu	menú infantil	me·noo een·fan·teel
family discount	descuento familiar	des·kwen·to fa·mee·lyar
highchair	trona	tro·na

Do you mind if I breastfeed here?
¿Le molesta que dé de pecho aquí?
le mo·les·ta ke de de pe·cho a·kee

Are children allowed?
¿Se admiten niños?
se ad·mee·ten nee·nyos

Is this suitable for ... year old children?
¿Es apto para niños de ... años?
es ap·to pa·ra nee·nyos de ... a·nyos

I need a ...	Necesito un...	ne·the·_see_·to oon ...
baby seat	asiento m de seguridad para bebés	a·_syen_·to de se·goo·ree·_da_ pa·ra be·_bes_
booster seat	asiento m de seguridad para niños	a·_syen_·to de se·goo·ree·_da_ pa·ra _nee_·nyos
potty	orinal m de niños	o·ree·_nal_ de _nee_·nyos
stroller	cochecito m	ko·che·_thee_·to
creche	guardería f	gwar·de·_ree_·a
park	parque m	_par_·ke
playground	parque m infantil	_par_·ke een·fan·_teel_
slide	tobogán m	to·bo·_gan_
swings	columpios m pl	ko·_loom_·pyos
theme park	parque m de atracciones	_par_·ke de a·trak·_thyo_·nes
toyshop	juguetería f	khoo·ge·te·_ree_·a

bless you!

In Spain, a polite way to respond to someone sneezing is by saying ¡Salud!, sa·_loo_, (health) or even ¡Jesús! khe·_soos_ (Jesus).

basics

lo básico

Yes.	*Sí.*	see
No.	*No.*	no
Please.	*Por favor.*	por fa·*vor*
Thank you (very much).	*(Muchas) Gracias.*	(*moo*·chas) *gra*·thyas
You're welcome.	*De nada.*	de *na*·da
Excuse me.	*Perdón/ Discúlpeme.*	per·*don*/ dees·*kool*·pe·me
Sorry.	*Lo siento.*	lo *syen*·to

greetings

los saludos

In Spain people are often quite casual in their interactions. It's fine to use the following expressions in both formal and informal situations.

Hello/HI.	*Hola.*	o·la
Good morning.	*Buenos días.*	*bwe*·nos *dee*·as
Good afternoon. (until 8pm)	*Buenas tardes.*	*bwe*·nas *tar*·des
Good evening.	*Buenas noches.*	*bwe*·nas *no*·ches
See you later.	*Hasta luego.*	*as*·ta *lwe*·go
Goodbye/Bye.	*Adiós.*	a·*dyos*
How are you?	*¿Qué tal?*	ke tal
Fine, thanks.	*Bien, gracias.*	byen *gra*·thyas

meeting people

What's your name?
  ¿Cómo te llamas? inf   ko·mo te lya·mas
  ¿Cómo se llama Usted? pol   ko·mo se lya·ma oos·te

My name is ...
  Me llamo ...   me lya·mo ...

I'd like to introduce you to ...
  Quisiera presentarte a ... inf   kee·sye·ra pre·sen·tar·te a ...
  Quisiera presentarle a ... pol   kee·sye·ra pre·sen·tar·le a ...

I'm pleased to meet you.
  Mucho gusto.   moo·cho goos·to

titles & addressing people

dirigiéndose a la gente

Señor and *Señora* tend to be used in everyday speech. *Doña*, although rare, is used as a mark of respect towards older women, while *Don* is sometimes used to address men. An elderly neighbour, for example, might be called *Doña Lola*.

Mr	*Señor*	se·nyor
Sir	*Don*	don
Miss	*Señorita*	se·nyo·ree·ta
Ms/Mrs	*Señora*	se·nyo·ra
Madam	*Doña*	do·nya

call a friend

You may hear friends calling each other *tío* m, tee·o, or *tía* f, tee·a, but these words are usually used when talking about others. They're a bit crass (a little like using 'sheila' to describe a girl in Australia). Guys use *colega*, ko·le·ga, and *hombre*, om·bre, to address their workmates or male friends. In the south, people call their friends *pixas*, pee·chas or *xoxos*, cho·chos.

making conversation

Spain is known for its distinct regional areas. A great conversation starter in Spain is to ask someone where they come from. Other good topics are sport, politics, history and travel.

Do you live here?
¿Vives aquí?   vee·ves a·kee

Where are you going?
¿Adónde vas?   a·don·de vas

What are you doing?
¿Qué haces?   ke a·thes

Are you waiting (for a city bus)?
¿Estás esperando   es·tas es·pe·ran·do
(un autobús)?   (oon ow·to·boos)

Can I have a light, please?
¿Tienes fuego, por favor?   tye·nes fwe·go por fa·vor

Do you like this?
¿Te gusta esto?   te goos·ta es·to

I love this.
Me encanta esto.   me en·kan·ta es·to

I'm here ...	*Estoy aquí ...*	es·toy a·kee ...
for a holiday	*de vacaciones*	de va·ka·thyo·nes
on business	*en viaje de*	en vya·khe de
	negocios	ne·go·thyos
to study	*estudiando*	es·tu·dyan·do
with my family	*con mi familia*	kon mee fa·mee·lya
with my partner	*con mi pareja* m&f	kon mee pa·re·kha

---

listen for ...

es·tas a·kee de va·ka·thyo·nes
¿Estás aquí de   **Are you here on**
vacaciones?   **holiday?**

meeting people

91

What's this called?
    ¿Cómo se llama esto?   ko·mo se *lya*·ma es·to

What do you think (about ...)?
    ¿Qué piensas (de ...)?   ke *pyen*·sas (de ...)

What a gorgeous baby!
    ¡Qué niño/a más   ke *nee*·nyo/a mas
    precioso/a! m/f   pre·*thyo*·so/a

Can I take a photo?
    ¿Puedo hacer una foto?   pwe·do a·*ther* oo·na *fo*·to

That's (beautiful), isn't it?
    ¿Es (precioso), no?   es (pre·*thyo*·so) no

How long are you here for?
    ¿Cuánto tiempo te vas   kwan·to *tyem*·po te vas
    a quedar?   a ke·*dar*

I'm here for ... weeks/days.
    Estoy aquí por ...   es·*toy* a·kee por ...
    semanas/días.   se·*ma*·nas/*dee*·as

This is my ...	*Éste/a es mi ...* m/f	es·te/a es mee ...
child	*hijo/a* m/f	ee·*kho*/a
colleague	*colega* m&f	ko·*le*·ga
friend	*amigo/a* m/f	a·*mee*·go/a
husband	*marido*	ma·*ree*·do
partner	*pareja* m&f	pa·*re*·kha
wife	*esposa*	es·*po*·sa

---

local talk

Drop a few casual expressions into your Spanish and see the difference it makes in interacting with locals:

Great!	*¡Cojonudo!*	ko·kho·*noo*·do
How cool!	*¡Qué guay!*	ke gwai
How interesting!	*¡Qué interesante!*	ke een·te·re·*san*·te
Really?	*¿De veras?*	de ve·ras
That's fantastic!	*¡Estupendo!*	es·too·*pen*·do
What's up?	*¿Qué hay?*	ke ai
You don't say!	*¡No me digas!*	no me *dee*·gas

nationalities

las nacionalidades

You'll find that many country names are similar to English. If you're not sure, try to say the name of your country with a Spanish flavour and it's more than likely you'll be understood.

Where are you from?
    ¿De dónde eres?   de *don*·de e·res

I'm from …	*Soy de …*	soy de …
Australia	*Australia*	ow·*stra*·lya
Canada	*Canadá*	ka·na·*da*
Sweden	*Suecia*	swe·thya

For more countries, see the **dictionary**.

age

la edad

How old …?	*¿Cuántos años …?*	kwan·tos a·nyos …
are you	*tienes*	*tye*·nes
is your son/	*tiene tu hijo/a* m/f	*tye*·ne too ee·*kho*/a
daughter		

I'm … years old.
    Tengo … años.   *ten*·go … a·nyos

He's/She's … years old.
    Tiene … años.   *tye*·ne … a·nyos

I'm younger than I look.
    Soy más joven de lo   soy mas *kho*·ven de lo
    que parezco.   ke pa·*reth*·ko

Too old!
    ¡Demasiado viejo!   de·ma·sya·do *vye*·kho

For your age, see **numbers**, page 29.

meeting people

occupations & study

What do you do?
¿A qué te dedicas?   a ke te de·*dee*·kas

What are you studying?
¿Qué estudias?   ke es·*too*·dyas

I'm self-employed.
Soy trabajador/   soy tra·ba·kha·*dor*/
trabajadora   tra·ba·kha·*do*·ra
autónomo/a. m/f   ow·*to*·no·mo/a

I'm a/an ...	*Soy ...*	soy ...
architect	*arquitecto/a* m/f	ar·kee·*tek*·to/a
mechanic	*mecánico/a* m/f	me·*ka*·nee·ko/a
writer	*escritor/*	es·kree·*tor*/
	escritora m/f	es·kree·*to*·ra
I work in ...	*Trabajo en ...*	tra·*ba*·kho en ...
education	*enseñanza*	en·se·*nyan*·tha
hospitality	*hostelería*	os·te·le·*ree*·a
I'm ...	*Estoy ...*	es·*toy* ...
retired	*jubilado/a* m/f	khoo·bee·*la*·do/a
unemployed	*en el paro*	en el *pa*·ro
I'm studying ...	*Estudio ...*	es·*too*·dyo ...
business	*comercio*	ko·*mer*·thyo
languages	*idiomas*	ee·*dyo*·mas
science	*ciencias*	*thyen*·thyas

I'm studying at ...	Estudio en ...	es·too·dyo en ...
college	el instituto	el eens·tee·too·to
school	el colegio	el ko·le·khyo
trade school	el instituto de formación profesional	el eens·tee·too·to de for·ma·thyon pro·fe·syo·nal
university	la universidad	la oo·nee·ver·see·da

For more occupations and studies, see the **dictionary**.

family

Do you have a ...?	¿Tienes ...?	tye·nes ...
I (don't) have a ...	(No) Tengo ...	(no) ten·go ...
brother	un hermano	oon er·ma·no
family	una familia	oo·na fa·mee·lya
partner	una pareja m&f	oo·na pa·re·kha

Do you live with your ...?
¿Vives con tu ...? vee·ves kon too ...

I live with my ...
Vivo con mi ... vee·vo kon mee ...

This is my ...
Éste/a es mi ... m/f es·te/a es mee ...

Are you married?
¿Estás casado/a? m/f es·tas ka·sa·do/a

I'm ...	Estoy ...	es·toy ...
married	casado/a m/f	ka·sa·do/a
separated	separado/a m/f	se·pa·ra·do/a

I'm single.
Soy soltero/a. m/f soy sol·te·ro/a

I live with someone.
Vivo con alguien. vee·vo kon al·gyen

children

When's your birthday?
¿Cuándo es tu cumpleaños?
kwan·do es too koom·ple·a·nyos

Do you go to school or kindergarten?
¿Vas al colegio o a la guardería?
vas al ko·le·khyo o a la gwar·de·ree·a

What grade are you in?
¿En qué curso estás?
en ke koor·so es·tas

Do you like ...?	*¿Te gusta …?*	te goos·ta ...
school	*el colegio*	el ko·le·khyo
sport	*el deporte*	el de·por·te
your teacher	*tu profesor/ profesora* m/f	too pro·fe·sor/ pro·fe·so·ra

What do you do after school?
¿Qué haces después del colegio?
ke a·thes des·pwes del ko·le·khyo

Do you learn English?
¿Aprendes inglés?
a·pren·des een·gles

I come from very far away.
Vengo de muy lejos.
ven·go de mooy le·khos

Are you lost?
¿Estás perdido/a? m/f
es·tas per·dee·do/a

Show me how to play.
Dime cómo se juega.
dee·me ko·mo se khwe·ga

Well done!
¡Muy bien!
mooy byen

farewells

Tomorrow is my last day here.
*Mañana es mi último
día aquí.*
ma·*nya*·na es mee *ool*·tee·mo
dee·a a·*kee*

It's been great meeting you.
*Me ha encantado
conocerte.*
me a en·kan·*ta*·do
ko·no·*ther*·te

Keep in touch!
*¡Nos mantendremos en
contacto!*
nos man·ten·*dre*·mos en
kon·*tak*·to

I'll send you copies of the photos.
*Te enviaré copias de
las fotos.*
te en·vee·a·*re* ko·pyas de
las *fo*·tos

---

spanish grannies

Even idioms translate across languages. Here are a few
golden oldies:

It's like casting pearls before swine.
*Es como echar
margaritas a los
cerdos.*
es ko·mo e·*char*
ma·ga·*ree*·tas a los
ther·dos

(lit: it's like feeding daisies to the pigs)

It doesn't rain, it pours.
*Éramos pocos y
parió la abuela.*
e·ra·mos *po*·kos y
pa·ree·o la a·*bwe*·la

(lit: there were a few of us and then granny gave birth)

This is like watching grass grow.
*Es más largo que un
día sin pan.*
es mas *lar*·go ke oon
dee·a seen pan

(lit: it's longer than a day without bread)

If you ever visit (Scotland) you can ...	Si algún día visitas (Escocia) ...	see al·goon dee·a vee·see·tas (es·ko·thya) ...
come and visit	ven a visitarnos	ven a vee·see·tar·nos
stay with me	te puedes quedar conmigo	te pwe·des ke·dar kon·mee·go

Here's my ...	Ésta es mi ...	es·ta es mee ...
What's your ...?	¿Cuál es tu ...?	kwal es too ...
address	dirección	dee·rek·thyon
email address	dirección de email	dee·rek·thyon de ee·mayl
fax number	número de fax	noo·me·ro de faks
mobile number	número de móvil	noo·me·ro de mo·veel
work number	número de teléfono en el trabajo	noo·me·ro de te·le·fo·no en el tra·ba·kho

For more on addresses, see **directions**, page 61.

brave new world

With Columbus' discovery of the New World in 1492 began an era of Spanish expansion in America, which is reflected in the language. *Patata*, *tomate*, *cacao* and *chocolate* are a few examples of words taken from the indigenous American languages. Bear in mind that Spanish has evolved differently and it's a good idea to take the *Latin American Spanish phrasebook* with you, rather than this one, if you're travelling there.

writing to people

If you want to impress your new friends by writing to them in Spanish when you get back home, here are some useful words and phrases:

Dear ...
Querido/a ... m/f

I'm sorry it's taken me so long to write.
Siento haber tardado tanto en escribir.

It was great to meet you.
Me encantó conocerte.

Thank you so much for your hospitality.
Muchísimas gracias por tu hospitalidad.

I miss you a lot.
Te echo mucho de menos.

I had a fantastic time in ...
Me lo pasé genial en ...

My favourite place was ...
Mi lugar preferido fue ...

I hope to visit ... again.
Espero visitar otra vez ...

Say 'hi' to ... (and ...) for me.
Saluda a ... (y a ...) de mi parte.

I'd love to see you again.
Tengo ganas de verte otra vez.

Write soon!
¡Escríbeme pronto!

With love,
Un beso,

Regards,
Saludos,

basque

Basque, or *Euskara*, is spoken at the western end of the Pyrenees and along the Bay of Biscay – from Bayonne in France to Bilbao in Spain, and then inland, almost to Pamplona.

No one quite knows its origin. Some have related it to the Sioux language, to Japanese, and even to the language of the Atlanteans. To complicate matters, dialects are also spoken in the Basque country, including Bizkaian, Gipuzkoan, High Navarrese, Aezkoan, Salazarese, Lapurdian, Low Navarrese and Suberoan. The most likely theory is that Basque is the lone survivor of a language family which once extended across Europe, and was wiped out by the languages of the Celts, the Germanic tribes and the Romans. It's amazing that Basque has survived so close to its original form.

Speaking Spanish in the Basque-speaking towns might be expected from a foreigner, but is not as warmly received as an attempt at one of the most ancient languages of Europe.

> greetings & civilities

Hi!	*Kaixo!*	kai·sho
Good morning.	*Egun on.*	e·goo non
Good afternoon/ evening.	*Arratsalde on.*	a·ra·chyal·de on
Goodbye.	*Agur.*	a·goor
Take care.	*Ondo ibili.*	on·do ee·beel·ee
How are you?	*Zer moduz?*	ser mo·doos
Fine, thank you.	*Ongi, eskerrik asko.*	on·gee e·ske·reek as·ko
Excuse me.	*Barkatu.*	bar·ka·too
Please.	*Mesedez.*	me·se·des
Thank you.	*Eskerrik asko.*	es·ke·reek kas·ko
You're welcome.	*Ez horregatik.*	es o·re·ga·teek

> language difficulties

Do you speak English?
Ingelesez ba al dakizu?
een·ge·le·ses ba al da·kee·soo

I know a little Basque.
Euskara apur bat badakit.
e·oos·ka·ra a·*poor* bat ba·da·*keet*

I don't understand.
Ez dut ulertzen.
es toot oo·*ler*·tzen

Could you speak in Castillian please?
Erdaraz egingo al didazu, mesedez?
er·da·ras e·*geen*·go al dee·*da*·soo me·se·des

How do you say that in Basque?
Nola esaten da hori euskaraz?
no·la e·sa·ten da o·ree e·oo·ska·*ras*

local talk

Hurray for us!
Gora gu 'ta gutarrak!
go·ra goo ta goo·ta·rak

The Basque Country's always partying!
Euskal Herrian beti jai!
e·oos·*kal* e·ree·an *be*·tee yai

catalan

Catalan is spoken by up to 10 million people in the north-east of Spain, a territory that comprises Catalonia, coastal Valencia and the Balearic Islands (Majorca, Minorca and Ibiza). Outside Spain, Catalan is also spoken in Andorra, the south of France and the town of Alguer in Sardinia.

Many famous creative types have been Catalan speakers: painters like Dalí, Miró and Picasso, architects like Gaudí and writers like Mercé Rodoreda.

Despite the fact that almost all Catalan speakers from Spain are bilingual, they appreciate it when visitors attempt to communicate, if even in the simplest way, in Catalan.

> greetings & civilities

Hello!	*Hola!*	o·la
Good morning.	*Bon dia.*	bon *dee*·a
Good afternoon.	*Bona tarda.*	*bo*·na *tar*·da
Good evening.	*Bon vespre.*	bon *bes*·pra
Goodbye.	*Adéu.*	a·*the*·oo
How are you?	*Com estàs?*	kom as·*tas*
(Very) Well.	*(Molt) Bé.*	(mol) be
Excuse me.	*Perdoni.*	par·*tho*·nee
Sorry.	*Ho sento.*	oo *sen*·to
Please.	*Sisplau.*	sees·*pla*·oo
Thank you.	*Gràcies.*	*gra*·see·as
Yes/No.	*Sí/No.*	see/no

Do you speak English?
Parla anglès?   par·la an·*gles*

Could you speak in Castilian please?
Pot parlar castellà   pot par·*la* kas·ta·*lya*
sisplau?   sees·*pla*·oo

I (don't) understand.
(No) Ho entenc.   (no) oo an·teng

How do you say ...?
Com es diu ...?   kom az *dee*·oo

---

local talk

No problem!
Això rai!   a·*sho* ra·ee

What a laugh!
Quin tip de riure!   kin tip da ri·a·oo·ra

---

galician

Galician, or *Galego*, is an official language of the Autonomous Community of Galicias and is also widely understood in neighbouring regions Asturias and Castilla-Léon. It's very similar to Portuguese, as the two languages have roots in Vulgar Latin.

Galicians are likely to revert to Spanish when addressing a stranger, especially a foreigner, but making a small effort to communicate in Galician will always be welcomed.

> greetings & civilities

Hello!	*Ola!*	o·la
Good day.	*Bon dia.*	bon *dee*·a
Good afternoon/ evening.	*Boa tarde.*	bo·a *tar*·de
Goodbye.	*Adeus.*	a·*de*·oos
	Até logo.	a·*te lo*·go
Excuse me.	*Perdón.*	per·*don*
Please.	*Por favor.*	por fa·*vor*
Thank you.	*Grácias.*	gra·see·as
Many thanks.	*Moitas grácias.*	*moy*·tas gra·see·as
That's fine.	*De nada.*	de *na*·da
Yes/No.	*Si/Non.*	see/non

> language difficulties

Do you speak English?
Fala inglés?   fa·la een·*gles*

Could you speak in Castilian please?
Pode falar en español,   po·de fa·la en e·spa·*nyol*
por favor?   por fa·*bor*

I (don't) understand.
(Non) Entendo.   (non) en·*ten*·do

What's this called in Galician?
Como se chama iso en   ko·mo se *cha*·ma *ee*·so en
galego?   ga·*le*·go

common interests

los intereses en común

What do you do in your spare time?

¿Qué te gusta hacer en tu tiempo libre?

ke te *goos*·ta a·*ther* en too *tyem*·po *lee*·bre

Do you like (travelling)?

¿Te gusta (viajar)?

te *goos*·ta (vya·*khar*)

I (don't) like …	(No) Me gusta …	(no) me *goos*·ta …
cooking	*cocinar*	ko·thee·*nar*
dancing	*ir a bailar*	eer a bai·*lar*
films	*el cine*	el *thee*·ne
gardening	*jardinería*	kha·dee·ne·*ree*·a
hiking	*el excursionismo*	el eks·koor·syo·*nees*·mo
music	*la música*	la *moo*·see·ka
painting	*la pintura*	la peen·*too*·ra
photography	*la fotografía*	la fo·to·gra·*fee*·a
pub crawls	*ir de bar en bar*	eer de bar en bar
reading	*leer*	le·*er*
shopping	*ir de compras*	eer de *kom*·pras
socialising	*salir*	sa·*leer*
sport	*el deporte*	el de·*por*·te

For sporting activities, see **sport**, page 129.

music

Do you like to ...?	¿Te gusta ...?	te *goos*·ta ...
go to concerts	ir a conciertos	eer a kon·*thyer*·tos
listen to music	escuchar música	es·koo·*char* moo·*see*·ka
play an instrument	tocar algún instrumento	to·kar al·*goon* eens·troo·*men*·to
sing	cantar	kan·tar

What ... do you like?	¿Qué ... te gusta/ gustan? sg/pl	ke ... te *goos*·ta/ *goos*·tan
music	música sg	moo·*see*·ka
bands	grupos pl	*groo*·pos

classical music	música f clásica	moo·*see*·ka *kla*·see·ka
electronic music	música f electrónica	moo·*see*·ka e·lek·*tro*·nee·ka
jazz	jazz m	khath
metal	metal m	me·*tal*
pop	música f pop	moo·*see*·ka pop
punk	música f punk	moo·*see*·ka poonk
rock	música f rock	moo·*see*·ka rok
R&B	rhythm and blues m	ree·dem and bloos
traditional music	música f popular	moo·*see*·ka po·pu·*lar*
world music	música f étnica	moo·*see*·ka et·nee·ka

art

When's the gallery open?
¿A qué hora abre la galería?   a ke o·ra *a*·bre la ga·le·*ree*·a

What's in the collection?
¿Qué hay en la colección?   ke ai en la ko·lek·*thyon*

What kind of art are you interested in?
   ¿Qué tipo de arte te interesa?
   ke *tee*·po de *ar*·te te een·te·*re*·sa

I'm interested in ...
   Me interesa/ interesan ... sg/pl
   me een·te·*re*·sa/ een·te·*re*·san ...

What do you think of ...?
   ¿Qué piensas de ...?
   ke *pyen*·sas de ...

It's a/an ... exhibition.
   Es una exposición de ...
   es *oo*·na eks·po·see·*thyon* de ...

I like the works of ...
   Me gustan las obras de ...
   me *goos*·tan las *o*·bras de ...

It reminds me of ...
   Me recuerda a ...
   me re·*kwer*·da a ...

... art	*arte* m ...	*ar*·te ...
graphic	*gráfico*	*gra*·fee·ko
impressionist	*impresionista*	eem·pre·syo·*nees*·ta
modernist	*modernista*	mo·der·*nees*·ta
Renaissance	*renacentista*	re·na·then·*tees*·ta

cinema & theatre

I feel like going to (a comedy).
Tengo ganas de ir
a (una comedia).
ten·go ga·nas de eer
a (oo·na ko·me·dya)

What's showing at the cinema (tonight)?
¿Qué película dan en el
cine (esta noche)?
ke pe·lee·koo·la dan en el
thee·ne (es·ta no·che)

Is it in English?
¿Es en inglés?
es en een·gles

Does it have (English) subtitles?
¿Tiene subtítulos
(en inglés)?
tye·ne soob·tee·too·los
(en een·gles)

I want to sell this ticket.
Quiero vender esta entrada.
kye·ro ven·der es·ta en·tra·da

Are those seats taken?
¿Están ocupados estos
asientos?
es·tan o·koo·pa·dos es·tos
a·syen·tos

Have you seen ...?
¿Has visto ...?
as vees·to ...

Who's in it?
¿Quién actúa?
kyen ak·too·a

It stars ...
Actúa ...
ak·too·a ...

Did you like the ...?	*¿Te gustó el ...?*	te goos·to el ...
ballet	*ballet*	ba·le
film	*cine*	thee·ne
play	*teatro*	te·a·tro

SOCIAL

108

I (don't) like ...
(No) me gusta/gustan ... sg/pl   (no) me *goos*·ta/*goos*·tan ...

I thought it was ...   *Pienso que fue ...*   *pyen*·so ke fwe ...
   excellent   *excelente*   eks·the·*len*·te
   long   *largo*   *lar*·go
   OK   *regular*   re·goo·*lar*

animated films	*películas* f pl *de*	pe·*lee*·koo·las de
	dibujos	dee·*boo*·khos
	animados	a·nee·*ma*·dos
comedy	*comedia* f	ko·*me*·dya
documentary	*documentales* m pl	do·koo·men·*ta*·les
drama	*drama* m	*dra*·ma
film noir	*cine* m *negro*	*thee*·ne ne·gro
(Spanish) cinema	*cine* m *(español)*	*thee*·ne (es·pa·*nyol*)
horror movies	*cine* m *de terror*	*thee*·ne de te·*ror*
sci-fi	*cine* m *de*	*thee*·ne de
	ciencia ficción	*thyen*·thya feek·*thyon*
short films	*cortos* m pl	*kor*·tos
thrillers	*cine* m *de*	*thee*·ne de
	suspenso	soos·*pen*·so

reading

What kind of books do you read?
   ¿Qué tipo de libros lees?   ke *tee*·po de *lee*·bros *le*·es

Which (Spanish) author do you recommend?
   ¿Qué autor (español)   ke ow·*tor* (es·pa·*nyol*)
   recomiendas?   re·ko·*myen*·das

Have you read ...?
   ¿Has leído ...?   as le·*ee*·do ...

On this trip I'm reading ...
   En este viaje estoy   en es·te vya·khe es·*toy*
   leyendo ...   le·*yen*·do ...

I'd recommend ...
   Recomiendo a ...   re·ko·*myen*·do a ...

Where can I exchange books?
   ¿Dónde puedo cambiar   *don*·de *pwe*·do kam·*byar*
   libros?   *lee*·bros

For more on books, see **shopping**, page 68.

---

dog in the manger

Proverbs are big in Spain. The Marques de Santilllana compiled a national collection in the second half of the 15th century, and one of the characters in *Don Qixote*, Sancho Panza, speaks almost entirely in proverbs.

The author Cervantes described these popular sayings as 'short sentences based on long experience', or is that long-windedness?

   ser como el perro del hortelano, que ni come las
   berzas, ni las deja comer al amo

(lit: to be like the market gardener's dog who doesn't eat the cabbages and won't let his master eat them either)

feelings

los sentimientos

Feelings are described with either nouns or adjectives: the nouns use 'have' in Spanish (eg, 'I have hunger') and the adjectives use 'be' (like in English).

I'm (not) ...	(No) Tengo ...	(no) ten·go ...
Are you ...?	¿Tienes ...?	tye·nes ...
cold	frío	free·o
hot	calor	ka·lor
hungry	hambre	am·bre
in a hurry	prisa	pree·sa
thirsty	sed	se

I'm (not) ...	(No) Estoy ...	(no) es·toy ...
Are you ...?	¿Estás ...?	es·tas ...
annoyed	fastidiado/a m/f	fas·tee·dya·do/a
embarrassed	avergonzado/a m/f	a·ver·gon·tha·do/a
horny	cachondo/a m/f	ka·chon·do/a
tired	cansado/a m/f	kan·sa·do/a
well	bien	byen

For health-related feelings, see **health**, page 182.

opinions

las opiniones

Did you like it?
¿Te gustó?   te goos·to

What did you think of it?
¿Qué pensaste de eso?   ke pen·sas·te de e·so

I thought it was ...	*Pienso que fue ...*	pyen·so ke fwe ...
It's ...	*Es ...*	es ...
beautiful	*bonito/a* m/f	bo·nee·to/a
bizarre	*raro/a* m/f	ra·ro/a
crap	*un coñazo/a* m/f	oon ko·nya·tho/a
crazy	*loco/a* m/f	lo·ko/a
entertaining	*entretenido/a* m/f	en·tre·te·nee·do/a
excellent	*fantástico/a* m/f	fan·tas·tee·ko/a
full on	*heavy*	khe·vee
horrible	*horrible*	o·ree·ble

by degrees

a little	*un poco*	oon po·ko
I'm a little sad.	*Estoy un poco triste.*	es·toy oon po·ko trees·te
quite	*bastante*	bas·tan·te
I'm quite disappointed.	*Estoy bastante decepcionado/a.* m/f	es·toy bas·tan·te de·thep·thyo·na·do/a
very	*muy*	mooy
I feel very lucky.	*Me siento muy afortunado/a.* m/f	me syen·to mooy a·for·too·na·do/a

politics & social issues

la política & los temas sociales

Who do you vote for?
¿A quién votas? a kyen vo·tas

I support the ... party.
Apoyo al partido ... a·po·yo al par·tee·do ...

Did you hear about ...?
  ¿Has oído que ...?   as o·ee·do ke ...

Are you in favour of ...?
  ¿Estás a favor de ...?   es·tas a fa·vor de ...

How do people feel about ...?
  ¿Cómo se siente la   ko·mo se syen·te la
  gente de ...?   khen·te de ...

drugs	*drogas* f pl	*dro·*gas
the economy	*economía* f	e·ko·no·*mee·*a
immigration	*inmigración* f	een·mee·gra·*thyon*
racism	*racismo* m	ra·*thees·*mo
unemployment	*desempleo* m	de·sem·*ple·*o

---

octopus in the garage

Keeping the attention of your audience can be a challenge in a foreign language. Try emphasising your opinion with some of these colourful expressions:

He's/She's the best.
  Es un trozo de pan.   es oon *tro·*tho de pan
  (lit: he's/she's a piece of bread)

**You can't make a silk purse
out of a sow's ear.**
  Aunque el mono se   a·*oon·*ke el *mo·*no se
  vista de seda,   *vees·*ta de *se·*da
  mono se queda.   *mo·*no se *ke·*da
  (lit: though the monkey may wear silk, it's still a monkey)

He's/She's a fish out of water.
  Se encuentra   se en·koo·*en·*tra
  como un pulpo en   ko·mo oon *pool·*po en
  un garaje.   oon ga·ra·khe
  (lit: he's/she's like an octopus in a garage)

the environment

Is there an environmental problem here?

¿Aquí hay un problema con el medio ambiente?	a·*kee* ai oon pro·*ble*·ma kon el *me*·dyo am·*byen*·te

Is this (forest) protected?

¿Está este (bosque) protegido?	es·*ta* es·te (*bos*·ke) pro·te·*khee*·do

biodegradable	*biodegradable*	bee·o·de·gra·*da*·ble
deforestation	*deforestación* f	de·fo·res·ta·*thyon*
hunting	*caza* f	*ka*·tha
oil spill	*fuga* f *de petróleo*	*foo*·ga de pe·*tro*·le·o
pollution	*contaminación* f	kon·ta·mee·na·*thyon*

perhaps, perhaps, perhaps

Don't feel you're limited to a plain 'yes' or 'no'.

Maybe.	*Quizás.*	kee·*thas*
OK.	*Vale.*	*va*·le
No way!	*¡De ningún modo!*	de neen·*goon mo*·do
It's/I'm OK.	*Está/Estoy bien.*	es·*ta*/es·*toy* byen
Just a minute.	*Un momento.*	oon mo·*men*·to
No problem.	*Sin problema.*	seen pro·*ble*·ma
Of course!	*¡Claro (que sí)!*	*kla*·ro (ke see)
Sure.	*Claro.*	*kla*·ro
You bet!	*¡Ya lo creo!*	ya lo *kre*·o
Just joking.	*Era broma.*	*e*·ra *bro*·ma

where to go

adónde ir

What's there to do in the evenings?
¿Qué se puede hacer   ke se *pwe*·de a·*ther*
por las noches?   por las *no*·ches

What's on ...?	*¿Qué hay ...?*	ke ai ...
locally	*en la zona*	en la *tho*·na
this weekend	*este fin de*	*es*·te feen de
	semana	se·*ma*·na
today	*hoy*	oy
tonight	*esta noche*	*es*·ta *no*·che

Where are ...?	*¿Dónde hay ...?*	*don*·de ai ...
gay venues	*lugares gay*	loo·*ga*·res gai
places to eat	*lugares para*	loo·*ga*·res *pa*·ra
	comer	ko·*mer*
pubs	*pubs*	poobs

Is there a local ...	*¿Hay una guía ...*	ai oo·na gee·a ...
guide?	*de la zona?*	de la *tho*·na
entertainment	*del ocio*	del o·thyo
film	*de cine*	de *thee*·ne
gay	*de lugares gay*	de loo·*ga*·res gai
music	*de música*	de *moo*·see·ka

read my lips

Foreign movies are usually dubbed into Spanish, but in bigger cities you'll find some films have Spanish subtitles. Look for *v.o.* (*version original*, 'original version') or *v.o.s.* (*version original subtitulada*, 'original version with subtitles') in listings.

I feel like going to a/the ...	Tengo ganas de ir ...	ten·go ga·nas de eer ...
ballet	al ballet	al ba·*le*
bar	a un bar	a oon bar
cafe	a un café	a oon ka·fe
concert	a un concierto	a oon kon·*thyer*·to
karaoke bar	a un bar de karaoke	a oon bar de ka·ra·o·ke
movies	al cine	al *thee*·ne
nightclub	a una discoteca	a *oo*·na dees·ko·te·ka
party	a una fiesta	a *oo*·na fyes·ta
restaurant	a un restaurante	a oon res·tow·*ran*·te
theatre	al teatro	al te·a·tro

invitations

las invitaciones

What are you doing this evening?
¿Qué haces esta noche?   ke *a*·thes es·ta *no*·che

What are you up to (right now)?
¿Qué haces (ahora)?   ke *a*·thes (a·o·ra)

Would you like to go for a ...?	¿Quieres que vayamos a ...?	kye·res ke va·ya·mos a ...
coffee	tomar un café	to·mar oon ka·fe
drink	tomar algo	to·mar al·go
meal	comer	ko·mer
walk	pasear	pa·se·ar

I feel like going ...	Me apetece ir a ...	me a·pe·te·the eer a ...
dancing	bailar	bai·*lar*
out somewhere	salir	sa·leer

My round.
Invito yo.   een·*vee*·to yo

Do you know a good restaurant?
¿Conoces algún buen   ko·*no*·thes al·*goon* bwen
restaurante?   res·tow·*ran*·te

Do you want to come to the (...) concert with me?
¿Quieres venir conmigo   *kye*·res ve·*neer* kon·*mee*·go
al concierto (de ...)?   al kon·*thyer*·to (de ...)

We're having a party.
Vamos a dar una fiesta.   *va*·mos a dar *oo*·na *fyes*·ta

Do you want to come?
¿Por qué no vienes?   por ke no *vye*·nes

Are you ready?
¿Estás listo/a? m/f   es·*tas lees*·to/a

are you my type?

If jobs, age and nationality don't really cut it when trying to describe yourself (and others), see if these words help:

activist	*activista* m&f	ak·tee·*vees*·ta
alcoholic	*alcohólico/a* m/f	al·ko·o·*lee*·ko/a
artistic	*artístico/a* m/f	ar·*tees*·tee·ko/a
creative	*creador/*	kre·a·*dor*/
	creadora m/f	kre·a·*do*·ra
daggy/dorky	*hortera* m&f	or·*te*·ra
goth	*siniestra* m&f	see·*nye*·stra
heavy	*heavy* m&f	*khe*·vee
intellectual	*intelectual* m&f	een·te·*lek*·twal
progressive	*progre* m&f	*pro*·gre
sporty	*deportivo/a* m/f	de·por·*tee*·vo/a
trendy/stylish	*moderno/a* m/f	mo·*der*·no/a
workaholic	*adicto/a* m/f	a·*deek*·to/a
	al trabajo	al tra·*ba*·kho
yuppie	*yupi* m&f	*yoo*·pee

responding to invitations

Sure!
¡Por supuesto!   por soo·*pwes*·to

Yes, I'd love to.
Me encantaría.   me en·kan·ta·*ree*·a

Where will we go?
¿A dónde vamos?   a *don*·de va·*mos*

That's very kind of you.
Es muy amable por   es mooy a·*ma*·ble por
tu parte.   *too par*·te

No, I'm afraid I can't.
Lo siento pero no puedo.   lo *syen*·to *pe*·ro no *pwe*·do

Sorry, I can't sing/dance.
Lo siento, no sé cantar/bailar.   lo *syen*·to no se kan·*tar*/bai·*lar*

What about tomorrow?
¿Qué tal mañana?   ke tal ma·*nya*·na

arranging to meet

What time shall we meet?
¿A qué hora quedamos?   a ke *o*·ra ke·*da*·mos

Where will we meet?
¿Dónde quedamos?   *don*·de ke·*da*·mos

Let's meet ...   *Quedamos ...*   ke·*da*·mos ...
  at (eight) o'clock   a *(las ocho)*   a (las *o*·cho)
  at the (entrance)   en *(la entrada)*   en (la en·*tra*·da)

I'll pick you up.
Paso a recogerte. · pa·so a re·ko·kher·te

I'll be coming later.
Iré más tarde. · ee·re mas tar·de

Where will you be?
¿Dónde estarás? · don·de es·ta·ras

If I'm not there by (nine), don't wait for me.
Si no estoy a (las nueve), · see no es·toy a (las nwe·ve)
no me esperes/esperéis. sg/pl · no me es·pe·res/es·pe·reys

OK!
¡Hecho! · e·cho

I'll see you then.
Nos vemos. · nos ve·mos

See you later/tomorrow.
Hasta luego/mañana. · as·ta lwe·go/ma·nya·na

I'm looking forward to it.
Tengo muchas ganas · ten·go moo·chas ga·nas
de ir. · de eer

Sorry I'm late.
Siento llegar tarde. · syen·to lye·gar tar·de

Never mind.
No pasa nada. · no pa·sa na·da

attention-getter		
Hey!	*¡Eh, tú!*	e too
Look!	*¡Mira!*	mee·ra
Listen (to this)!	*¡Escucha (esto)!*	es·koo·cha (es·to)

nightclubs & bars

Where can we go (salsa) dancing?
¿Dónde podemos ir a
bailar (la salsa)?
don·de po·de·mos eer a
bai·lar (la sal·sa)

How do I get there?
¿Cómo se llega?
ko·mo se lye·ga

What type of music do you like?
¿Qué tipo de música
prefieres?
ke tee·po de moo·see·ka
pre·fye·res

I really like (reggae).
Me encanta (el reggae).
me en·kan·ta (el re·gai)

Come on!
¡Vamos!
va·mos

This place is great!
¡Este lugar me encanta!
es·te loo·gar me en·kan·ta

drugs

I don't take drugs.
No consumo ningún
tipo de drogas.
no kon·soo·mo neen·goon
tee·po de dro·gas

I take … occasionally.
Tomo … de vez en cuando.
to·mo … de veth en kwan·do

Do you want to have a smoke?
¿Nos fumamos un porro?
nos foo·ma·mos oon po·ro

I'm high.
Estoy colocado/a. m/f
es·toy ko·lo·ka·do/a

For more on bars, drinks and partying, see **eating out**, page 150.

asking someone out

saliendo con alguien

Don't be surprised if invitations come late in the day. Social life in Spain continues well into the night: sometimes people begin to eat dinner at 10pm and many clubs open at midnight.

Would you like to do something (tonight)?
¿Quieres hacer algo (esta noche)?
kye·res a·ther al·go (es·ta no·che)

Yes, I'd love to.
Me encantaría.
me en·kan·ta·ree·a

I'm busy.
Estoy ocupado/a. m/f
es·toy o·koo·pa·do/a

local talk

He's/She's hot.
Él/Ella es cachondo/a. m/f
el/e·lya es ka·chon·do/a

What a babe.
Vaya hembra.
va·ya em·bra

He/She gets around.
Se va a la cama con cualquiera.
se va a la ka·ma kon kwal·kye·ra

pick-up lines

frases para ligar

Would you like a drink?
¿Te apetece una copa?
te a·pe·te·the oo·na ko·pa

Do you have a light?
¿Tienes fuego?
tye·nes fwe·go

You're great.

Eres estupendo/a. m/f   e·res es·too·*pen*·do/a

**You mustn't come here much, because
I would have noticed you sooner.**

No debes venir mucho   no *de*·bes ve·*neer* moo·cho
por aquí porque me habría   por a·*kee* por·ke me a·*bree*·a
fijado en ti antes.   fee·*kha*·do en tee *an*·tes

**I've been watching you for a while, and
you're (the best-looking girl) here.**

Hace rato que te observo y   a·the *ra*·to ke te ob·*ser*·vo ee
eres (la chica mas guapa)   e·res (la *chee*·ka mas *gwa*·pa)
aqui.   a·*kee*

rejections

I'm here with my boyfriend/girlfriend.

Estoy aquí con mi   es·*toy* a·*kee* kon mee
novio/a. m/f   *no*·vyo/a

Excuse me, I have to go now.

Lo siento, pero me tengo   lo *syen*·to *pe*·ro me *ten*·go
que ir.   ke eer

Leave me alone!

Déjame en paz.   *de*·kha·me en path

Hey, I'm not interested in talking to you.

Mira tío/a, es que no me   *mee*·ra *tee*·o/a es ke no me
interesa hablar   een·te·*re*·sa ab·*lar*
contigo. m/f   kon·*tee*·go

Listen, why don't you go and get fucked.

Oye rico/a, por qué no   o·ye *ree*·ko/a por ke no
te vas a tomar por   te vas a to·*mar* por
el culo. m/f   el *koo*·lo

getting closer

Can I kiss you?
  ¿Te puedo besar?   te *pwe*·do be·*sar*

Do you want to come inside for a drink?
  ¿Quieres entrar a   *kye*·res en·*trar* a
  tomar algo?   to·*mar* al·go

Do you want a massage?
  ¿Quieres un masaje?   *kye*·res oon ma·*sa*·khe

Let's go to bed!
  ¡Vámonos a la cama!   va·*mo*·nos a la *ka*·ma

sex

el sexo

Kiss me!
  ¡Dame un beso!   *da*·me oon *be*·so

I want you.
  Te deseo.   te de·*se*·o

I want to make love to you.
Quiero hacerte el amor.   kye·ro a·*ther*·te el a·*mor*

Do you have a condom?
¿Tienes un condón?   tye·nes oon kon·*don*

Touch me here.
Tócame aquí.   to·ka·me a·*kee*

Do you like this?
¿Esto te gusta?   es·to te *goos*·ta

I (don't) like that.
Eso (no) me gusta.   e·so (no) me *goos*·ta

I think we should stop now.
Pienso que deberíamos   *pyen*·so ke de·be·*ree*·a·mos
parar.   pa·*rar*

Oh yeah!
¡Así!   a·*see*

faster	*rápido*	ra·*pee*·do
harder	*fuerte*	*fwer*·te
slower	*despacio*	des·*pa*·thyo
softer	*suave*	*swa*·ve

I can't get it up, sorry.
Lo siento, no puedo   lo *syen*·to no *pwe*·do
levantarla.   le·van·*tar*·la

Don't worry, I'll do it myself.
No te preocupes, lo hago yo.   no te pre·o·*koo*·pes lo a·go yo

endearments

heart	*corazon* m&f	ko·*ro*·thon
little love	*amorcito/a* m/f	a·mor·*thee*·to/a
my life	*mi vida* m&f	mee *vee*·da
my love	*mi amor* m&f	mee a·*mor*
sky	*cielo* m&f	*thye*·lo
treasure	*tesoro* m&f	te·*so*·ro

That was amazing.
    Eso fue increíble.   e·so fwe een·kre·ee·ble

Are you sleepy?
    ¿Tienes sueño?   tye·nes swe·nyo

Can I stay over?
    ¿Puedo quedarme?   pwe·do ke·dar·me

I love you.
    Te quiero.   te kye·ro

I think we're good together.
    Creo que estamos   kre·o ke es·ta·mos
    muy bien juntos.   mooy byen khoon·tos

problems

Are you seeing someone else?
    ¿Me estás engañando   me es·tas en·ga·nyan·do
    con alguien?   kon al·gyen

I never want to see you again.
    No quiero volver a verte.   no kye·ro vol·ver a ver·te

He's just a friend.
    Es un amigo   es oon a·mee·go
    nada más.   na·da mas

She's just a friend.
    Es una amiga   es oo·na a·mee·ga
    nada más.   na·da mas

I want to stay friends.
   Me gustaría que   me goos·ta·*ree*·a ke
   quedáramos como   ke·*da*·ra·mos *ko*·mo
   amigos.   a·*mee*·gos

We'll work it out.
   Lo resolveremos.   lo re·sol·ve·*re*·mos

passionate language

That's not true!	*¡Eso no es verdad!*	e·so no es ver·*da*
In your dreams!	*¡En sueños!*	en *swe*·nyos
Come off it!	*¡No me jodas!*	no me *kho*·das
Damn!	*¡Hostia!*	os·tya
Fuck!	*¡Joder!*	kho·*der*
Shit!	*¡Mierda!*	*myer*·da

beliefs & cultural differences
creencias & diferencias culturales

religion

la religión

What's your religion?
¿Cuál es tu religión?   kwal es too re·lee·*khyon*

Can I pray here?
¿Puedo rezar aquí?   pwe·do re·*thar* a·*kee*

I'm (not) ...	(No) Soy ...	(no) soy ...
agnostic	*agnóstico/a* m/f	ag·*nos*·tee·ko/a
Buddhist	*budista*	boo·*dees*·ta
Catholic	*católico/a* m/f	ka·to·lee·ko/a
Christian	*cristiano/a* m/f	krees·*tya*·no/a
Hindu	*hindú*	een·*doo*
Jewish	*judío/a* m/f	khoo·*dee*·o/a
Muslim	*musulmán/*	moo·sool·*man/*
	musulmána m/f	moo·sool·*ma*·na
practising	*practicante*	prak·tee·*kan*·te
religious	*religioso/a* m/f	re·lee·*khyo*·so/a

I (don't) believe in ...	(No) Creo en ...	(no) *kre*·o en ...
God	*Dios*	dyos
destiny/fate	*el destino*	el des·*tee*·no

cultural differences

las diferencias culturales

Is this a local or national custom?
¿Esto es una costumbre   es·to es oo·na kos·*toom*·bre
local o nacional?   lo·*kal* o na·thyo·*nal*

I'm not used to this.
No estoy acostumbrado/a   no es·*toy* a·kos·toom·*bra*·do/a
a esto. m/f   a *es*·to

This is (very) ...	*Esto es (muy) ...*	es·to es (mooy) ...
fun	*divertido*	dee·ver·tee·do
interesting	*interesante*	een·te·re·san·te
different	*diferente*	dee·fe·ren·te

I'm sorry, it's against my beliefs.

| *Lo siento, eso va en* | lo syen·to e·so va en |
| *contra de mis creencias.* | kon·tra de mees kre·en·thyas |

I don't mind watching, but I'd rather not join in.

No me importa mirar,	no me eem·por·ta mee·rar
pero prefiero no	pe·ro pre·fye·ro no
participar.	par·tee·thee·par

I'll try it.

| *Lo probaré.* | lo pro·ba·re |

Sorry, I didn't mean to do something wrong.

| *Lo siento, lo hice* | lo syen·to lo ee·the |
| *sin querer.* | seen ke·rer |

sporting interests

los intereses deportivos

What sport do you play?
¿Qué deporte practicas?   ke de·*por*·te prak·*tee*·kas

What sport do you follow?
¿A qué deporte eres   a ke de·*por*·te e·res
aficionado/a? m/f   a·fee·thyo·*na*·do/a

I play/do ...
Practico ...   prak·*tee*·ko ...

I follow ...
Soy aficionado/a al ... m/f   soy a·fee·thyo·*na*·do/a al ...

basketball	*baloncesto* m	ba·lon·*thes*·to
cycling	*ciclismo* m	thee·*klees*·mo
football (soccer)	*fútbol* m	*foot*·bol
tennis	*tenis* m	*te*·nis
volleyball	*voleibol* m	bo·*lei*·bol

Do you like sport?
¿Te gustan los deportes?   te *goos*·tan los de·*por*·tes

Yes, very much.
Me encantan.   me en·*kan*·tan

Not really.
En realidad, no mucho.   en re·a·lee·*da* no *moo*·cho

I like watching it.
Me gusta mirar.   me *goos*·ta mee·*rar*

Who's your favourite sportsperson?

¿Quién es tu deportista favorito/a? m/f   kyen es too de·por·tees·ta fa·vo·ree·to/a

What's your favourite team?

¿Cuál es tu equipo favorito?   kwal es too e·kee·po fa·vo·ree·to

going to a game

ir al partido

Would you like to go to a (basketball) game?

¿Te gustaría ir a un partido de (baloncesto)?   te goos·ta·ree·a eer a oon par·tee·do de (ba·lon·thes·to)

Who are you supporting?

¿Con qué equipo vas?   kon ke e·kee·po vas

scoring

What's the score?	*¿Cómo van?*	ko·mo van
draw/even	*empatados*	em·pa·ta·dos
love (zero)	*cero*	the·ro
match-point	*match point*	mach poyn
nil (zero)	*cero*	the·ro

How much time is left?

¿Cuánto tiempo queda de partido?   kwan·to tyem·po ke·da de par·tee·do

Who's ...?	*¿Quién ...?*	kyen ...
playing	*juega*	khwe·ga
winning	*va ganando*	va ga·nan·do

That was a ... game!	*¡Ese partido fue ...!*	e·se par·tee·do fwe ...
boring	*aburrido*	a·boo·ree·do
great	*cojonudo*	ko·kho·noo·do

playing sport

Do you want to play?
¿Quieres jugar?
kye·res khoo·gar

Can I join in?
¿Puedo jugar?
pwe·do khoo·gar

Yeah, that'd be great.
Sí, me encantaría.
see me en·kan·ta·ree·a

Not at the moment, thanks.
Ahora mismo no, gracias.
a·o·ra mees·mo no gra·thyas

I have an injury.
Tengo una lesión.
ten·go oo·na le·syon

Where's the best place to run around here?
¿Cuál es el mejor sitio
para hacer footing por
aquí cerca?
kwal es el me·khor see·tyo
pa·ra a·ther foo·teen por
a·kee ther·ka

Do I have to be a member to attend?
¿Hay que ser socio/a
para entrar? m/f
ai ke ser so·thyo/a
pa·ra en·trar

Is there a women-only pool?
¿Hay alguna piscina
sólo para mujeres?
ai al·goo·na pees·thee·na
so·lo pa·ra moo·khe·res

Where are the change rooms?
¿Dónde están los
vestuarios?
don·de es·tan los
ves·twa·ryos

Can I have a locker?
¿Puedo usar una
taquilla?
pwe·do oo·sar oo·na
ta·kee·lya

Where's the nearest ...?	*¿Dónde está ...* *más cercano/a?* m/f	don·de es·ta ... mas ther·ka·no/a
gym	*el gimnasio* m	el kheem·na·syo
swimming pool	*la piscina* f	la pees·thee·na
tennis court	*la pista* f *de tenis*	la pees·ta de te·nees

What's the charge per ...?	¿Cúanto cobran por ...?	kwan·to ko·bran por ...
day	día	dee·a
game	partida	par·tee·da
hour	hora	o·ra
visit	visita	vee·see·ta
Can I hire a ...?	¿Es posible alquilar una ...?	es po·see·ble al·kee·lar oo·na ...
ball	pelota	pe·lo·ta
bicycle	bicicleta	bee·thee·kle·ta
court	cancha	kan·cha
racquet	raqueta	ra·ke·ta

fair play?

I disagree!	No estoy de acuerdo!	no es·toy de a·kwer·do
Yeah, sure!	Sí hombre!	see om·bre
Yes, but ...	Sí pero ...	see pe·ro ...
Whatever.	Lo que sea.	lo ke se·a

diving

el buceo

I'd like to (go) ...	Me gustaría ...	me goos·ta·ree·a ...
explore wrecks	explorar naufragios	eks·plo·rar now·fra·khyos
learn to dive	aprender a bucear	a·pren·der a boo·the·ar
scuba diving	hacer submarinismo	a·ther soob·ma·ree·nees·mo
snorkelling	bucear con tubo	boo·the·ar kon too·bo

Where are some good diving sites?

¿Dónde hay buenos lugares   don·de ai *bwe*·nos loo·ga·res
para bucear?   pa·ra boo·the·*ar*

Are there jellyfish?

¿Hay medusas?   ai me·*doo*·sas

Where can we hire ...?

¿Dónde se puede alquilar ...?   don·de se *pwe*·de al·kee·*lar* ...

diving course	*curso* m *de buceo*	*koor*·so de boo·*the*·o
diving equipment	*equipo* m *de buceo*	e·*kee*·po de boo·*the*·o
flippers	*aletas* f pl	a·*le*·tas
mask	*gafas* f pl	*ga*·fas
wetsuits	*trajes* m pl	*tra*·khes
	isotérmicos	ee·so·*ter*·mee·kos

extreme sports

los deportes extremos

Are you sure this is safe?

¿De verdad que esto es   de ver·*da* ke es·to es
seguro?   se·*goo*·ro

Is the equipment secure?

¿Está seguro el equipo?   es·ta se·*goo*·ro el e·*kee*·po

This is insane!

¡Esto es una locura!   es·to es oo·na lo·*koo*·ra

abseiling	*rappel* m	ra·*pel*
bungy-jumping	*puenting* m	*pwen*·teen
caving	*espeleología* f	es·pe·le·o·lo·*khee*·a
game fishing	*pesca* f *deportiva*	*pes*·ka de·por·*tee*·va
mountain biking	*ciclismo* m *de*	thee·*klees*·mo de
	montaña	mon·*ta*·nya
rock-climbing	*escalada* f	es·ka·*la*·da

soccer

el fútbol

Who plays for (Real Madrid)?
*¿Quién juega en el
(Real Madrid)?*

kyen *khwe*·ga en el
(re·*al* ma·*dree*)

What a terrible team!
¡Qué equipo más espantoso!

ke e·*kee*·po mas es·pan·*to*·so

He's a great player.
Es un gran jugador.

es oon gran khoo·ga·*dor*

**He played brilliantly in the match
against (Italy).**
*Jugó de fenomenal
en el partido contra
(Italia).*

khoo·*go* de fe·no·me·*nal*
en el par·*tee*·do *kon*·tra
(ee·*ta*·lya)

Which team is at the top of the league?
*¿Qué equipo está en
primera posición en
la liga?*

ke e·*kee*·po es·*ta* en
pree·*me*·ra po·see·*thyon* en
la *lee*·ga

corner	saque m de esquina	sa·ke de es·kee·na
free kick	tiro m libre	tee·ro lee·bre
goalkeeper	portero m	por·te·ro
offside	fuera de juego	fwe·ra de khwe go
penalty	penalty m	pe·nal·tee

sports talk

What a ...!	¡Qué ...!	ke ...
goal	gol	gol
pass	pase	pa·se

Your/My point.
Tu/Mi punto. — too/mee *poon*·to

Kick it to me!
¡Pásamelo! — pa·sa·me·lo

You're a good player.
Juegas bien. — khwe·gas byen

Thanks for the game.
Gracias por el partido. — gra·thyas por el par·tee·do

tennis

el tenis

Would you like to play tennis?
¿Quieres jugar al tenis? — kye·res khoo·gar al te·nees

Can we play at night?
¿Se puede jugar de noche? — se pwe·de khoo·gar de no·che

Game, Set, Match.
Juego, set y partido. — khwe·go set ee par·tee·do

ace	ace m	eys
advantage	ventaja f	ven·ta·kha
fault	falta f	fal·ta
play doubles	jugar dobles	khoo·gar do·bles
(against)	(contra)	(kon·tra)
serve	saque m	sa·ke

walking & mountaineering

trekking & alpinismo

For language on hiking, see **outdoors**, page 137.

water sports

los deportes acuáticos

Can I book a lesson?
¿Puedo reservar una clase? pwe·do re·ser·var oo·na kla·se

Is safety gear provided?
¿Proporcionan el equipo pro·por·thyo·nan el e·kee·po
de seguridad? de se·goo·ree·da

Are there any ...?	*¿Hay ...?*	ai ...
reefs	*arrecifes*	a·re·thee·fes
rips	*corrientes*	ko·ryen·tes
water hazards	*peligros en*	pe·lee·gros en
	el agua	el a·gwa

motorboat	*lancha* f *motora*	lan·cha mo·to·ra
sail	*vela* f	ve·la
surfboard	*tabla* f *de surf*	ta·bla de soorf
surfing	*surf* m	soorf
water-skis	*esquís* m pl *acuáticos*	es·kees a·kwa·tee·kos
wave	*ola* f	o·la

local sports

If you hear the sounds of bat, ball and exertion, it may be *pelotari*, pelota players, enjoying the traditional game of *pelota vasca,* a type of handball. It's also known as *jai-alai* in Basque.

ball	*pelota* f	pe·lo·ta
striker	*delantero/a* m/f	de·lan·te·ro/a
wall	*frontón* m	fron·ton

hiking

el excursionismo

There's plenty of walking, hiking and mountaineering to do in Spain. A recognised cross-country walking trail is known as *Gran Recorrido* (GR), gran re·ko·ree·do, while the shorter walking paths scattered throughout the country are called *Pequeños Recorridos* (PR), pe·ke·nyos re·ko·ree·dos.

Where can I ...?	¿Dónde puedo ...?	*don·de pwe·do ...*
buy supplies	*comprar viveres*	kom·*prar* vee·ver·es
find someone	*encontrar a*	en·kon·*trar* a
who knows	*alguien que*	*al*·gyen ke
this area	*conozca el área*	ko·*noth*·ka el a·re·a
get a map	*obtener un*	ob·te·*ner* oon
	mapa	*ma*·pa
hire hiking	*alquilar un*	al·kee·*lar* oon
gear	*equipo para ir*	e·*kee*·po pa·ra eer
	de excursion	de eks·koor·*syon*

signs

Por Aquí a ...	por a·*kee* a ...	**This Way To ...**
Terreno de Cámping	te·*re*·no de *kam*·peen	**Camping Ground**
Prohibido Acampar	pro·ee·*bee*·do a·kam·*par*	**No Camping**

Where can I find out about hiking trails?

¿Dónde hay información sobre caminos rurales de la zona?		don·de ai een·for·ma·*thyon* so·bre ka·*mee*·nos roo·*ra*·les de la *tho*·na

How long is the trail?

¿Cuántos kilómetros tiene el camino?

kwan·tos kee·*lo*·me·tros *tye*·ne el ka·*mee*·no

How high is the climb?

¿A qué altura se escala?

a ke al·*too*·ra se es·*ka*·la

Do we need a guide?

¿Se necesita un guía?

se ne·the·*see*·ta oon *gee*·a

Are there guided treks?

¿Se organizan excursiones guiadas?

se or·ga·*nee*·than eks·koor·*syo*·nes gee·a·das

Do we need to take ...?	¿Se necesita llevar ...?	se ne·the·*see*·ta lye·var ...
bedding	algo en que dormir	*al*·go en ke dor·*meer*
food	comida	ko·*mee*·da
water	agua	a·gwa
Is the track ...?	¿Es ... el sendero?	es ... el sen·*de*·ro
(well-)marked	(bien) marcado	(byen) mar·*ka*·do
open	abierto	a·*byer*·to
scenic	pintoresco	peen·to·*res*·ko
Which is the ... route?	¿Cuál es el camino más ...?	kwal es el ka·*mee*·no mas ...
easiest	fácil	*fa*·theel
shortest	corto	*kor*·to

Where's a ...?	¿Dónde hay ...?	don·de ai ...
camping site	un cámping	oon kam·peen
village	un pueblo	oon pwe·blo

Where are the ...?	¿Dónde hay ...?	don·de ai ...
showers	duchas	doo·chas
toilets	servicios	ser·vee·thyos

Where have you come from?
¿De dónde vienes?   de don·de vye·nes

How long did it take?
¿Cuánto ha tardado?   kwan·to a tar·da·do

Does this path go to ...?
¿Este camino va a ...?   es·te ka·mee·no va a ...

Can we go through here?
¿Se puede pasar por aquí?   se pwe·de pa·sar por a·kee

Is the water OK to drink?
¿Se puede beber el agua?   se pwe·de be·ber el a·gwa

I'm lost.
Estoy perdido/a. m/f   es·toy per·dee·do/a

Is It safe?
¿Es seguro?   es se·goo·ro

Is there a hut there?
¿Hay una cabaña allí?   ai oo·na ka·ba·nya a·lyee

When does it get dark?
¿A qué hora oscurece?   a ke o·ra os·koo·re·the

signs

¡Prohibido	pro·ee·bee·do	**No Swimming!**
Nadar!	na·dar	

outdoors

139

at the beach

Where's the ...	¿Dónde está la	don·de es·ta la
beach?	playa ...?	pla·ya ...
best	mejor	me·khor
nearest	más cercana	mas ther·ka·na
nudist	nudista	noo·dees·ta

Is it safe to dive/swim here?
  ¿Es seguro bucear/   es se·goo·ro boo·the·ar/
  nadar aquí?   na·dar a·kee

What time is high/low tide?
  ¿A qué hora es la marea   a ke o·ra es la ma·re·a
  alta/baja?   al·ta/ba·kha

Do we have to pay?
  ¿Hay que pagar?   ai ke pa·gar

How much to	¿Cuánto por	kwan·to por
rent ...?	alquilar ... ?	al·kee·lar ...
a chair	una silla	oo·na see·lya
a hut	una cabaña	oo·na ka·ba·nya
an umbrella	un parasol	oon pa·ra·sol

listen for ...

kwee·da·do kon la re·sa·ka	
Cuidado con la	**Be careful of the**
resaca.	**undertow.**
es pe·lee·gro·so	
¡Es peligroso!	**It's dangerous!**
e·res mo·de·lo	
¿Eres modelo?	**Are you a model?**

weather

What's the weather like?
   ¿Qué tiempo hace?   ke *tyem*·po a·the

Today it's ...	*Hoy hace ...*	oy a·the ...
Will it be ...	*Mañana*	ma·*nya*·na
tomorrow?	*hará ...?*	a·ra ...
cold	*frío*	*free*·o
freezing	*un frío*	oon *free*·o
	que pela	ke *pe*·la
hot	*calor*	ka·*lor*
sunny	*sol*	sol
warm	*calor*	ka·*lor*
windy	*viento*	*vyen*·to

(Today) It's raining.
   (Hoy) Está lloviendo.   (oy) es·*ta* lyo·*vyen*·do

(Tomorrow) It will be raining.
   (Mañana) Lloverá.   (ma·*nya*·na) lyo·ve·*ra*

Where can I	*¿Dónde puedo*	*don*·de *pwe*·do
buy ...?	*comprar ...?*	kom·*prar* ...
a rain	*un*	oon
jacket	*impermeable*	eem·per·me·*a*·ble
sunblock	*crema solar*	*kre*·ma so·*lar*
an umbrella	*un paraguas*	oon pa·*ra*·gwas
hail	*granizo* m	gra·*nee*·tho
storm	*tormenta* f	tor·*men*·ta
sun	*sol* m	sol

flora & fauna

What ... is that?	¿Qué ... es ése/ésa? m/f	ke ... es e·se/e·sa
animal	animal m	a·nee·mal
flower	flor f	flor
plant	planta f	plan·ta
tree	árbol m	ar·bol

What's it used for?
¿Para qué se usa?   pa·ra ke se oo·sa

Can you eat the fruit?
¿Se puede comer la fruta?   se pwe·de ko·mer la froo·ta

Is it endangered?
¿Está en peligro   es·ta en pe·lee·gro
de extinción?   de eks·teen·thyon

Is it ...?	¿Es ...?	es ...
common	común	ko·moon
dangerous	peligroso/a m/f	pe·lee·gro·so/a
protected	protegido/a m/f	pro·te·khee·do/a

For geographical and agricultural terms, and names of animals and plants, see the **dictionary**.

key language

The main meal in Spain, 'lunchtime' is called *la hora de comer*, la o·ra de ko·mer. It's served between 1.30pm and 4.30pm.

breakfast	*desayuno* m	de·sa·yoo·no
lunch	*comida* f	ko·mee·da
dinner	*cena* f	the·na
snack	*tentempié* m	ten·tem·pye
eat	*comer*	ko·mer
drink	*beber*	be·ber
Please.	*Por favor.*	por fa·vor
Thank you.	*Gracias.*	gra·thyas
I'd like ...	*Quisiera ...*	kee·sye·ra ...
I'm starving!	*¡Estoy*	es·toy
	hambriento/a! m/f	am·bryen·to/a

finding a place to eat

Can you recommend a ...?	*¿Puede recomendar un/una ...?* m/f	pwe·de re·ko·men·dar oon/oo·na ...
bar	*bar* m	bar
cafe	*café* m	ka·fe
coffee bar	*cafetería* f	ka·fe·te·ree·a
restaurant	*restaurante* m	res·tow·ran·te

Are you still serving food?

  ¿Siguen sirviendo comida? — see·gen seer·vyen·do ko·mee·da

How long is the wait?
　　¿Cuánto hay que esperar?　　kwan·to ai ke es·pe·rar

Where would you go for (a) ...?	*¿Adónde se va para ...?*	a·don·de se va pa·ra ...
celebration	*celebrar*	sel·e·brar
cheap meal	*comer barato*	ko·mer ba·ra·to
local specialities	*comer comida típica*	ko·mer ko·mee·da tee·pee·ka

I'd like to reserve a table for ...	*Quisiera reservar una mesa para ...*	kee·sye·ra re·ser·var oo·na me·sa pa·ra ...
(two) people	*(dos) personas*	(dos) per·so·nas
(eight) o'clock	*las (ocho)*	las (o·cho)

listen for ...

lo syen·to e·mos the·ra·do	
Lo siento, hemos cerrado.	**Sorry, we're closed.**
no te·ne·mos me·sa	
No tenemos mesa.	**We have no tables.**
oon mo·men·to	
Un momento.	**One moment.**

I'd like ..., please.	*Quisiera ..., por favor.*	kee·sye·ra ... por fa·vor
a table for (five)	*una mesa para (cinco)*	oo·na me·sa pa·ra (theen·ko)
the (non-) smoking section	*(no) fumadores*	(no) foo·ma·do·res
the drink list	*la lista de bebidas*	la lees·ta de be·bee·das
the menu	*el menú*	el me·noo

Do you have ... ?	*¿Tienen ... ?*	tye·nen ...
children's meals	*comidas para niños*	ko·mee·das pa·ra nee·nyos
a menu in English	*un menú en inglés*	oon me·noo en een·gles

at the restaurant

Is it self-serve?
¿Es de autoservicio?   es de ow·to·ser·vee·thyo

Is service included in the bill?
¿La cuenta incluye   la kwen·ta een·kloo·ye
servicio?   ser·vee·thyo

What would you recommend?
¿Qué recomienda?   ke re·ko·myen·da

I'll have what they're having.
Tomaré lo mismo que ellos.   to·ma·re lo mees·mo ke e·lyos

Does it take long to prepare?
¿Tarda mucho en   tar·da moo·cho en
prepararse?   pre·pa·rar·se

What's in that dish?
¿Que lleva ese plato?   ke lye·va e·se pla·to

For more on special diets, see **vegetarian & special meals**, page 159, and **health**, page 184.

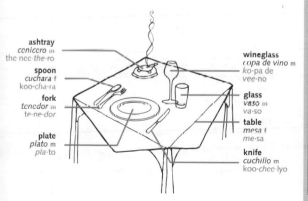

ashtray
cenicero m
the·nee·the·ro

spoon
cuchara f
koo·cha·ra

fork
tenedor m
te·ne·dor

plate
plato m
pla·to

wineglass
copa de vino m
ko·pa de
vee·no

glass
vaso m
va·so

table
mesa f
me·sa

knife
cuchillo m
koo·chee·lyo

Are these complimentary?
  ¿Éstos son gratis? es·tos son *gra*·tees

We're just having drinks.
  Sólo queremos tomar algo. *so*·lo ke·re·mos to·*mar al*·go

I'd like a local speciality.
  Quisiera un plato kee·*sye*·ra oon *pla*·to
  típico. *tee*·pee·ko

signs		
Reservado	re·ser·va·do	**Reserved**

at the table

a la mesa

Please bring ...	*Por favor nos trae ...*	por fa·*vor* nos *tra*·e ...
the bill	*la cuenta*	la *kwen*·ta
a glass	*un vaso*	oon *va*·so
a serviette	*una servilleta*	oo·na ser·vee·*lye*·ta
a wineglass	*una copa*	oo·na *ko*·pa
	de vino	de *vee*·no

For more words you might find on a menu, see the **culinary reader**, page 161.

listen for ...	
le *goos*·ta ...	
¿Le gusta ...?	**Do you like ...?**
re·ko·*myen*·do ...	
Recomiendo ...	**I suggest the ...**
ko·mo lo *kye*·re pre·pa·*ra*·do	
¿Cómo lo quiere	**How would you like**
preparado?	**that cooked?**

FOOD

146

Aperitivos	a·pe·ree·tee·vos	Appetisers
Caldos	kal·dos	Soups
Cervezas	ther·ve·thas	Beers
De Entrada	de en·tra·da	Entrees
Digestivos	dee·khes·tee·vos	Digestifs
Ensaladas	en·sa·la·das	Salads
Licores	lee·ko·res	Spirits
Postres	pos·tres	Desserts
Refrescos	re·fres·kos	Soft Drinks
Segundos Platos	se·goon·dos pla·tos	Main Courses
Vinos Blancos	vee·nos blan·kos	White Wines
Vinos Dulces	vee·no dool·thes	Dessert Wines
Vinos Espumosos	vee·nos es·poo·mo·sos	Sparkling Wines
Vinos Tintos	vee·nos teen·tos	Red Wines

talking food

hablando de comida

I love this dish.
  Me encanta este plato.   me en·kan·ta es·te pla·to

We love the local cuisine.
  Nos encanta la comida   nos en·kan·ta la ko·mee·da
  típica de la zona.   tee·pee·ka de la tho·na

That was delicious!
  ¡Estaba buenísimo!   es·ta·ba bwe·nee·see·mo

My compliments to the chef.
  Mi enhorabuena al   mee en·o·ra·bwe·na al
  cocinero.   ko·thee·ne·ro

I'm full.   *Estoy lleno/a.* m/f   es·toy lye·no/a

This is ...   *Esto está ...*   es·to es·ta ...
  burnt   *quemado*   ke·ma·do
  (too) cold   *(muy) frío*   (mooy) free·o
  superb   *exquisito*   eks·kee·see·to

meals

> breakfast

What's a typical Spanish (breakfast)?

¿Cómo es un típico (desayuno) español?	ko·mo es oon tee·pee·ko (de·sa·yoo·no) es·pa·nyol

omelette	tortilla	tor·tee·lya
muesli	muesli	mwes·lee
toast	tostadas	tos·ta·das

For typical dishes, see the **culinary reader**, page 161, and for other food items see the **dictionary**.

> light meals

What's that called?	¿Cómo se llama eso?	ko·mo se lya·ma e·so
I'd like ..., please.	Quisiera ..., por favor.	kee·sye·ra ... por fa·vor
a piece	un trozo	oon tro·tho
a sandwich	un sándwich	oon san·weech
one slice	una loncha	oo·na lon·cha
that one	ése/a m/f	e·se/a
two	dos	dos

> condiments

Is there any ...?	¿Hay ...?	ai ...
chilli sauce	salsa f de guindilla	sal·sa de geen·dee·lya
pepper	pimienta f	pee·myen·ta
salt	sal f	sal
tomato sauce/ ketchup	salsa f de tomate	sal·sa de to·ma·te
vinegar	vinagre m	vee·na·gre

methods of preparation

los métodos de cocción

I'd like it ...	Lo quiero ...	lo kye·ro ...
I don't want it ...	No lo quiero ...	no lo kye·ro ...
deep-fried	frito en aceite abundante	free·to en a·they·te a·boon·dan·te
medium	no muy hecho	no mooy e·cho
rare	vuelta y vuelta	vwel·ta ee vwel·ta
re-heated	recalentado	re·ka·len·ta·do
steamed	al vapor	al va·por
well-done	muy hecho	mooy e·cho
with the dressing on the side	con el aliño aparte	kon el a·lee·nyo a·par·te
without ...	sin ...	seen ...

in the bar

Excuse me!	¡Oiga!	*oy*·ga
I'm next.	Ahora voy yo.	a·*o*·ra voy yo
I'll have ...	Para mí ...	*pa*·ra mee ...

Same again, please.
    Otra de lo mismo.   *o*·tra de lo *mees*·mo

No ice, thanks.
    Sin hielo, gracias.   seen *ye*·lo *gra*·thyas

I'll buy you a drink.
    Te invito a una copa.   te een·*vee*·to a *oo*·na *ko*·pa

What would you like?
    ¿Qué quieres tomar?   ke *kye*·res to·*mar*

It's my round.
    Es mi ronda.   es mee *ron*·da

You can get the next one.
    La próxima la pagas tú.   la *prok*·see·ma la *pa*·gas too

How much is that?
    ¿Cuánto es eso?   *kwan*·to es *e*·so

Do you serve meals here?
    ¿Sirven comidas aquí?   *seer*·ven ko·*mee*·das a·*kee*

listen for ...

a·*kee* tye·ne
    ¡Aquí tiene!   **Here you go!**

don·de le gus·ta·*ree*·a sen·*tar*·se
    ¿Dónde le gustaría   **Where would you like**
    sentarse?   **to sit?**

en ke le *pwe*·do ser·*veer*
    ¿En qué le puedo servir?   **What can I get for you?**

kye·re to·*mar* al·go *myen*·tras es·*pe*·ra
    ¿Quiere tomar algo   **Would you like a**
    mientras espera?   **drink while you wait?**

tapas

Tapas are scrumptious cooked bar snacks, available pretty much around the clock at bars and some clubs. You'll find they're free in some places, laid out in the bar for you to choose from. This follows village tradition at the turn of the century in the whole of Andalusia, as well as in Extremadura, Low Castile, Murcia and the working-class districts of Madrid and Barcelona.

Other places will rotate the dishes. Listen for ...

da·me oo·na pree·*me*·ra
  ¡Dame una primera!   **Give me a starter!**

oo·na se·*goon*·da
  ¡Una segunda!   **Give me a main dish!**

... as the bar attendant orders a different speciality each time from the cook. See if you can stay on your stool long enough to get back to number one again.

• how hungry are you?

banderilla/	ban·de·*ree*·lya/	small tapa serving
moruno/	mo·*roo*·no/	on bread or a
pinchito	peen·*chee*·to	toothpick
ración	ra·*thyon*	large tapa serving

• common tapas:

montadito	mon·ta·*deet*·o	bread-topped tapa
pan tumaca	pan too·*ma*·ka	tapa of toasted bread rubbed with tomatoes & garlic, served with oil
queso en	*ke*·soh en	cheese in olive oil,
aceite	a·*say*·tay	served as a tapa

• regional tapas:

naveganta	na·ve·*gan*·ta	in Burgos
pintxo	*peen*·cho	in Basque Country

nonalcoholic drinks

las bebidas no alcohólicas

I don't drink alcohol.
No bebo alcohol.   no *be*·bo al·ko·*hol*

(cup of) coffee ...	*(taza de) café* m ...	*(ta*·tha de) ka·*fe* ...
(cup of) tea ...	*(taza de) té* m ...	*(ta*·tha de) te ...
with milk	*con leche*	kon *le*·che
without sugar	*sin azúcar*	seen a·*thoo*·kar
soft drink	*refrescos* m	re·*fres*·ko
... water	*agua* f ...	*a*·gwa ...
boiled	*hervida*	er·*vee*·da
mineral	*mineral*	mee·ne·*ral*
(sparkling)	*(con gas)*	(kon gas)

alcoholic drinks

las bebidas alcohólicas

beer	*cerveza* f	ther·*ve*·tha
brandy	*coñac* m	ko·*nyak*
champagne	*champán* m	cham·*pan*
cocktail	*combinado* m	kom·bee·*na*·do
sangria (red-wine punch)	*sangría* f	san·*gree*·a
a shot of ...	*un chupito* m de ...	oon choo·*pee*·to de ...
gin	*ginebra* f	khee·*ne*·bra
rum	*ron* m	ron
tequila	*tequila* m	te·*kee*·la
vodka	*vodka* m	*vod*·ka
whisky	*güisqui* m	gwees·*kee*

a big fan of the mini

Many Spanish bars provide massive plastic beakers of beer to cater for young revellers. It's cut with water and average tasting – but cheap and free flowing! These fountains of froth are called *minis*.

Other words you'll need when ordering a brew:

cerveza f ...	ther·ve·tha ...	... beer
de barril	de ba·*ril*	draught
negra	*neg*·ra	dark
rubia	roo·bee·a	light
sin alcohol	sin al·kol	nonalcoholic
botellín m	bo·tel·yin	small bottle of beer (250 ml)
litrona f	lee·*tro*·na	litre bottle of beer
mediana f	me·dee·a·na	bottle of beer (300 ml)

a bottle/glass of ... wine	*una botella/ copa de vino ...*	oo·na bo·*te*·lya/ *ko*·pa de *vee*·no ...
dessert	*dulce*	*dool*·the
red	*tinto*	*teen*·to
rose	*rosado*	ro·*sa*·do
sparkling	*espumoso*	es·poo·*mo*·so
white	*blanco*	*blan*·ko
a ... of beer	*una ... de cerveza*	oo·na ... de ther·ve·tha
glass	*caña*	*ka*·nya
jug	*jarra*	*kha*·ra
pint	*pinta*	*peen*·ta

one too many?

Cheers!
¡Salud!
sa·*loo*

Thanks, but I don't feel like it.
Lo siento, pero no me apetece.
lo *syen*·to *pe*·ro no me a·pe·*te*·the

This is hitting the spot.
Me lo estoy pasando muy bien.
me lo es·*toy* pa·*san*·do mooy byen

I'm tired, I'd better go home.
Estoy cansado/a, mejor me voy a casa. m/f
es·*toy* kan·*sa*·do/a me·*khor* me voy a *ka*·sa

Where's the toilet?
¿Dónde está el lavabo?
don·de es·*ta* el la·*va*·bo

I'm feeling drunk.
Esto me está subiendo mucho.
es·to me es·*ta* soo·*byen*·do *moo*·cho

I feel fantastic!
¡Me siento fenomenal!
me *syen*·to fe·no·me·*nal*

I really, really love you.
Te quiero muchísimo.
te *kye*·ro moo·*chee*·see·mo

I think I've had one too many.
Creo que he tomado demasiado.
kre·o ke e to·*ma*·do de·ma·*sya*·do

Can you call a taxi for me?
¿Me puedes pedir un taxi?
me *pwe*·des pe·*deer* oon *tak*·see

I don't think you should drive.
No creo que deberías conducir.
no *kre*·o ke de·be·*ree*·as kon·doo·*theer*

I'm pissed.
Estoy borracho/a. m/f
es·*toy* bo·*ra*·cho/a

I feel ill.
Me siento mal.
me *syen*·to mal

key language

lenguaje clave

A piece.	*Un trozo.*	oon *tro*·tho
A slice.	*Una loncha.*	*oo*·na *lon*·cha
That one.	*Ése.*	*e*·se
This.	*Esto.*	*es*·to
A bit more.	*Un poco más.*	oon *po*·ko mas
Less.	*Menos.*	*me*·nos
Enough!	*¡Basta!*	*ba*·sta
cooked	*cocido/a* m/f	ko·*thee*·do/a
dried	*seco/a* m/f	*se*·ko/a
fresh	*fresco/a* m/f	*fres*·ko/a
frozen	*congelado/a* m/f	kon·khe·*la*·do/a
raw	*crudo/a* m/f	*kroo*·do/a

buying food

comprando comida

How much?
¿Cuánto?　　　　　*kwan*·to

How many?
¿Cuántos?　　　　　*kwan*·tos

How much is (a kilo of cheese)?
¿Cuánto vale (un kilo　*kwan*·to va·le (oon *kee*·lo
de queso)?　　　　　de *ke*·so)

What's the local speciality?
¿Cuál es la especialidad　kwal es la es·pe·thya·lee·*da*
de la zona?　　　　de la *tho*·na

What's that?
¿Qué es eso?　　　　ke es *e*·so

Can I taste it?
¿Puedo probarlo/a? m/f   *pwe*·do pro·*bar*·lo/a

Can I have a bag, please?
¿Me da una bolsa, por favor?   me da oo·na *bol*·sa por fa·*vor*

I'd like ...	*Póngame ...*	*pon*·ga·me ...
(three) pieces	*(tres) piezas*	(tres) *pye*·thas
(six) slices	*(seis) lonchas*	(seys) *lon*·chas
(two) kilos	*(dos) kilos*	(dos) *kee*·los
(200) grams	*(doscientos) gramos*	(dos·*thyen*·tos) *gra*·mos

Do you have ...?	*¿Tiene ... ?*	*tye*·ne ...
anything cheaper	*algo más barato*	*al*·go mas ba·*ra*·to
any other kinds	*otros tipos*	*ot*·ros *tee*·pos

Where can I find the ... section?	*¿Dónde está la sección de ...?*	*don*·de es·*ta* la sek·*thyon* de ...
dairy	*productos lácteos*	pro·*dook*·tos *lak*·te·os
frozen goods	*productos congelados*	pro·*dook*·tos kon·khe·*la*·dos
fruit and vegetable	*frutas y verduras*	*froo*·tas ee ver·*doo*·ras
meat	*carne*	*kar*·ne
poultry	*aves*	*a*·ves

cooking utensils

utensilios de cocina

Could I please borrow a/an ...?
¿Me puede prestar ...?   me *pwe*·de pres·*tar* ...

Where's a/an ...?
¿Dónde hay ...?   *don*·de ai ...

bottle opener	*abrebotellas* m	a·bre·bo·*te*·lyas
bowl	*bol* m	bol
can opener	*abrelatas* m	a·bre·*la*·tas
chopping board	*tabla* f *para cortar*	*tab*·la pa·ra kor·*tar*
cup	*taza* f	*ta*·tha
corkscrew	*sacacorchos* m	sa·ka·*kor*·chos
fork	*tenedor* m	ten·ne·*dor*
fridge	*nevera* m	ne·*ve*·ra
frying pan	*sartén* f	sar·*ten*
glass	*vaso* m	*va*·so
knife	*cuchillo* m	koo·*chee*·lyo
oven	*horno* m	*or*·no
plate	*plato* m	*pla*·to
saucepan	*cazo* m	*ka*·tho
spoon	*cuchara* f	koo·*cha*·ra
toaster	*tostadora* f	tos·ta·*do*·ra

listen for ...

e·so es (oon man·*che*·go)
Eso es (un manchego).   That's (a manchego).

no *ke*·da mas
No queda más.   There's none left.

e·so es (*theen*·ko e·oo·ros)
Eso es (cinco euros).   That's (five euros).

al·go mas
¿Algo más?   Would you like anything else?

useful amounts

Please give me ...	Por favor, deme ...	por fa·vor de·me ...
(100) grams	(cien) gramos	(thyen) gra·mos
half a dozen	una media docena	oo·na me·dya do·the·na
half a kilo	un medio kilo	oon me·dyo kee·lo
a kilo	un kilo	oon kee·lo
a bottle (of ...)	una botella (de ...)	oo·na bo·te·lya (de ...)
a jar	una jarra	oo·na kha·ra
a packet	un paquete	oon pa·ke·te
a tin	una lata	oo·na la·ta
(just) a little	(sólo) un poquito	(so·lo) oon po·kee·to
many	muchos/as m/f	moo·chos/as
more	más	mas
some	algunos/as m/f	al·goo·nos/as
less	menos	me·nos

FOOD

158

vegetarian & special meals
comidas vegetarianas & platos especiales

ordering food

I'm vegetarian.
Soy vegetariano/a. m/f soy ve·khe·ta·rya·no/a

Is there a (vegetarian) restaurant near here?
¿Hay un restaurante ai oon res·tow·ran·te
(vegetariano) por aquí? (ve·khe·ta·rya·no) por a·kee

Do you have ... *¿Tienen comida ...?* tye·nen ko·mee·da ...
food?

halal	halal	a·lal
kosher	kosher	ko·sher
vegan	vegetariana	ve·khe·ta·rya·na
	estricta	es·trik·ta

I don't eat red meat.
No como carne roja. no ko·mo kar·ne ro·kha

Is it cooked in/with butter?
¿Esta cocinado es·ta ko·thee·na·do
en/con mantequilla? en/kon man·te·kee·lya

Could you	*¿Me puede*	me pwe·de
prepare a meal	*preparar una*	pre·pa·rar oo·na
without ...?	*comida sin ...?*	ko·mee·da seen ...
eggs	huevo	we·vo
fish	pescado	pes·ka·do
meat/fish	caldo de carne/	kal·do de kar·ne/
stock	pescado	pes·ka·do
pork	cerdo	ther·do
poultry	aves	a·ves

Is this ...?	¿Esto es ...?	es·to es ...
free of animal produce	sin productos de animales	seen pro·*dook*·tos de a·nee·*ma*·les
free-range	de corral	de *ko*·ral
genetically modified	transgénico	trans·*khe*·nee·ko
gluten-free	sin gluten	seen *gloo*·ten
low in sugar	bajo en azúcar	ba·kho en a·*thoo*·kar
low-fat	bajo en grasas	ba·kho en gra·sas
organic	orgánico	or·ga·nee·ko
salt-free	sin sal	seen sal

special diets & allergies

regímenes especiales & alergias

I'm on a special diet.
Estoy a régimen especial.   es·toy a re·khee·men es·pe·thyal

I'm allergic to ...	Soy alérgico/a ... m/f	soy a·ler·khee·ko/a ...
dairy produce	a los productos lácteos	a los pro·*dook*·tos *lak*·te·os
honey	al miel	al myel
MSG	al glutamato monosódico	al gloo·ta·*ma*·to mo·no·so·dee·ko
nuts	a las nueces	a las *nwe*·thes
seafood	a los mariscos	a los ma·*rees*·kos
shellfish	a los crustáceos	a los kroos·*ta*·thyos

For a more detailed version of this glossary, see Lonely Planet's *World Food Spain*.

A

acebuche ⓜ a·the·*boo*·che wild olive

acedía ⓕ a·the·*dee*·a plaice/flounder

aceite ⓜ a·*they*·te oil
— **de girasol** de khee·ra·*sol* sunflower oil
— **de oliva** de o·*lee*·va olive oil
— **de oliva virgen extra** de o·*lee*·va veer·khen eks·tra extra virgin olive oil

aceituna ⓕ a·they·*too*·na olive
— **negra** ne·gra black olive
— **verde** ver·de green olive

ácido/a ⓜ/ⓕ a·*thee*·do/a tart (of fruit)

adobo ⓜ a·*do*·bo marinade

agrios ⓜ pl a·gryos citrus fruits

aguacate ⓜ a·gwa·*ka*·te avocado

aguaturma ⓕ a·gwa·*toor*·ma Jerusalem artichoke

ajiaco ⓜ a·*khya*·ko spicy potato dish

ajoaceite ⓜ a·kho·a·*they*·te garlic & oil sauce • garlic mayonnaise

ajohariha ⓕ a·*kho*·a·ree·na potatoes stewed in garlic sauce

ajoarriero (al) a·kho·a·*rye*·ro (al) 'mule-driver's garlic' - anything cooked in a sauce of onions, garlic & chilli

ala ⓕ *a*·la (chicken) wing

alajú ⓜ a·la·*khoo* honey & almond cake

albaricoque ⓜ al·ba·ree·ko·ke apricot
— **seco** se·ko dried apricot

albóndigas ⓕ pl al·*bon*·dee·gas meatballs
— **de pescado** de pes·ka·do fish balls

alcachofas ⓕ pl al·ka·cho·fas artichokes
— **guisadas a la española** gee·sa·das a la es·pa·*nyo*·la artichokes in wine
— **rellenas** re·*lye*·nas stuffed artichokes

alcaparra ⓕ al·ka·pa·ra caper

alioli ⓜ a·lee·o·*lee* garlic mayonnaise

almejas ⓕ pl al·*me*·khas clams – superb eaten raw
— **a la marinera** a la ma·ree·ne·ra clams in white wine
— **al horno** al or·no baked clams

almendrado ⓜ al·men·*dra*·do almond cake or biscuit • chocolate covered ice cream bar

almendras ⓕ pl al·*men*·dras almonds

alubia ⓕ a·*loo*·bya haricot bean

anacardo ⓜ a·na·*kar*·do cashew nut

anchoas ⓕ pl an·*cho*·as anchovies – mostly eaten fresh, grilled or fried

angelote ⓜ an·khe·*lo*·te monkfish

anguila ⓕ an·*gee*·la adult eel

angulas ⓕ pl an·goo·las baby eels – prized as a delicacy, they resemble vermicelli
— **en all i pebre** en al *ee* pe·bre baby eels with pepper & garlic

apio ⓜ a·pyo celery

arándano ⓜ a·*ran*·da·no blueberry

arenque ⓜ a·ren·ke herring
— **ahumado** a·oo·ma·do kipper

arroz ⓜ a·*roth* rice
— **a la Alcireña** a la al·thee·re·nya baked rice dish
— **abanda (de València)** a·ban·da (de va·*len*·thya) fish paella
— **con leche** kon le·che rice pudding
— **con pollo** kon po·lyo chicken & rice
— **integral** een·te·*gral* brown rice
— **marinera** ma·ree·ne·ra seafood rice
— **salvaje** sal·va·khe wild rice

asadillo ⓜ a·sa·*dee*·lyo roasted red capsicums

asados ⓜ pl a·sa·dos *roast meats*

atún ⓜ a·toon *tuna – often served marinated & raw*

— **al horno** al or·no *baked tuna*

avellana ⓕ a·ve·lya·na *hazelnut*

aves ⓕ pl a·ves *poultry*

azúcar ⓜ a·thoo·kar *sugar*

B

bacalao ⓜ ba·ka·low *cod – usually salted & dried*

— **a la vizcaína** a la veeth·ka·ee·na *cod with chillies & capsicums*

— **del convento** del kon·ven·to *cod with potatoes & spinach in broth*

bacón ⓜ ba·kon *bacon*

barbo ⓜ bar·bo *red mullet*

barra ⓕ ba·ra *long stick of bread*

batata ⓕ ba·ta·ta *sweet potato*

beicon ⓜ bey·kon *streaky bacon rashers*

berberechos ⓜ pl ber·be·re·chos *cockles*

— **en vinagre** en vee·na·gre *cockles in vinegar*

berenjenas ⓕ pl be·ren·khe·nas *eggplants*

— **a la mallorquina** a la ma·lyor·kee·na *eggplants with garlic mayonnaise*

— **con setas** kon se·tas *eggplants with mushrooms*

berza ⓕ ber·tha *cabbage*

— **a la andaluza** a la an·da·loo·tha *cabbage & meat hotpot*

besugo ⓜ be·soo·go *red bream*

— **a la Donostiarra** a la do·nos·tya·ra *barbecued red bream with garlic & paprika*

— **estilo San Sebastián** es·tee·lo san se·bas·tyan *barbecued red bream with garlic & paprika*

bienmesabe ⓜ byen·me·sa·be *sponge cake, egg & almond confection*

bisbe ⓜ bees·be *black & white blood sausage*

bistec ⓜ bees·tek *steak*

— **con patatas** kon pa·ta·tas *steak with chips*

bizcocha ⓕ **manchega** beeth·ko·cha man·che·ga *cake soaked in milk, sugar, vanilla & cinnamon*

bizcocho ⓜ beeth·ko·cho *sponge cake*

— **de almendra** de al·men·dra *almond cake*

— **de avellana** de a·ve·lya·na *hazelnut cake*

bizcochos ⓜ pl **borrachos** beeth·ko·chos bo·ra·chos *cake soaked in liqueur*

bocadillo ⓜ bo·ka·dee·lyo *bread roll with a filling*

bocas ⓕ pl **de la isla** bo·kas de la ees·la *large crab claws*

bogavante ⓜ bo·ga·van·te *lobster*

bollo ⓜ bo·lyo *crusty bread roll*

bonito ⓜ bo·nee·to *white fleshy tuna*

boquerón ⓜ bo·ke·ron *whitebait*

boquerones ⓜ pl bo·ke·ro·nes *anchovies marinated in wine vinegar*

— **fritos** free·tos *fried anchovies*

brama ⓕ bra·ma *sea bream*

bróculi ⓜ bro·ko·lee *broccoli*

budín ⓜ **de atún** boo·deen de a·toon *baked tuna pudding*

bull ⓜ **de atún** bool de a·toon *rabbit with garlic & tuna boiled with potatoes*

buñuelitos ⓜ pl boo·nywe·lee·tos *small cheese or ham fritters*

— **de San José** de san kho·se *lemon & vanilla crepes*

buñuelo ⓜ boo·nywe·lo *fried pastry*

burrida ⓕ **de ratjada** boo·ree·da de rat·kha·da *fish soup with almonds*

butifarra ⓕ **(blanca)** boo·tee·fa·ra (blan·ka) *cured pork sausage*

— **con setas** kon se·tas *Catalan sausage with mushrooms*

C

caballa ⓕ ka·ba·lya *mackerel*

cabra ⓕ ka·bra *goat*

cabracho ⓜ ka·bra·cho *scorpion fish • mullet*

cacahuete ⓜ ka·ka·we·te *peanut*

cachelos ⓜ pl ka·che·los *potatoes with spicy sausage & pork*

cádiz ⓜ ka·deeth *fresh goats' milk cheese*

calabacín ⓜ ka·la·ba·theen *zucchini*

calabaza ⓕ ka·la·ba·tha *pumpkin*

calamares ⓜ pl ka·la·ma·res *calamari – popular fried or stuffed*
— **fritos a la romana** free·tos a la ro·ma·na *squid rings fried in batter*
— **rellenos** re·lye·nos *stuffed squid*

calçots ⓜ pl kal·sots *spring onion-like vegetables chargrilled and eaten with a romesco dipping sauce*

caldeirada ⓕ kal·dey·ra·da *salted cod & potatoes in a paprika sauce • fish soup*

caldereta ⓕ kal·de·re·ta *stew*
— **asturiana** as·too·rya·na *fish stew*
— **de cordero** de kor·de·ro *lamb stew*

caldillo de perro kal·dee·lyo de pe·ro *'puppy dog soup' – stew of onions, fresh fish & orange juice*

caldo ⓜ kal·do *broth • clear soup • stock*
— **al estilo del Mar Menor** al es·tee·lo del mar me·nor *fish stew from the Mar Menor*
— **gallego** ga·lye·go *broth with haricot beans, ham & sausage*

callos ⓜ pl ka·lyos *tripe*

camarones fritos ⓜ pl ka·ma·ro·nes free·tos *deep-fried prawns*

canagroc ka·na·grok *mushroom*

cañaillas ⓕ pl **de la Isla** ka·nyay·lyas de la ees·la *boiled sea snails*

canelones ⓜ pl ka·na·lo·nes *squares of pasta for making cannelloni*
— **con espinaca** kon es·pee·na·ka *cannelloni with spinach, anchovies & bechamel*
— **con pescado** kon pes·ka·do *cannelloni with cod, eggs & mushrooms*

canapés ⓜ pl **de fiambres** ka·na·pes de fee·am·bres *mini hors d'oeuvres with ham, anchovies or cheese*

cangrejo ⓜ kan·gre·kho *large-clawed crab usually eaten steamed or boiled*

cantalupo ⓜ kan·ta·loo·po *cantaloupe*

canutillos ⓜ pl ka·noo·tee·lyos *cream biscuits*

capones ⓜ pl **de Villalba** ka·po·nes de vee·lyal·ba *Christmas dish of chicken marinated in brandy*

caracoles ⓜ pl ka·ra·ko·les *snails*

caramelos ⓜ pl ka·ra·me·los *caramels • confection*

cardos ⓜ pl **fritos** kar·dos free·tos *fried thistles*

carne ⓕ kar·ne *meat*
— **de membrillo** de mem·bree·lyo *quince 'cheese'*
— **molida** mo·lee·da *minced meat*

cassolada ⓕ ka·so·la·da *potato & vegetable stew with bacon & ribs*

castaña ⓕ kas·ta·nya *chestnut*

caviar ⓜ ka·vyar *caviar*

caza ⓕ ka·tha *game*

cazón ⓜ ka·thon *dogfish or shark with a sweet scallop-like flavour*

cazuelitas ⓕ pl **de langostinos San Rafael** ka·thwe·lee·tas de lan·gos·tee·nos san ra·fa·el *baked rice with seafood*

cebolla ⓕ the·bo·lya *onion*

cecina ⓕ the·thee·na *cured meat*

cerdo ⓜ ther·do *pork*

cereales ⓜ pl the·re·a·les *cereal*

cereza ⓕ the·re·tha *cherry*
— **silvestre** seel·ves·tre *wild cherry*

ciervo ⓜ thyer·vo *deer*

cigala ⓕ thee·ga·la *crayfish*

ciruela ⓕ thee·rwe·la *plum*
— **pasa** pa·sa *prune*

civet ⓜ **de llebre** see·vet de le·bre *hare stew*

cochifrito de cordero ko·chee·free·to de kor·de·ro *lamb fried with garlic & lemon*

cochinillo ⓜ ko·chee·nee·lyo *suckling pig*
— **asado** a·sa·do *roast suckling pig*
— **de pelotas** de pe·lo·tas *meatball stew*
coco ⓜ ko·ko *coconut*
codornices ① pl **a la plancha** ko·dor·nee·thes a la *plan*·cha *grilled quail*
codorniz ① ko·dor·neeth *quail*
— **con pimientos** kon pee·*myen*·tos *capsicums stuffed with quail*
col ① kol *cabbage*
— **lombarda** lom·bar·da *red cabbage*
coles ① pl **de bruselas** ko·les de broo·se·las *Brussels sprouts*
coliflor ① ko·lee·flor *cauliflower*
conejo ⓜ ko·ne·kho *rabbit*
— **de monte** de mon·te *wild rabbit*
coquina ① ko·kee·na *large clam*
corazón ⓜ ko·ra·thon *heart*
cordero ⓜ kor·de·ro *lamb*
— **al chilindrón** al chee·leen·dron *lamb in tomato & capsicum sauce*
— **con almendras** kon al·men·dras *lamb in almond sauce*
costillas ① pl kos·tee·lyas *ribs*
crema ① kre·ma *cream*
— **catalana** ka·ta·la·na *creme brulee*
— **de espinacas** de es·pee·na·kas *cream of spinach soup*
— **de naranja** de na·ran·kha *orange cream dessert*
— **de San José** de san kho·se *egg custard flavoured with cinnamon*
— **de verduras** de ver·doo·ras *cream of vegetable soup*
crocante ⓜ kro·kan·te *ice cream with chopped nuts & chocolate*

CH

chalote ⓜ cha·lo·te *shallot*
champiñones ⓜ pl cham·pee·nyo·nes *cultivated white mushrooms*
chanquetes ⓜ pl chan·ke·tes *whitebait • baby anchovies*

chilindrón (al) chee·leen·dron (al) *cooked in a tomato & red pepper sauce*
chipirón ⓜ chee·pee·ron *baby squid – very popular in the Basque Country*
chocolate ⓜ cho·ko·la·te *chocolate*
— **caliente** ka·lee·en·te *thick hot chocolate*
chocos ⓜ pl cho·kos *squid*
chorizo ⓜ cho·ree·tho *spicy red cooked sausage, similar to salami*
— **de Pamplona** de pam·plo·na *fine-textured, hard chorizo*
— **de Salamanca** de sa·la·man·ka *chunky chorizo from Salamanca*
chuletas ① pl choo·le·tas *chops • cutlets*
— **al sarmiento** al sar·myen·to *chops prepared over wood from vines*
— **de buey** de bwey *ox chops*
— **de cerdo a la aragonesa** de ther·do a la a·ra·go·ne·sa *baked pork chops with wine & onion*
churros ⓜ choo·ros *fried doughnut strips bought from street-sellers or in cafes*

D

de soja de so·kha *with soya*
despojos ⓜ pl des·po·khos *offal*
dorada ① **a la sal** do·ra·da a la sal *salted sea bream*
dulce ⓜ dool·the *sweet*
— **de batata** de ba·ta·ta *sweet potato pudding from Málaga*
dulces ⓜ pl dool·thes *sweets*
— **de las monjas** dool·thes de las mon·khas *confectionery made by nuns & sold in convents or cake shops*

E

embutidos ⓜ pl em·boo·tee·dos *generic name for cured sausages*
empanada ① em·pa·na·da *savoury pie*
— **de carne** de kar·ne *spicy meat pie*
— **de espinaca** de es·pee·na·ka *spinach pie*

empanadilla ① em·pa·na·*dee*·lya *small pie, either sweet or savoury*

empanado ⓜ em·pa·*na*·do *coated in bread crumbs*

emparedado ⓜ em·pa·re·*da*·do *sandwich*
— **de jamón y espárragos** de kha·*mon* ee es·pa·ra·gos *fried ham & asparagus rolls*

empiñonado ⓜ em·pee·nyo·*na*·do *small marzipan-filled pastry with pinenuts*

en salsa verde en *sal*·sa ver·de *in a parsley & garlic sauce*

encurtidos ⓜ pl en·koor·*tee*·dos *pickles*

ensaimada ① **mallorquina** en·sai·*ma*·da ma·lyor·*kee*·na *spiral-shaped bun made with lard*

ensalada ① en·sa·*la*·da *salad*
— **de frutas** de *froo*·tas *fruit salad*
— **de patatas** de pa·*ta*·tas *potato salad*
— **del tiempo** del *tyem*·po *seasonal salad*
— **mixta** *meeks*·ta *mixed salad*

escaldadillas ① pl es·kal·da·*dee*·lyas *dough soaked in orange juice & fried*

escalivada ① es·ka·lee·va·da *roasted red capsicums in olive oil*

escalopes ⓜ pl **de ternera rellenos** es·ka·*lo*·pes de ter·*ne*·ra re·*lye*·nos *deep fried veal cutlets stuffed with egg & cheese*

espaguetis ⓜ pl es·pa·ge·tees *spaghetti*

espárragos ⓜ pl es·*pa*·ra·gos *asparagus*
— **con dos salsas** kon dos *sal*·sas *asparagus & tomato or paprika mayonnaise*
— **en vinagreta** en vee·na·gre·ta *asparagus in vinaigrette*

espinacas ① pl es·pee·*na*·kas *spinach*
— **a la catalana** a la ka·ta·*la*·na *spinach with pinenuts & raisins*

esqueixada ① es·kee·*sha*·da *cod dressed with olives, tomato & onion*

etxeko kopa e·*che*·ko ko·pa *ice cream dessert*

F

fabada ① **asturiana** fa·*ba*·da as·too·rya·na *stew made with pork, blood sausage & white beans*

faisán ⓜ fai·*san* *pheasant*

faves ① pl **a la catalana** fa·ves a la ka·ta·*la*·na *broad beans with ham*

fiambres ⓜ pl fee·*am*·bres *cold meats*
— **surtidos** soor·*tee*·dos *selection of cold meats*

fideos ⓜ pl fee·*de*·os *pasta noodles*

fideua ① fee·*de*·wa *rice or noodles with fish & shellfish*

fideus ⓜ pl **a la cassola** fee·*de*·oos a la ka·so·la *Catalan noodle dish*

filete ⓜ fee·*le*·te *steak* • *any boneless slice of meat*
— **a la parrilla** a la pa·*ree*·lya *grilled beef steak*
— **de ternera** de ter·*ne*·ra *veal steak*

filloas ① pl fee·*lyo*·as *Galician pancakes filled with cream*

flan ⓜ flan *creme caramel*

flaó ① fla·o *sweet cheese flan*

flor manchega ① flor man·*che*·ga *deep-fried sweet wafers*

frambuesa ① fram·*bwe*·sa *raspberry*

frangellos ⓜ pl fran·*khe*·lyos *sweet made from cornmeal, milk & honey*

fresa ① *fre*·sa *strawberry*

tricandó ⓜ **de langostinos** free·kan·do de lan·gos·*tee*·nos *shrimp in almond sauce*

frite ⓜ free·te *lamb stew, served on festive occasions*

fritos ⓜ pl *free*·tos *fritters*
— **con miel** kon myel *honey-roasted fritters*

fritura ① free·*too*·ra *mixed fried fish*

fruta ① *froo*·ta *fruit*
— **variada** va·ree·a·da *selection of fresh fruit*

frutas ① pl **en almíbar** *froo*·tas en al·*mee*·bar *fruit in syrup*

frutos ⓜ pl **secos** *froo*·tos se·kos *nuts & dried fruit*

fuet ① foo·*et* *thin pork sausage*

G

gachas ① pl **manchegas** ga·chas man·che·gas *flavoured porridge*

galleta ① ga·lye·ta *biscuit*

gambas ① gam·bas *prawns*
— **a la plancha** a la plan·cha *grilled prawns*
— **en gabardina** en ga·bar·dee·na *prawns in batter*

Gamonedo ⓜ ga·mo·ne·do *sharp-tasting cheese, smoked & cured*

garbanzos ⓜ pl gar·ban·thos *chickpeas*
— **con cebolla** kon the·bo·lya *chickpeas in onion sauce*
— **tostados** tos·ta·dos *roasted chickpeas (sold as a snack)*

garbure ① gar·boo·re *green vegetable soup • pork & ham dish*

garúm ⓜ ga·room *olive & anchovy dip*

Gata-Hurdes ga·ta·oor·des *cheese*

gazpacho ⓜ gath·pa·cho *cold tomato soup*
— **andaluz** an·da·looz *cold tomato soup with chopped salad vegetables*
— **pastoril** pas·to·reel *rabbit stew with tomato & garlic*

gazpachos ⓜ pl **manchegos** gath·pa·chos man·che·gos *game & vegetable hotpot*

Gaztazarra ⓜ gath·ta·tha·ra *cheese*

gitano ⓜ khee·ta·no *Andalusian chickpea & tripe stew*

gofio ⓜ go·fyo *toasted cornmeal or barley*

granadilla ① gra·na·dee·lya *passion fruit*

grano ⓜ gra·no *grain*
— **largo** lar·go *long-grain (rice)*

gratinado ⓜ **de berenjenas** gra·tee·na·do de be·ren·khe·nas *eggplant gratin*

Grazalema ① gra·tha·le·ma *semi-cured sheep's milk cheese*

guindilla ① geen·dee·lya *mild green chilli*

guisado ⓜ gee·sa·do *stew*
— **de cordero** de kor·de·ro *lamb ragout*
— **de ternera** de ter·ne·ra *veal ragout*

guisante ⓜ gee·san·te *pea*
— **seco** se·ko *split pea*
— **mollar** mo·lyar *snow pea*

guisantes ⓜ pl **con jamón a la española** gee·san·tes kon kha·mon a la es·pa·nyo·la *pea & ham dish*

guisat ⓜ **de marisco** gee·sat de ma·rees·ko *stew made with seafood*

guiso ⓜ **de conejo estilo canario** gee·so de ko·ne·kho es·tee·lo ka·na·ryo *rabbit stew*

guiso ⓜ **de rabo de toro** gee·so de ra·bo de to·ro *stewed bull's tail with potatoes*

H

habas ① pl a·bas *broad beans*
— **a la granadina** a la gra·na·dee·na *broad beans with eggs & ham*
— **fritas** free·tas *fried broad beans (sold as a snack)*

habichuela ① a·bee·chwe·la *white bean*

hamburguesa ① am·boor·ge·sa *hamburger*

harina ① a·ree·na *flour*
— **integral** een·te·gral *wholemeal flour*

helado ⓜ e·la·do *ice cream*

hígado ⓜ ee·ga·do *liver*

higo ⓜ ee·go *fig*
— **seco** se·ko *dried fig*

hogaza ① o·ga·tha *dense, thick-crusted bread*

hoja ① **de parra** o·kha de pa·ra *vine leaf*

hojaldres ⓜ pl o·khal·dres *small flaky pastries covered in sugar*

hojas ① pl **verdes** o·khas ver·des *green vegetables*

hornazo ⓜ or·na·tho *bread stuffed with sausage*

hortalizas ① pl or·ta·lee·thas *vegetables*

huevo ⓜ we·vo egg
— **cocido** ko·thee·do boiled egg
— **de chocolate** de cho·ko·la·te chocolate egg
— **frito** free·to fried egg
huevos ⓜ pl we·vos egg dishes
— **a la flamenca** a la fla·men·ka baked vegetables with egg & ham
— **al estilo Sóller** al es·tee·lo so·lyer fried eggs served with a milk & vegetable sauce
— **en salsa agria** en sal·sa a·grya boiled eggs in wine & vinegar
— **escalfados** es·kal·fa·dos poached eggs
— **revueltos** re·vwel·tos scrambled eggs

J

jabalí ⓜ kha·ba·lee wild boar
— **con castaños** kon sal·sa de kas·ta·nyos wild boar in chestnut sauce
jamón ⓜ kha·mon ham
— **cocido** ko·thee·do cooked ham
— **ibérico** ee·ber·ik·o ham from the Iberian pig, said to be the best in Spain
— **serrano** se·ra·no cured mountain ham
jengibre ⓜ khen·gee·bre ginger
jerez (al) khe·reth (al) in a sherry sauce
judía ⓘ khoo·dee·a fresh green bean • dried kidney bean
judias ⓘ pl **del tío Lucas** khoo·dee·as del tee·o loo·kas bean stew with garlic & bacon
judias ⓘ pl **verdes a la castellana** khoo·dee·as ver·des a la kas·te·lya·na fried capsicums, garlic & green beans
judiones ⓜ pl **de la granja** kho·dee·o·nes de la gran·kha pork & bean stew

K

kiskilla kees·kee·lya shrimp (also spelled quisquilla)

L

langosta ⓘ lan·gos·ta lobster
— **a la ibicenca** a la ee·bee·then·ka lobster with stuffed squid
langostinos ⓜ pl lan·gos·tee·nos king prawns
— **a la plancha** a la plan·cha grilled king prawns
lavanco ⓜ la·van·ko wild duck
lechuga ⓘ le·choo·ga lettuce
legumbres ⓘ pl le·goom·bres pulses • vegetables • vegetable dishes
— **secas** se·kas dried pulses
leguminosas ⓘ pl le·goo·mee·no·sas legumes
lengua ⓘ len·gwa tongue
— **a la aragonesa** a la a·ra·go·ne·sa tongue in tomato & capsicum sauce
lenguado ⓜ len·gwa·do sole
— **al chacolí con hongos** al cha·ko·lee kon on·gos sole with white wine & mushrooms
lenguados ⓜ pl **al plato** len·gwa·dos al pla·to sole & mushroom casserole
lenguas ⓘ pl **con salsa de almendras** len·gwas kon sal·sa de al·men·dras tongue in almond sauce
lentejas ⓘ pl len·te·khas lentils
liebre ⓘ lye·bre hare
— **con castañas** kon kas·ta·nyas hare with chestnuts
— **estofada** es·to·fa·da stewed hare
lima ⓘ lee·ma lime
limón ⓜ lee·mon lemon
lomo ⓜ lo·mo fillet • loin • sirloin
— **curado** koo·ra·do cured pork sausage
— **de cerdo** de ther·do loin of pork
longaniza ⓘ lon·ga·nee·tha chorizo, long & skinny sausage
lubina ⓘ loo·bee·na sea bass
— **a la marinera** a la ma·ree·ne·ra sea bass in parsley sauce
lucio ⓜ loo·thyo pike

LL

llagostí m **a l'allioli** lyan·gos·*tee* a la·*lye*·o·lee *grilled prawns in garlic mayonnaise*

llenguado m **a la nyoca** lyen·*gwa*·do a la *nyo*·ka *sole with pine nuts & raisins*

M

macedonia f **de frutas** ma·the·*do*·nya de *froo*·tas *fruit salad*

macedonia f **de verduras** ma·the·*do*·nya de ver·*doo*·ras *mixed vegetables*

magdalena f ma·da·*le*·na *small fairy cake to dunk in coffee*

magras f pl *ma*·gras *fried eggs, ham, cheese & tomato*

maíz m ma·*eeth* *maize • corn*
— **tierno** *tyer*·no *sweetcorn*

mandarina f man·da·*ree*·na *tangerine • mandarin*

mango m *man*·go *mango*

manitas f pl **de cerdo** ma·*nee*·tas de *ther*·do *pig's trotters*

manitas f pl **de cordero** ma·*nee*·tas de kor·*de*·ro *leg of lamb*

manteca f man·*te*·ka *lard*

mantecado m man·te·*ka*·do *a soft lard biscuit • dairy ice cream*

mantequilla f man·te·*kee*·lya *butter*
— **sin sal** seen sal *unsalted butter*

manzana f man·*tha*·na *apple*

manzanas f **asadas** man·*tha*·nas a·*sa*·das *baked apples*

margarina f mar·ga·*ree*·na *margarine*

marinera (a la) ma·ree·*ne*·ra (a la) *cooked or served in a white wine sauce*

mariscos m ma·*rees*·kos *shellfish • seafood*

marmitako mar·mee·*ta*·ko *fresh tuna & potato casserole*

marrano m ma·*ra*·no *pork*

mar y cel m mar ee sel *dish of sausages, rabbit, shrimp & angler fish*

masa f *ma*·sa *pastry (dough)*

mayonesa f ma·yo·*ne*·sa *mayonnaise*

medallones m pl **de merluza** me·da·*lyo*·nes de mer·*loo*·tha *hake steaks*

mejillones m pl me·khee·*lyo*·nes *mussels*
— **al vino blanco** al *vee*·no *blan*·ko *mussels in white wine*
— **con salsa** kon *sal*·sa *mussels with tomato sauce*

mel f **i mató** mel ee ma·*to* *a dessert of curd cheese with honey*

melocotón m me·lo·ko·*ton* *peach*

melocotones m pl **al vino** me·lo·ko·*to*·nes al *vee*·no *peaches in red wine*

melón m me·*lon* *melon*

membrillo m mem·*bree*·lyo *quince*

menestra f me·*nes*·tra *mixed vegetable stew*
— **de pollo** de *po*·lyo *chicken & vegetable stew*

merengue m me·*ren*·ge *meringue*

merluza f mer·*loo*·tha *hake*

mermelada f mer·me·*la*·da *marmalade*

mero m *me*·ro *halibut • grouper • sea bass*

miel f myel *honey*
— **de azahar** de a·tha·*ar* *orange blossom honey*
— **de caña** de *ka*·nya *treacle*

migas f pl *mee*·gas *fried cubes of bread with capsicums*
— **a la aragonesa** a la a·ra·go·*ne*·sa *fried bread with bacon rashers in tomato sauce*
— **mulatas** moo·*la*·tas *cubes of bread soaked in chocolate & fried*

mojarra f mo·*kha*·ra *type of sea bream*

moje m **manchego** mo·*khe* man·*che*·go *cold broth with black olives*

mojete m mo·*khe*·te *dipping sauce for bread, made from potatoes, garlic, tomatoes & paprika*
— **murciano** moor·*thya*·no *fish & capsicum dish*

mojo m *mo*·kho *spicy capsicum sauce*

mollejas f pl mo·*lye*·khas *sweetbreads*

mollete ⓜ mo·*lye*·te *soft round bap roll*

monas ⓕ pl **de pascua** *mo*·nas de *pas*·kwa *Easter cakes • figures made of chocolate*

mongetes ⓕ pl **seques i butifarra** mon·*zhe*·tes se·kes ee boo·tee·*fa*·ra *haricot beans with roasted pork sausage*

mora ⓕ *mo*·ra *blackberry*

moraga ⓕ **de sardina** mo·*ra*·ga de sar·*dee*·na *fresh anchovies on a spit*

morcilla ⓕ mor·*thee*·lya *black pudding, often stewed with beans & vegetables*

mortadela ⓕ mor·ta·*de*·la *mortadella sausage*

morteruelo ⓜ mor·te·*rwe*·lo *pate dish containing offal, game & spices*

mostachones ⓜ pl mos·ta·*cho*·nes *small cakes for dipping in coffee or hot chocolate (also spelled* mostatxones*)*

mostaza ⓕ mos·*ta*·tha *mustard*
— **en grano** en *gra*·no *mustard seed*

múgil ⓜ *moo*·kheel *grey mullet*

mujol ⓜ **guisado** moo·*khol* gee·sa·do *red mullet*

mus ⓜ **de chocolate** moos de cho·ko·*la*·te *chocolate mousse*

muslo ⓜ *moos*·lo *(chicken) leg & thigh*

N

nabo ⓜ *na*·bo *root vegetable • turnip*

naranja ⓕ na·*ran*·kha *orange*

nata ⓕ *na*·ta *cream*
— **agria** *a*·grya *sour cream*
— **montada** mon·*ta*·da *whipped cream*

natillas ⓕ pl na·*tee*·lyas *creamy custard dessert*
— **de chocolate** de cho·ko·*la*·te *chocolate custard*

navaja ⓕ na·va·kha *razor clam*

nécora ⓕ *ne*·ko·ra *small crab*

nueces ⓕ pl *new*·thes *nuts*

nuez ⓕ nweth *nut*
— **de América** de a·*me*·ree·ka *pecan nut*
— **de nogal** de no·*gal* *walnut*

Ñ

ñora ⓕ *nyo*·ra *sweet red capsicum (usually dried)*

O

oca ⓕ *o*·ka *goose*

olla ⓕ *o*·lya *meat & vegetable stew • cooking pot*

oreja ⓕ **de mar** o·*re*·kha de mar *abalone*

ostiones ⓜ pl **a la gaditana** os·*tyo*·nes a la ga·dee·*ta*·na *Cádiz oysters with garlic, parsley & bread crumbs*

ostra ⓕ *os*·tra *oyster*

oveja ⓕ o·*ve*·kha *mutton*

P

pá ⓜ **amb oli** pa amb o·*lee* *toasted bread with garlic & olive oil*

pacana ⓕ pa·*ka*·na *pecan*

paella ⓕ pa·*e*·lya *rice dish which has many regional variations*
— **marinera** ma·ree·*ne*·ra *paella with fish & seafood*
— **zamorana** tha·mo·*ra*·na *paella with meat*

palitos ⓜ pl **de queso** pa·*lee*·tos de *ke*·so *cheese straws*

palmera ⓕ pal·*me*·ra *leaf-shaped flaky pastry, often coated in chocolate*

palomitas ⓕ pl pa·lo·*mee*·tas *popcorn*

pan ⓜ pan *bread*
— **aceite** a·*they*·te *flat round bread*
— **árabe** *a*·ra·be *pita bread*
— **de Alá** de a·*la* *'Allah's Bread' – dessert*
— **de boda** de *bo*·da *sculpted bread traditionally made for weddings*
— **de centeno** de then·*te*·no *rye bread*
— **duro** *doo*·ro *stale bread, used for toasting & eating with olive oil*
— **integral** een·te·*gral* *wholemeal bread*

panaché ⓜ pa·na·*che* mixed vegetable stew

panallets ⓜ pl pa·na·*lyets* marzipan sweets

panceta ⓕ pan·*the*·ta salt-cured, streaky bacon

panchineta ⓕ pan·chee·*ne*·ta almond tart

panecillo ⓜ pa·ne·*thee*·lyo small bread roll

panojas ⓕ pl **malagueñas** pa·*no*·khas ma·la·ge·*nyas* sardine dish

papas ⓕ pl **arrugadas** *pa*·pas a·roo·*ga*·das potatoes boiled in their jackets

pargo ⓜ *par*·go sea bream

parrillada ⓕ pa·ree·*lya*·da grilled meat
— **de mariscos** de ma·*rees*·kos seafood grill

pastel ⓜ pas·*tel* cake
— **de boda** de *bo*·da wedding cake
— **de chocolate** de cho·ko·*la*·te chocolate cake
— **de cierva** de *thyer*·va meat pie
— **de cumpleaños** de koom·ple·a·*nyos* birthday cake

pastelitos ⓜ pl **de miel** pas·te·*lee*·tos de myel honey fritters

pataco ⓜ pa·*ta*·ko tuna & potato stew

patatas ⓕ pl pa·*ta*·tas potatoes
— **a la riojana** a la ree·o·*kha*·na potatoes with chorizo & paprika
— **alioli** a·lee·o·*lee* potatoes in garlic mayonnaise
— **bravas** *bra*·vas potatoes in spicy tomato sauce
— **con chorizo** kon cho·*ree*·tho potatoes with chorizo
— **estofadas** es·to·*fa*·das boiled potatoes

pato ⓜ *pa*·to duck
— **a la sevillana** a la se·vee·*lya*·na duck with orange sauce
— **alcaparrada** al·ka·pa·*ra*·da duck with capers & almonds

pavo ⓜ *pa*·vo turkey

pececillos ⓜ pl pe·pe·the·*thee*·lyos small fish

pechina ⓕ pe·*chee*·na scallop

pecho ⓜ *pe*·cho breast of lamb

pechuga ⓕ pe·*choo*·ga breast of poultry

pepinillo ⓜ pe·pee·*nee*·lyo gherkin

pepino ⓜ pe·*pee*·no cucumber

pepitoria ⓕ pe·pee·to·*rya* sauce made with egg & almond

pepitos ⓜ pl pe·*pee*·tos chocolate eclair cakes filled with custard

pera ⓕ *pe*·ra pear

La Peral ⓕ la pe·*ral* soft cheese

perca ⓕ *per*·ka perch

perdices ⓕ pl per·*dee*·thes partridges
— **a la manchega** a la man·*che*·ga partridge in red wine & capsicums
— **con chocolate** kon cho·ko·*la*·te partridge with chocolate

perdiz ⓕ per·*deeth* partridge

peregrina ⓕ pe·re·*gree*·na scallop

pericana ⓕ pe·ree·*ka*·na dish of olives, cod oil, capsicums & garlic

perrito ⓜ **caliente** pe·*ree*·to ka·lee·*en*·te hot dog

pescada ⓕ **á galega** pes·*ka*·da a ga·*le*·ga hake fried in olive oil & served with garlic & paprika sauce

pescadilla ⓕ pes·ka·*dee*·lya whiting • young hake

pescaditos ⓜ pl **rebozados** pes·ka·*dee*·tos re·bo·*tha*·dos small fish fried in batter

pescado ⓜ pes·*ka*·do fish
— **a l'all cremat** a lal kre·*mat* fish in burnt garlic

pescaíto ⓜ **frito** pes·ka·*ee*·to *free*·to tiny fried fish

pestiños ⓜ pl pes·*tee*·nyos honey-coated aniseed pastries, fried with filling

pez ⓕ **espada** peth es·*pa*·da swordfish
— **frito** *free*·to fried swordfish steaks on a skewer

picada ① pee·ka·da *mixture of garlic, parsley, toasted almonds & nuts, often used to thicken sauces*

picadillo ⑩ pee·ka·dee·lyo *salad consisting of diced vegetables*
— **de atún** de a·toon *salad made with diced tuna & capsicums*
— **de ternera** de ter·ne·ra *minced veal*

pichón ⑩ pee·chon *pigeon*

pichones ⑩ pl **asados** pee·cho·nes a·sa·dos *roast pigeons*

pilotes ① pl pee·lo·tes *Catalan meatballs*

pimiento ⑩ pee·myen·to *capsicum*
— **amarillo** a·ma·ree·lyo *yellow capsicum*
— **rojo** ro·kho *red capsicum*
— **verde** ver·de *green capsicum*

pimientos ⑩ pl pee·myen·tos *capsicums (the ones from El Bierzo are especially good)*
— **a la riojana** a la ree·o·kha·na *roast red capsicum fried in oil & garlic*
— **al chilindrón** al chee·leen·dron *capsicum casserole*

piña ① pee·nya *pineapple*

pinchito ⑩ **moruno** peen·chee·to mo·roo·no *lamb & chicken kebabs*

piñón ⑩ pee·nyon *pinenut*

pinta ① peen·ta *pinto bean*

pintada ① peen·ta·da *guinea fowl*

piquillo ⑩ pee·kee·lyo *sweet & spicy capsicums*

pistacho ⑩ pees·ta·cho *pistachio nut*

pisto ⑩ **manchego** pees·to man·che·go *zucchini with capsicum & tomato, fried or stewed*

plátano ⑩ pla·ta·no *banana*

pochas ① pl po·chas *beans*
— **a la riojana** à la ree·o·kha·na *beans with chorizo in spicy paprika sauce*
— **con almejas** kon al·me·khas *beans with clams*

pollo ⑩ po·lyo *chicken*
— **asado** a·sa·do *roast chicken*
— **con samfaina** kon sam·fai·na *chicken with mixed vegetables*
— **en escabeche** en es·ka·be·che *marinated chicken*
— **en salsa de ajo** en sal·sa de a·kho *chicken in garlic sauce*
— **granadina** gra·na·dee·na *chicken with wine & ham*
— **y langosta** ee lan·gos·ta *chicken with crayfish*

pulpo ⑩ **a feira** pool·po a fey·ra *spicy boiled octopus*

polvorón ⑩ pol·vo·ron *almond shortbread, often eaten at Christmas*

pomelo ⑩ po·me·lo *grapefruit*

postre ⑩ pos·tre *dessert*
— **de naranja** de na·ran·kha *cream-filled oranges*

potaje ⑩ po·ta·khe *broth*
— **castellano** kas·te·lya·no *broth with beans & sausages*
— **de garbanzos** de gar·ban·thos *broth with chickpeas*
— **de lentejas** de len·te·khas *lentil broth*

pote ⑩ **gallego** po·te ga·lye·go *stew*

potito ⑩ po·tee·to *jar of baby food*

pringada ① preen·ga·da *bread dipped in sauce • a marinated sandwich*

productos ⑩ pl **biológicos** pro·dook·tos bee·o·lo·khee·kos *organic produce*

productos ⑩ pl **del mar** pro·dook·tos del mar *seafood products*

productos ⑩ pl **lácteos** pro·dook·tos lak·te·os *dairy products*

puchero ⑩ poo·che·ro *casserole*

pudin ⑩ poo·din *pudding*

puerco ⑩ pwer·ko *pork*

puerro ⑩ pwe·ro *leek*

pulpo ⑩ pool·po *octopus*

punta ① **de diamante** poon·ta de dya·man·te *confection from Valencia*

porrusalda ① po·roo·sal·da *cod & potato stew*

culinary reader

Q

queso ⓜ *ke·so* cheese
— **azul** *a·thool* blue cheese
— **crema** *kre·ma* cream cheese
quisquilla ⓕ *kees·kee·lya* shrimp
(also spelled kiskilla)

R

rábano ⓜ *ra·ba·no* radish
rabas ⓕ **en salsa verde** *ra·bas en sal·sa
ver·de* squid in green sauce
rabassola ⓕ *ra·ba·so·la* mushroom
rape ⓜ *ra·pe* monkfish
— **a la gallega** *a la ga·lye·ga* monkfish
with potatoes & garlic sauce
— **a la Monistrol** *a la mo·nees·trol*
monkfish with bechamel sauce
redondo ⓜ *re·don·do* round (of beef)
— **al horno** *al or·no* roast beef
regañaos ⓜ pl *re·ga·nya·os* pastry
stuffed with sardines &
red capsicum
relleno ⓜ *re·lye·no* stuffing
remolacha ⓕ *re·mo·la·cha* beetroot
reo ⓜ *re·o* sea trout
repollo ⓜ *re·po·lyo* cabbage
repostería ⓕ *re·pos·te·ree·a*
confectionery
requesón ⓜ *re·ke·son*
cottage cheese
riñón ⓜ *ree·nyon* kidney
róbalo ⓜ *ro·ba·lo* haddock • sea bass
rodaballo ⓜ *ro·da·ba·lyo* turbot • brill
romero ⓜ *ro·me·ro* rosemary
romesco ⓜ *ro·mes·ko* sweet red
capsicum, almond & garlic sauce
rosca ⓕ *ros·ka de kar·ne*
meatloaf wrapped in bacon
rosco ⓜ *ros·ko* small sweet bun
rossejat ⓜ *ro·se·dyat* rice with fish &
shellfish
rovellons ⓜ pl **a la plancha** *ro·ve·lyons
a la plan·cha* garlic mushrooms
ruibarbo ⓜ *roo·ee·bar·bo* rhubarb

S

salchicha ⓕ *sal·chee·cha* pork sausage
salchichón ⓜ *sal·chee·chon* cured &
peppery white sausage
salmón ⓜ *sal·mon* salmon
— **a la ribereña** *a la ree·be·re·nya*
salmon in a cider sauce
— **ahumado** *a·oo·ma·do* smoked
salmon
salmonete ⓜ *sal·mo·ne·te* red mullet
salmorejo ⓜ *sal·mo·re·kho* thick
gazpacho soup made from tomato,
bread, olive oil, vinegar, garlic &
green capsicum
— **de Córdoba** *de kor·do·ba* gazpacho
soup made with more vinegar than
usual
salpicón ⓜ *sal·pee·kon* fish or meat
salad
salsa ⓕ *sal·sa* sauce
— **alioli** *a·lee·o·lee* garlic & olive oil
vinaigrette • garlic mayonnaise
— **de holandesa** *de o·lan·de·sa*
hollandaise sauce
— **de mayonesa** *de ma·yo·ne·sa*
mayonnaise sauce
— **de tomate** *de to·ma·te* tomato sauce
— **inglesa** *een·gle·sa* Worcestershire
sauce
— **tártara** *tar·ta·ra* tartar sauce
— **verde** *ver·de* parsley & garlic sauce
samfaina ⓕ *sam·fai·na* grilled
vegetable sauce
sancocho ⓜ *san·ko·cho* fish dish
served with potatoes
sandía ⓕ *san·dee·a* watermelon
sándwich ⓜ *san·weech* sandwich
— **mixto** *meeks·to* toasted ham &
cheese sandwich
sanocho ⓜ **canario** *sa·no·cho ka·na·ryo*
baked monkfish with potatoes
sardinas ⓕ *sar·dee·nas* sardines
— **a la parrilla** *a la pa·ree·lya* sardines
grilled
— **en cazuela** *en ka·thwe·la* sardines
served in a clay pot

sargo m sar·go *bream*

sepia f se·pya *cuttlefish*

sesos m pl se·sos *brains*

setas f pl se·tas *wild mushrooms*
— **a la kashera** a la ka·she·ra *sauteed wild mushrooms*
— **rellenas** re·lye·nas *mushrooms stuffed*

sofrit pagés m so·freet pa·zhes *vegetable stew*

sofrito m so·free·to *fried tomato sauce*

soja f so·kha *soya bean*

soldaditos m pl **de Pavía** sol·da·dee·tos de pa·vee·a *cod fritters*

solomillo m so·lo·mee·lyo *fillet*

sopa f so·pa *soup*
— **del día** del dee·a *soup of the day*

sopas f pl **de leche** so·pas de le·che *pieces of bread soaked in milk & cinnamon*

sopas f pl **engañadas** so·pas en·ga·nya·das *soup made from capsicum, onion shoots, vinegar, figs & grapes*

sorbete m sor·be·te *sorbet*

sorropután m so·ro·poo·toon *tuna casserole*

suizo m swee·tho *sugared bun*

sukaldi soo·kal·dee *beef stew*

suquet m soo·ket *clams in almond sauce*

suquet de peix m soo·ket de peysh *fish stew*

suspiros m pl **de monja** soos·pee·ros de mon·kha *'nun's sighs' – custard sweets*

T

tallarines m pl ta·lya·ree·nes *pasta noodles*

tarta f tar·ta *cake • tart*
— **de almendra** de al·men·dra *almond tart*
— **de manzana** de man·tha·na *apple tart*

tartaleta f tar·ta·le·ta *tartlet*

tartaletas f pl **de huevos revueltos** tar·ta·le·tas de we·vos re·vwel·tos *scrambled egg tartlets*

ternera f ter·ne·ra *veal*
— **a la sevillana** a la se·vee·lya·na *veal served with whole olives*
— **en cazuela con berenjenas** en ka·thwe·la kon be·ren·khe·nas *veal & eggplant casserole*

tocino m to·thee·no *salted pork • bacon*
— **del cielo** del thye·lo *creamy dessert made with egg yolk & sugar, with a caramel topping*

tocrudo m to·kroo·do *'everything raw'– salad of meat, garlic, onion & green capsicum*

tomate m to·ma·te *tomatoes*
— **(de) pera** (de) pe·ra *plum tomato*
— **frito** free·to *tinned tomato sauce*

tomates m pl to·ma·tes
— **enteros y pelados** en·te·ros ee pe·la·dos *tinned whole tomatoes*
— **rellenos de atún** re·lye·nos de a·toon *tomatoes stuffed with tuna*

toro m to·ro *bull meat*

torrefacto m to·re·fak·to *dark-roasted coffee beans*

torrija f to·ree·kha *French toast*

torta f tor·ta *pie • tart • flat bread*
— **de aceite** de a·they·te *sweet, flat cake or biscuit made with oil*
— **pascualina** pas·kwa·lee·na *spinach & egg pie, eaten at Easter*

tortilla f tor·tee·lya *omelette*
— **española** es·pa·nyo·la *potato & onion omelette*
— **francesa** fran·the·sa *plain omelette*

tortillas f pl **de camarones** tor·tee·lyas de ka·ma·ro·nes *shrimp fritters*

tortita f tor·tee·ta *waffle*

tostada f tos·ta·da *toasted bread*

tocino m to·thee·no *bacon*

tripas f pl tree·pas *intestines • guts*

trucha f troo·cha *trout*
— **a la marinera** a la ma·ree·ne·ra *trout in a white wine sauce*

truchas ① pl *troo·*chas *trout*
— **a la navarra** a la na·va·ra *trout with ham*
— **con vino y romero** kon *vee·*no ee ro·*me·*ro *trout with red wine & rosemary*
trufa ① *troo·*fa *truffle*
— **tarta** *tar·*ta *chocolate truffle cake*
tumbet (de peix) ⓜ toom·*bet* (de peysh) *vegetable souffle, sometimes containing fish*
turrón ⓜ too·*ron Spanish nougat*

U

uva ① *oo·*va *grape*
— **de corinto** de ko·*reen·*to *currant*
— **pasa** *pa·*sa *raisin*
— **sultana** sool·*ta·*na *sultana*

V

vacuno ⓜ va·*koo·*no *beef*
venado ⓜ ve·*na·*do *venison*

verduras ① ver·*doo·*ras *vegetables*
vieira ① vee·*ey·*ra *scallop*
villagodio ⓜ vee·*lya·*go·dyo *large steak*
vinagre ⓜ vee·*na·*gre *vinegar*
visita ① vee·*see·*ta *almond cake*

Y

yemas ① pl *ye·*mas *small round cakes*
yogur ⓜ yo·*goor yogurt*

Z

zanahoria ① tha·na·*o·*rya *carrot*
zarangollo ⓜ tha·ran·*go·*lyo *fried zucchini*
zarzamora ① thar·tha·*mo·*ra *blackberry*
zarzuela ① **de mariscos** thar·*thwe·*la de ma·*rees·*kos *spicy shellfish stew*
zarzuela ① **de pescado** thar·*thwe·*la de pes·*ka·*do *fish in almond sauce*
zurrukutano thoo·roo·koo·*ta·*no *cod & green capsicum soup*

emergencies

emergencias

Help!	¡Socorro!	so·ko·ro
Stop!	¡Pare!	pa·re
Go away!	¡Váyase!	va·ya·se
Thief!	¡Ladrón!	lad·ron
Fire!	¡Fuego!	fwe·go
Watch out!	¡Cuidado!	kwee·da·do

It's an emergency.
  Es una emergencia.   es oo·na e·mer·khen·thya

Call the police!
  ¡Llame a la policía!   lya·me a la po·lee·thee·a

Call a doctor!
  ¡Llame a un médico!   lya·me a oon me·dee·ko

Call an ambulance!
  ¡Llame a una   lya·me a oo·na
  ambulancia!   am·boo·lan·thya

I'm ill.
  Estoy enfermo/a. m/f   es·toy en·fer·mo/a

My friend is ill.
  Mi amigo/a está   mee a·mee·go/a es·ta
  enfermo/a. m/f   en·fer·mo/a

Could you help me, please?
  ¿Me puede ayudar,   me pwe·de a·yoo·dar
  por favor?   por fa·vor

I have to use the telephone.
Necesito usar el
teléfono.
ne·the·*see*·to oo·*sar* el
te·*le*·fo·no

I'm lost.
Estoy perdido/a. m/f
es·*toy* per·*dee*·do/a

Where are the toilets?
¿Dónde están los
servicios?
don·de es·*tan* los
ser·*vee*·thyos

---

the underground

Petty crime is particularly common in Madrid and Barcelona. Try not to stand near the train doors and keep money out of sight. If someone attempts to rob you, try screaming these phrases at the top of your lungs:

Leave me alone!	*¡Déjame en paz!*	de·kha·me en path
Help, thief!	*¡Socorro, al ladron!*	so·ko·ro al lad·ron

---

police

la policia

In an emergency, call the police, who will then put you through to other emergency services (fire brigade and ambulance). For more on making a call, see **communications**, page 72.

Where's the police station?
¿Dónde está la
comisaría?
don·de es·*ta* la
ko·mee·sa·*ree*·a

I want to report an offence.
Quiero denunciar un
delito.
kye·ro de·noon·*thyar* oon
de·*lee*·to

He/She tried to assault me.
Él/Ella intentó
asaltarme.
el/e·lya een·ten·*to*
a·sal·*tar*·me

He/She tried to rob me.
Él/Ella intentó robarme.   el/e·lya een·ten·to ro·bar·me

I've been robbed.
Me han robado.   me an ro·ba·do

I've been raped.
He sido violado/a. m/f   e see·do vee·o·la·do/a

My ... was stolen.
Mi ... fue robado/a. m/f   mee ... fwe ro·ba·do/a

My ... were stolen.
Mis ... fueron robados/as. m/f   mee ... fwe·ron ro·ba·dos/as

I've lost my ...	*He perdido ...*	e per·dee·do ...
bags	*mis maletas*	mees ma·le·tas
money	*mi dinero*	mee dee·ne·ro
passport	*mi pasaporte*	mee pa·sa·por·te

I apologise.
Lo siento.   lo syen·to

I didn't realise I was doing anything wrong.
No sabía que estaba   no sa·bee·a ke es·ta·ba
haciendo algo mal.   a·thyen·do al·go mal

I'm innocent.
Soy inocente.   soy ee·no·then·te

I (don't) understand.
(No) Entiendo.   (no) en·tyen·do

I want to contact my embassy/consulate.
Quiero ponerme en   kye·ro po·ner·me en
contacto con mi   kon·tak·to kon mee
embajada/consulado.   em·ba·kha·da/kon·soo·la·do

Can I call a lawyer?
¿Puedo llamar a un   pwe·do lya·mar a oon
abogado?   a·bo·ga·do

I need a lawyer who speaks English.

Necesito un abogado   ne·the·*see*·to oon a·bo·*ga*·do
que hable inglés.   ke *a*·ble een·*gles*

Can I pay an on-the-spot fine?

¿Podemos pagar una   po·*de*·mos pa·*gar* oo·na
multa al contado?   *mool*·ta al kon·*ta*·do

This drug is for personal use.

Esta droga es para uso   es·ta *dro*·ga es *pa*·ra oo·so
personal.   per·so·*nal*

I have a prescription for this drug.

Tengo receta para esta   *ten*·go re·*the*·ta *pa*·ra es·ta
droga.   *dro*·ga

What am I accused of?

¿De qué me acusan?   de ke me a·*ku*·san

the police may say ...

You have overstayed your visa.

El plazo de tu   el *pla*·tho de too
visado se ha pasado.   vee·*sa*·do se a pa·*sa*·do

You'll be charged with ...

Será acusado/a de ... m/f   se·*ra* a·koo·*sa*·do/a de ...

He'll/She'll be charged with ...

Él/Ella será acusado/a   el/e·lya se·*ra* a·koo·*sa*·do/a
de ...   de ...

assault	*asalto*	a·*sal*·to
possession	*posesión*	po·se·*syon*
(of illegal	*(de sustancias*	(de soos·*tan*·thyas
substances)	*ilegales)*	ee·le·*ga*·les)
shoplifting	*ratería*	ra·te·*ree*·a
speeding	*exceso de*	eks·*the*·so de
	velocidad	ve·lo·thee·*da*

SAFE TRAVEL

178

doctor

el médico

Where's the nearest ...?	¿Dónde está ... más cercano/a? m/f	don·de es·ta ... mas ther·ka·no/a
chemist	la farmacia f	la far·ma·thya
dentist	el dentista m	el den·tees·ta
doctor	el médico m	el me·dee·ko
hospital	el hospital m	el os·pee·tal
medical centre	el consultorio m	el kon·sool·to·ryo
optometrist	el oculista m	el o·koo·lees·ta

I've been vaccinated for ...	Estoy vacunado/a contra ... m/f	es·toy va·koo·na·do/a kon·tra ...
He's/She's been vaccinated for ...	Está vacunado/a contra ... m/f	es·ta va·koo·na·do/a kon·tra ...
tetanus	el tétano m	el te·ta·no
typhoid	la tifus	la tee·foos
hepatitis	la hepatitis	la e·pa·tee·tees
A/B/C	A/B/C	a/be/the
... fever	la fiebre ...	la fye·bre ...

I need a doctor (who speaks English).
Necesito un doctor (que hable inglés).   ne·the·see·to oon dok·tor (ke a·ble een·gles)

I'm sick.
Estoy enfermo/a. m/f   es·toy en·fer·mo/a

Could I see a female doctor?
¿Puede examinarme una doctora?   pwe·de ek·sa·mee·nar·me oo·na dok·to·ra

For women's medical issues, see **women's health**, page 183.

the doctor may say ...

What's the problem?
¿Qué le pasa?   ke le *pa*·sa

Where does it hurt?
¿Dónde le duele?   *don*·de le *dwe*·le

Do you have a temperature?
¿Tiene fiebre?   *tye*·ne *fye*·bre

How long have you been like this?
¿Desde cuándo se   *des*·de *kwan*·do se
siente así?   *syen*·te a·*see*

Have you had this before?
¿Ha tenido esto antes?   a te·*nee*·do es·to *an*·tes

Have you had unprotected sex?
¿Ha tenido relaciones   a te·*nee*·do re·la·*thyo*·nes
sexuales sin   sek·*swa*·les seen
protección?   pro·tek·*thyon*

Are you allergic?
¿Tiene usted alergias?   *tye*·ne oos·te a·*ler*·khyas

Are you on medication?
¿Se encuentra   se en·*kwen*·tra
bajo medicación?   *ba*·kho me·dee·ka·*thyon*

You need to be admitted to hospital.
Necesita ingresar   ne·the·*see*·ta een·gre·*sar*
en un hospital.   en oon os·pee·*tal*

How long are you travelling for?
Por cuánto tiempo   por *kwan*·to *tyem*·po
está viajando.   es·*ta* vya·*khan*·do

You should have it checked when you go home.
Debería revisarlo   de·be·*ree*·a re·vee·*sar*·lo
cuando vuelva a casa.   *kwan*·do *vwel*·va a *ka*·sa

Do you ...?	¿Usted ...?	oos·te ...
drink	bebe	*be*·be
smoke	fuma	*foo*·ma
take drugs	toma drogas	*to*·ma *dro*·gas

I've run out of my medication.
Se me terminaron los   se me ter·mee·*na*·ron los
medicamentos.   me·dee·ka·*men*·tos

This is my usual medicine.
Éste es mi medicamento   es·te es mee me·dee·ka·*men*·to
habitual.   a·bee·too·*al*

My prescription is ...
Mi receta es ...   mee re·*the*·ta es ...

I don't want a blood transfusion.
No quiero que me hagan   no *kye*·ro ke me a·gan
una transfusión de   oo·na trans·foo·*syon* de
sangre.   san·gre

Please use a new syringe.
Por favor, use una   por fa·*vor* oo·se oo·na
jeringa nueva.   khe·*reen*·ga nwe·va

I need new ...	*Necesito ...*	ne·the·*see*·to ...
	nuevas.	nwe·vas
glasses	*gafas*	ga·fas
contact	*lentes de*	*len*·tes de
lenses	*contacto*	kon·*tak*·to

For cost & receipts, see **shopping**, page 64

symptoms & conditions

los síntomas & las condiciones

I have ...
Tengo ...   ten·go ...

I've recently had ...
Hace poco he tenido ...   a·the po·ko e te·nee·do ...

There's a history of ...
Hay antecedentes de ...   ai an·te·the·*den*·tes de ...

I'm on regular medication for ...
Estoy bajo   es·*toy* ba·kho
medicación para ...   me·dee·ka·*thyon* pa·ra ...

asthma	asma m	as·ma
diarrhoea	diarrea f	dee·a·re·a
fever	fiebre f	fye·bre
infection	infección f	in·fek·thyon
sprain	torcedura f	tor·the·doo·ra

It hurts here.
Me duele aquí. — me dwe·le a·kee

I've been injured.
He sido herido/a. m/f — e see·do e·ree·do/a

I've been vomiting.
He estado vomitando. — e es·ta·do vo·mee·tan·do

I'm dehydrated.
Estoy deshidratado/a. m/f — es·toy de·seed·ra·ta·do/a

I can't sleep.
No puedo dormir. — no pwe·do dor·meer

I think it's the medication I'm on.
Me parece que son los medicamentos que estoy tomando. — me pa·re·the ke son los me·dee·ka·men·tos ke es·toy to·man·do

I feel ...	Me siento ...	me syen·to ...
better	mejor	me·khor
depressed	deprimido/a m/f	de·pree·mee·do
dizzy	mareado/a m/f	ma·re·a·do
shivery	destemplado/a m/f	des·tem·pla·do
strange	raro/a m/f	ra·ro
weak	débil	de·beel
worse	peor	pe·or

For more symptoms & conditions, see the **dictionary**.

women's health

la salud femenina

I think I'm pregnant.
  Creo que estoy embarazada. kre·o ke es·*toy* em·ba·ra·*tha*·da

I haven't had my period for ... weeks.
  Hace ... semanas que no a·the ... se·*ma*·nas ke no
  me viene la regla. me *vye*·ne la *reg*·la

I need a pregnancy test.
  Necesito una prueba ne·the·*see*·to *oo*·na *prwe*·ba
  de embarazo. de em·ba·*ra*·tho

I'm on the Pill.
  Tomo la píldora. to·mo la *peel*·do·ra

I've noticed a lump here.
  He notado que tengo e no·*ta*·do ke *ten*·go
  un bulto aquí. oon *bool*·to a·*kee*

I need ...	*Quisiera ...*	kee·*sye*·ra ...
contraception	*usar algún*	oo·*sar* al·*goon*
	método anti-	*me*·to·do an·tee·
	conceptivo	kon·thep·*tee*·vo
the morning-	*tomar la*	to·*mar* la
after pill	*píldora del*	*peel*·do·ra del
	día siguiente	*dee*·a see·*gyen*·te

the doctor may say ...

Are you pregnant?
  ¿Está embarazada? es·*ta* em·ba·ra·*tha*·da

You're pregnant.
  Está embarazada. es·*ta* em·ba·ra·*tha*·da

When did you last have your period?
  ¿Cuándo le vino la *kwan*·do le *vee*·no la
  regla por última vez? *reg*·la por *ool*·tee·ma veth

Are you using contraception?
  ¿Usa anticonceptivos? oo·sa an·tee·kon·thep·*tee*·vos

Do you have your period?
  ¿Tiene la regla? *tye*·ne la *reg*·la

allergies

I'm allergic to ...	Soy alérgico/a ... m/f	soy a·ler·khee·ko/a ...
He's/She's allergic to ...	Es alérgico/a ... m/f	es a·ler·khee·ko/a ...
antibiotics	a los antibióticos	a los an·tee·byo·tee·kos
anti-inflammatories	a los anti-inflamatorios	a los an·tee·een·fla·ma·to·ryos
aspirin	a la aspirina	a la as·pee·ree·na
bees	a las abejas	a las a·be·khas
codeine	a la codeina	a la ko·de·ee·na
nuts	a las nueces	a las nwe·thes
peanuts	a los cacahuetes	a los ka·ka·we·tes
penicillin	a la penicilina	a la pe·nee·thee·lee·na
pollen	al polen	al po·len

For more food-related allergies, see **vegetarian & special meals** page 160.

I have a skin allergy.
Tengo una alergia en la piel.
ten·go oo·na a·ler·khya en la pyel

I'm on a special diet.
Estoy a régimen especial.
es·toy a re·khee·men es·pe·thyal

inhaler	inhalador m	een·a·la·dor
injection	inyección f	een·yek·thyon
antihistamines	antihista-mínicos m pl	an·tees·ta-mee·nee·kos

alternative treatments

tratamientos alternativos

I don't use Western medicine.
No uso la medicina occidental.

no *oo*·so la me·dee·*thee*·na ok·thee·den·*tal*

I prefer ...
Prefiero ...

pre·*fye*·ro ...

Can I see someone who practises ...?
¿Puedo ver a alguien que practique ...?

pwe·do ver al·gyen ke prak·*tee*·ke ...

parts of the body

las partes del cuerpo

My ... hurts.
Me duele ...

me *dwe*·le ...

I can't move my ...
No puedo mover ...

no *pwe*·do mo·ver ...

I have a cramp in my ...
Tengo calambres en ...

ten·go ka·*lam*·bres en ...

My ... is swollen.
Mi ... está hinchado.

mee ... es·ta een·*cha*·do

health

185

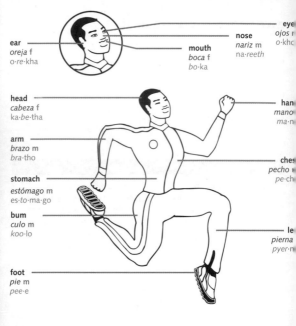

eye
ojos m
o·kho

nose
nariz m
na·reeth

mouth
boca f
bo·ka

ear
oreja f
o·re·kha

head
cabeza f
ka·be·tha

han
mano
ma·n

arm
brazo m
bra·tho

stomach
estómago m
es·to·ma·go

che
pecho
pe·ch

bum
culo m
koo·lo

le
pierna
pyer·n

foot
pie m
pee·e

chemist

la farmacia

Is there a (night) chemist nearby?
¿Hay una farmacia (de
guardía) por aquí?

ai oo·na far·ma·thya (de
gwar·dee·a) por a·kee

I need something for ...
Necesito algo para ...

ne·the·see·to al·go pa·ra ...

Do I need a prescription for ...?
¿Necesito receta
para ...?

ne·the·see·to re·the·ta
pa·ra ...

I have a prescription.
  Tengo receta médica.   ten·go re·*the*·ta me·dee·ka

How many times a day?
  ¿Cuántas veces al día?   kwan·tas ve·thes al *dee*·a

dentist

el dentista

I have a broken tooth.
  Se me ha roto un diente.   se me a *ro*·to oon *dyen*·te

I have a toothache.
  Me duele una muela.   me *dwe*·le *oo*·na *mwe*·la

health

187

I've lost a filling.
Se me ha caído un
empaste.

se me a ka·*ee*·do oon
em·*pas*·te

My gums hurt.
Me duelen las encías.

me *dwe*·len las en·*thee*·as

I don't want it extracted.
No quiero que me lo saquen.

no *kye*·ro ke me lo *sa*·ken

I need a/an ...	*Necesito ...*	ne·the·*see*·to ...
anaesthetic	*una anestesia*	*oo*·ne a·nes·*te*·sya
filling	*un empaste*	oon em·*pas*·te

signs		
Asistencia Sanitaria	a·see·*sten*·thee·a sa·nee·*ta*·ree·a	**First Aid**
Farmacia	far·ma·*thee*·a	**Pharmacy/ Drug Store**
Horas de Visita	o·ras de vee·see·ta	**Visiting Hours**
Hospital	o·spee·*tal*	**Hospital**
Médico	*me*·dee·ko	**Doctor**
Planta	*plan*·ta	**Ward**
Urgencias	ur·*khen*·thee·as	**Casualty/ Emergency**

SUSTAINABLE TRAVEL

As the climate change debate heats up, the matter of sustainability becomes an important part of the travel vernacular. In practical terms, this means assessing our impact on the environment and local cultures and economies – and acting to make that impact as positive as possible. Here are some basic phrases to get you on your way …

communication & cultural differences

Would you like me to teach you some English?
¿Quieres que te enseñe   kye·res ke te en·se·nye
algo de inglés?   al·go de een·gles

Is this a local or national custom?
¿Esto es una costumbre   es·to es oo·na kos·toom·bre
local o nacional?   lo·kal o na·thyo·nal

I respect your customs.
Respeto sus costumbres.   res·pe·to soos kos·toom·bres

community benefit & involvement

What sorts of issues is this community facing?
¿A qué tipo de problemas se   a ke tee·po de pro·ble·mas se
enfrenta esta comunidad?   en·fren·ta es·ta ko·moo·nee·da

climate change	*cambio*	*kam*·byo
	climático m	klee·*ma*·tee·ko
freedom of	*libertad de*	lee·ber·*ta* de
religion	*religión* f	re·lee·*khyon*
interregional	*tirantez*	tee·ran·*teth*
tension	*interregional* f	een·ter·re·khyo·*nal*
racism	*racismo* m	ra·*thees*·mo
unemployment	*desempleo* m	des·em·*ple*·o

I'd like to volunteer my skills.

*Me gustaría ofrecer mis
conocimientos.*

me goos·ta·ree·a o·fre·*ther* mees
ko·no·thee·*myen*·tos

Are there any volunteer programs available in the area?

*¿Hay programas de
voluntariado en la zona?*

ai pro·*gra*·mas de
vo·loon·ta·*rya*·do en la *tho*·na

environment

Where can I recycle this?

*¿Dónde se puede
reciclar esto?*

don·de se *pwe*·de
re·thee·*klar* es·to

transport

Can we get there by public transport?

*¿Se puede ir en transporte
público?*

se *pwe*·de eer en trans·*por*·te
poo·blee·ko

Can we get there by bike?

¿Se puede ir en bici?

se *pwe*·de eer en *bee*·thee

I'd prefer to walk there.

Prefiero ir a pie.

pre·*fye*·ro eer a pye

accommodation

I'd like to stay at a locally-run hotel.

*Me gustaría alojarme
en un hotel del barrio.*

me goos·ta·*ree*·a a·lo·*khar*·me
en oon o·*tel* del *ba*·ryo

Are there any ecolodges here?

*¿Hay algún ecolodge
por aquí?*

ai al·*goon* e·ko·loch
por a·*kee*

Can I turn the air conditioning off and open the window?

*¿Puedo apagar el aire
acondicionado y abrir
la ventana?*

pwe·do a·pa·*gar* el *ai*·re
a·kon·dee·thyo·*na*·do ee a·*breer*
la ven·*ta*·na

There's no need to change my sheets.

No hace falta cambiar no a·the *fal*·ta kam·*byar*
las sábanas. las *sa*·ba·nas

shopping

Where can I buy locally produced goods/souvenirs?

¿Dónde puedo comprar *don*·de *pwe*·do kom·*prar*
recuerdos de la zona? re·*kwer*·dos de la *tho*·na

Do you sell Fair Trade products?

¿Se venden productos de se *ven*·den pro·*dook*·tos de
comercio equitativo? ko·*mer*·thyo e·kee·ta·*tee*·vo

food

Do you sell ...?	¿Se venden ...?	se *ven*·den ...
locally produced food	*comestibles de la zona*	ko·mes·*tee*·bles de la *tho*·na
organic produce	*productos agrícolas biológicos*	pro·*dook*·tos a·*gree*·ko·las bee·o·*lo*·khee·kos

Can you tell me which traditional foods I should try?

¿Que platos típicos ke *pla*·tos *tee*·pee·kos
debería probar? de·be·*ree*·a pro·*bar*

sightseeing

Are cultural tours available?

¿Se pueden hacer se *pwe*·den a·*ther*
recorridos culturales? re·ko·*ree*·dos kool·too·*ra*·les

Does the guide speak any of the regional languages?

¿El guía habla alguna el *gee*·a a·bla al·*goo*·na
lengua regional? *len*·gwa re·*khyo*·nal

Basque	euskera m	e·oos·ke·ra
Catalan	catalán m	ka·ta·lan
Galician	gallego m	ga·lye·go
Does your company ...?	Su empresa ...?	soo em·pre·sa ...
donate money to charity	hace donativos a organizaciones benéficas	a·the do·na·ti·vos a or·ga·nee·tha·thyo·nes be·ne·fee·kas
hire local guides	contrata a guías de la zona	kon·tra·ta a gee·as de la tho·na
visit local businesses	visita a negocios locales	vee·see·ta a ne·go·thyos lo·ka·les

Nouns in the dictionary have their gender indicated by ⓜ or ⓕ. If it's a plural noun, you'll also see pl. Where a word that could be either a noun or a verb has no gender indicated, it's a verb.

A

(to be) able *poder* po·der
aboard *a bordo* a bor·do
abortion *aborto* ⓜ a·bor·to
about *sobre* so·bre
above *arriba* a·ree·ba
abroad *en el extranjero* en el eks·tran·khe·ro
accept *aceptar* a·thep·tar
accident *accidente* ⓜ ak·thee·den·te
accommodation *alojamiento* ⓜ a·lo·kha·myen·to
across *a través* a tra·ves
activist *activista* ⓜ&ⓕ ak·tee·vees·ta
acupuncture *acupuntura* ⓕ a·koo·poon·too·ra
adaptor *adaptador* ⓜ a·dap·ta·dor
address *dirección* ⓕ dee·rek·thyon
administration *administración* ⓕ ad·mee·nees·tra·thyon
admission price *precio* ⓜ *de entrada* pre·thyo de en·tra·da
admit *admitir* ad·mee·teer
adult *adulto* ⓜ a·dool·to
advertisement *anuncio* ⓜ a·noon·thyo
advice *consejo* ⓜ kon·se·kho
aerobics *aeróbic* ⓜ ai·ro·beek
Africa *África* ⓕ a·free·ka
after *después de* des·pwes de
aftershave *bálsamo de aftershave* bal·sa·mo de ahf·ter·sha·eev
again *otra vez* o·tra veth
age *edad* ⓕ e·da
aggressive *agresivo/a* ⓜ/ⓕ a·gre·see·vo/a

agree *estar de acuerdo* es·tar de a·kwer·do
agriculture *agricultura* ⓕ a·gree·kul·too·ra
AIDS *SIDA* ⓜ see·da
air *aire* ⓜ ai·re
air mail *por vía aérea* por vee·a a·e·re·a
air-conditioned *con aire acondicionado* kon ai·re a·kon·dee·thyo·na·do
air-conditioning *aire* ⓜ *acondicionado* ai·re a·kon·dee·thyo·na·do
airline *aerolínea* ⓕ ay·ro·lee·nya
airport *aeropuerto* ⓜ ay·ro·pwer·to
airport tax *tasa* ⓕ *del aeropuerto* ta·sa del ay·ro·pwer·to
alarm clock *despertador* ⓜ des·per·ta·dor
alcohol *alcohol* ⓜ al·col
all *todo* to·do
allergy *alergia* ⓕ a·ler·khya
allow *permitir* per·mee·teer
almonds *almendras* ⓕ pl al·men·dras
almost *casi* ka·see
alone *solo/a* ⓜ/ⓕ so·lo/a
already *ya* ya
also *también* tam·byen
altar *altar* ⓜ al·tar
altitude *altura* ⓕ al·too·ra
always *siempre* syem·pre
amateur *amateur* ⓜ&ⓕ a·ma·ter
ambassador *embajador/embajadora* ⓜ/ⓕ em·ba·kha·dor/em·ba·kha·do·ra
among *entre* en·tre
anarchist *anarquista* ⓜ&ⓕ a·nar·kees·ta
ancient *antiguo/a* ⓜ/ⓕ an·tee·gwo/a
and *y* ee
angry *enfadado/a* ⓜ/ⓕ en·fa·da·do/a

animal *animal* ⓜ a·nee·mal
ankle *tobillo* ⓜ to·bee·lyo
answer *respuesta* ⓕ res·pwes·ta
answering machine *contestador* ⓜ
   automático kon·tes·ta·dor
   ow·to·ma·tee·ko
ant *hormiga* ⓕ or·mee·ga
anthology *antología* ⓕ an·to·lo·khee·a
antibiotics *antibióticos* ⓜ pl
   an·tee·byo·tee·kos
antinuclear *antinuclear* an·tee·noo·kle·ar
antique *antigüedad* ⓕ an·tee·gwe·da
antiseptic *antiséptico* ⓜ
   an·tee·sep·tee·ko
any *alguno/a* ⓜ/ⓕ al·goo·no/a
appendix *apéndice* ⓜ a·pen·dee·the
apple *manzana* ⓕ man·tha·na
appointment *cita* ⓕ thee·ta
apricot *albaricoque* ⓜ al·ba·ree·ko·ke
archaeological *arqueológico/a* ⓜ/ⓕ
   ar·keo·lo·khee·ko/a
architect *arquitecto/a* ⓜ/ⓕ
   ar·kee·tek·to/a
architecture *arquitectura* ⓕ
   ar·kee·tek·too·ra
argue *discutir* dees·koo·teer
arm *brazo* ⓜ bra·tho
army *ejército* ⓜ e·kher·thee·to
arrest *detener* de·te·ner
arrivals *llegadas* ⓕ pl lye·ga·das
arrive *llegar* lye·gar
art *arte* ⓜ ar·te
art gallery *museo* ⓜ *de arte* moo·se·o
   de ar·te
artichoke *alcachofa* ⓕ al·ka·cho·fa
artist *artista* ⓜ&ⓕ ar·tees·ta
ashtray *cenicero* ⓜ the·nee·the·ro
Asia *Asia* ⓕ a·sya
ask (a question) *preguntar* pre·goon·tar
ask (for something) *pedir* pe·deer
aspirin *aspirina* ⓕ as·pee·ree·na
assault *asalto* ⓜ a·sal·to
asthma *asma* ⓜ as·ma
athletics *atletismo* ⓜ at·le·tees·mo
atmosphere *atmósfera* ⓕ at·mos·fe·ra
aubergine *berenjena* ⓕ be·ren·khe·na
aunt *tía* ⓕ tee·a

Australia *Australia* ⓕ ow·stra·lya
Australian Rules football *fútbol* ⓜ
   australiano foot·bol ow·stra·lya·no
automatic teller machine *cajero* ⓜ
   automático ka·khe·ro
   ow·to·ma·tee·ko
autumn *otoño* ⓜ o·to·nyo
avenue *avenida* ⓕ a·ve·nee·da
avocado *aguacate* ⓜ a·gwa·ka·te

B

B&W (film) *blanco y negro* blan·ko
   ee ne·gro
baby *bebé* ⓜ be·be
baby food *comida* ⓕ *de bebé*
   ko·mee·da de be·be
baby powder *talco* ⓜ tal·ko
babysitter *canguros* ⓜ kan·goo·ros
back (of body) *espalda* ⓕ es·pal·da
back (of chair) *respaldo* ⓜ res·pal·do
backpack *mochila* ⓕ mo·chee·la
bacon *tocino* ⓜ to·thee·no
bad *malo/a* ⓜ/ⓕ ma·lo/a
bag *bolso* ⓜ bol·so
baggage *equipaje* ⓜ e·kee·pa·khe
baggage allowance *límite de*
   equipaje lee·mee·te de e·kee·pa·khe
baggage claim *recogida* ⓕ *de*
   equipajes re·ko·khee·da de
   e·kee·pa·khes
bakery *panadería* ⓕ pa·na·de·ree·a
balance (account) *saldo* ⓜ sal·do
balcony *balcón* ⓜ bal·kon
ball *pelota* ⓕ pe·lo·ta
ballet *ballet* ⓜ ba·le
banana *plátano* ⓜ pla·ta·no
band *grupo* ⓜ groo·po
bandage *vendaje* ⓜ ven·da·khe
band-aids *tiritas* ⓕ pl tee·ree·tas
bank *banco* ⓜ ban·ko
bank account *cuenta* ⓕ *bancaria*
   kwen·ta ban·ka·rya
banknotes *billetes* ⓜ pl *(de banco)*
   bee·lye·tes (de ban·ko)
baptism *bautizo* ⓜ bow·tee·tho

bar *bar* ⓜ bar
bar (with music) *pub* ⓜ poob
bar work *trabajo* ⓜ *de camarero/a* ⓜ/ⓕ tra·*ba*·kho de ka·ma·*re*·ro/a
baseball *béisbol* ⓜ beys·bol
basket *canasta* ⓕ ka·*nas*·ta
basketball *baloncesto* ⓜ ba·lon·*thes*·to
bath *bañera* ⓕ ba·*nye*·ra
bathing suit *bañador* ⓜ ba·nya·*dor*
bathroom *baño* ⓜ *ba*·nyo
battery (car) *batería* ⓕ ba·te·*ree*·a
battery (small) *pila* ⓕ *pee*·la
be *ser* ser • *estar* es·*tar*
beach *playa* ⓕ *pla*·ya
bean sprouts *brotes* ⓜ pl *de soja* *bro*·tes de so·kha
beans *judías* khoo·*dee*·as
beautiful *hermoso/a* ⓜ/ⓕ er·*mo*·so/a
beauty salon *salón* ⓜ *de belleza* sa·*lon* de be·*lye*·tha
because *porque* por·*ke*
bed *cama* ⓕ *ka*·ma
bedding *ropa* ⓕ *de cama* *ro*·pa de *ka*·ma
bedroom *habitación* ⓕ a·bee·ta·*thyon*
bee *abeja* ⓕ a·*be*·kha
beef *carne* ⓕ *de vaca* *kar*·ne de *va*·ka
beer *cerveza* ⓕ ther·*ve*·tha
beetroot *remolacha* ⓕ re·mo·*la*·cha
before *antes* *an*·tes
beggar *mendigo/a* ⓜ/ⓕ men·*dee*·go/a
begin *comenzar* ko·men·*thar*
behind *detrás de* de·*tras* de
below *abajo* a·*ba*·kho
best *lo mejor* lo me·*khor*
bet *apuesta* ⓕ a·*pwes*·ta
better *mejor* me·*khor*
between *entre* *en*·tre
bible *biblia* ⓕ *bee*·blya
bicycle *bicicleta* ⓕ bee·thee·*kle*·ta
big *grande* *gran*·de
bike *bici* ⓕ *bee*·thee
bike chain *cadena* ⓕ *de bici* ka·*de*·na de *bee*·thee
bike path *camino* ⓜ *de bici* ka·*mee*·no de *bee*·thee
bill *cuenta* ⓕ *kwen*·ta

biodegradable *biodegradable* bee·o·de·gra·*da*·ble
biography *biografía* ⓕ bee·o·gra·*fee*·a
bird *pájaro* ⓜ *pa*·kha·ro
birth certificate *partida* ⓕ *de nacimiento* par·*tee*·da de na·thee·*myen*·to
birthday *cumpleaños* ⓜ koom·ple·a·nyos
birthday cake *pastel* ⓜ *de cumpleaños* pas·*tel* de koom·ple·a·nyos
biscuit ⓕ *galleta* ga·*lye*·ta
bite (dog) *mordedura* ⓕ mor·de·*doo*·ra
bite (food) *bocado* ⓜ bo·*ka*·do
bite (insect) *picadura* ⓕ pee·ka·*doo*·ra
black *negro/a* ⓜ/ⓕ *ne*·gro/a
blanket *manta* ⓕ *man*·ta
bleed *sangrar* san·*grar*
blind *ciego/a* ⓜ/ⓕ *thye*·go/a
blister *ampolla* ⓕ am·*po*·lya
blocked *atascado/a* ⓜ/ⓕ a·tas·*ka*·do/a
blood *sangre* ⓕ *san*·gre
blood group *grupo* ⓜ *sanguíneo* *groo*·po san·*gee*·neo
blood pressure *presión* ⓕ *arterial* pre·*syon* ar·te·*ryal*
blood test *análisis* ⓜ *de sangre* a·*na*·lee·sees de *san*·gre
blue *azul* a·*thool*
board (ship, etc) *embarcarse* em·bar·*kar*·se
boarding house *pensión* ⓕ pen·*syon*
boarding pass *tarjeta* ⓕ *de embarque* tar·*khe*·ta de em·*bar*·ke
bone *hueso* ⓜ *we*·so
book *libro* ⓜ *lee*·bro
book (make a reservation) *reservar* re·ser·*var*
booked out *lleno/a* ⓜ/ⓕ *lye*·no/a
bookshop *librería* ⓕ lee·bre·*ree*·a
boots *botas* ⓕ pl bo·tas
border *frontera* ⓕ fron·*te*·ra
boring *aburrido/a* ⓜ/ⓕ a·boo·*ree*·do/a
borrow *tomar prestado* to·*mar* pres·*ta*·do
botanic garden *jardín* ⓜ *botánico* khar·*deen* bo·*ta*·nee·ko
both *dos* ⓜ/ⓕ pl dos

bottle *botella* ① bo·te·lya
bottle opener *abrebotellas* ⑩ a·bre·bo·te·lyas
bowl *bol* ⑩ bol
box *caja* ① ka·kha
boxer shorts *calzones* ⑩ pl kal·tho·nes
boxing *boxeo* ⑩ bo·se·o
boy *chico* ⑩ chee·ko
boyfriend *novio* ⑩ no·vyo
bra *sujetador* ⑩ soo·khe·ta·dor
Braille *Braille* ⑩ brai·lye
brakes *frenos* ⑩ pl fre·nos
branch office *sucursal* ① soo·koor·sal
brandy *coñac* ⑩ ko·nyak
brave *valiente* va·lyen·te
bread *pan* ⑩ pan
  brown bread *pan moreno* pan mo·re·no
  bread rolls *bollos* bo·lyos
  rye *pan de centeno* pan de then·te·no
  sourdough *pan de masa fermentada* pan de ma·sa fer·men·ta·da
  white bread *pan blanco* pan blan·ko
  wholemeal *integral* een·te·gral
break *romper* rom·per
break down *descomponerse* des·kom·po·ner·se
breakfast *desayuno* ⑩ des·a·yoo·no
breasts *senos* ⑩ pl se·nos
breathe *respirar* res·pee·rar
bribe *soborno* ⑩ so·bor·no
bribe *sobornar* so·bor·nar
bridge *puente* ⑩ pwen·te
briefcase *maletín* ⑩ ma·le·teen
brilliant *cojonudo/a* ⑩/① ko·kho·noo·do/a
bring *traer* tra·er
brochure *folleto* ⑩ fo·lye·to
broken *roto/a* ⑩/① ro·to/a
bronchitis *bronquitis* ⑩ bron·kee·tees
brother *hermano* ⑩ er·ma·no
brown *marrón* ma·ron
bruise *cardenal* ⑩ kar·de·nal
brussels sprouts *coles* ⑩ pl *de Bruselas* ko·les de broo·se·las

bucket *cubo* ⑩ koo·bo
Buddhist *budista* ⑩&① boo·dees·ta
buffet *buffet* ⑩ boo·fe
bug *bicho* ⑩ bee·cho
build *construir* kons·troo·eer
building *edificio* ⑩ e·dee·fee·thyo
bull *toro* ⑩ to·ro
bullfight *corrida* ① ko·ree·da
bullring *plaza* ① *de toros* pla·tha de to·ros
bum (of body) *culo* ⑩ koo·lo
burn *quemadura* ① ke·ma·doo·ra
bus *autobús* ⑩ ow·to·boos
bus (intercity) *autocar* ⑩ ow·to·kar
bus station *estación de autobuses/autocares* ① es·ta·thyon de ow·to·boo·ses/ow·to·ka·res
bus stop *parada* ① *de autobús* pa·ra·da de ow·to·boos
business *negocios* ⑩ pl ne·go·thyos
business class *clase* ① *preferente* kla·se pre·fe·ren·te
business person *comerciante* ⑩&① ko·mer·thyan·te
busker *artista callejero/a* ⑩/① ar·tees·ta ka·lye·khe·ro/a
busy *ocupado/a* ⑩/① o·koo·pa·do/a
but *pero* pe·ro
butcher's shop *carnicería* ① kar·nee·the·ree·a
butter *mantequilla* ① man·te·kee·lya
butterfly *mariposa* ① ma·ree·po·sa
buttons *botones* ⑩ pl bo·to·nes
buy *comprar* kom·prar

C

cabbage *col* kol
cable *cable* ⑩ ka·ble
cable car *teleférico* ⑩ te·le·fe·ree·ko
café *café* ⑩ ka·fe
cake *pastel* ⑩ pas·tel
cake shop *pastelería* ① pas·te·le·ree·a
calculator *calculadora* ① kal·koo·la·do·ra
calendar *calendario* ⑩ ka·len·da·ryo

calf *ternero* ⑩ ter·ne·ro

camera *cámara* ① (fotográfica)
ka·ma·ra (fo·to·gra·fee·ka)

camera shop *tienda* ① *de fotografía*
tyen·da de fo·to·gra·fee·a

camp *acampar* a·kam·par

camping store *tienda* ① *de*
provisiones de cámping tyen·da de
pro·vee·syo·nes de kam·peen

campsite *cámping* ⑩ kam·peen

can *lata* ① la·ta

can (be able) *poder* po·der

can opener *abrelatas* ⑩ a·bre·la·tas

Canada *Canadá* ⑩ ka·na·da

cancel *cancelar* kan·the·lar

cancer *cáncer* ⑩ kan·ther

candle *vela* ① ve·la

cantaloupe *cantalupo* ⑩ kan·ta·loo·po

capsicum (red/green) *pimiento* ⑩
rojo/verde pee·myen·to ro·kho/
ver·de

car *coche* ⑩ ko·che

car hire *alquiler* ⑩ *de coche* al·kee·ler
de ko·che

car owner's title *papeles* ⑩ pl *del*
coche pa·pe·les del ko·che

car registration *matrícula* ①
ma·tree·koo·la

caravan *caravana* ① ka·ra·va·na

cards *cartas* ① pl kar·tas

care (about something) *preocuparse*
por pre·o·koo·par·se por

care (for someone) *cuidar de* kwee·dar de

caring *bondadoso/a* ⑩/①
bon·da·do·so/a

carpark *aparcamiento* ⑩ a·par·ka·myen·to

carpenter *carpintero/a* ⑩/①
kar·peen·te·ro/a

carrot *zanahoria* ① tha·na·o·rya

carry *llevar* lye·var

carton *cartón* ⑩ kar·ton

cash *dinero* ⑩ *en efectivo* dee·ne·ro en
e·fek·tee·vo

cash (a cheque) *cambiar (un cheque)*
kam·byar (oon che·ke)

cash register *caja* ① *registradora*
ka·kha re·khees·tra·do·ra

cashew nut *anacardo* ⑩ a·na·kar·do

cashier *caja* ① ka·kha

casino *casino* ⑩ ka·see·no

cassette *casete* ⑩ ka·se·te

castle *castillo* ⑩ kas·tee·lyo

casual work *trabajo* ⑩ *eventual*
tra·ba·kho e·ven·twal

cat *gato/a* ⑩/① ga·to/a

cathedral *catedral* ① ka·te·dral

Catholic *católico/a* ⑩/① ka·to·lee·ko/a

cauliflower *coliflor* ① ko·lee·flor

caves *cuevas* ① pl kwe·vas

CD *cómpact* ⑩ kom·pakt

celebrate (an event) *celebrar* the·le·brar

celebration *celebración* ①
the·le·bra·thyon

cemetery *cementerio* ⑩ the·men·te·ryo

cent *centavo* ⑩ then·ta·vo

centimetre *centímetro* ⑩ then·tee·me·tro

central heating *calefacción* ① *central*
ka·le·fak·thyon then·tral

centre *centro* ⑩ then·tro

ceramic *cerámica* ① the·ra·mee·ka

cereal *cereales* ⑩ pl the·re·a·les

certificate *certificado* ⑩
ther·tee·fee·ka·do

chair *silla* ① see·lya

champagne *champán* ⑩ cham·pan

chance *oportunidad* ① o·por·too·nee·da

change (money) *cambio* ⑩ kam·byo

change *cambiar* kam·byar

changing rooms *vestuarios* ⑩ pl
ves·twa·ryos

charming *encantador/encantadora* ⑩/①
en·kan·ta·dor/en·kan·ta·do·ra

chat up *ligar* lee·gar

cheap *barato/a* ⑩/① ba·ra·to/a

cheat *tramposo/a* ⑩/① tram·po·so/a

check *revisar* re·vee·sar

check (bank) *cheque* ⑩ che·ke

check-in *facturación* ① *de equipajes*
fak·too·ra·thyon de e·kee·pa·khes

checkpoint *control* ⓜ kon·*trol*
cheese *queso* ⓜ *ke*·so
chef *cocinero* ⓜ ko·thee·*ne*·ro
chemist (person) *farmacéutico/a* ⓜ/ⓕ far·ma·the·oo·ti·ko/a
chemist (shop) *farmacia* ⓕ far·ma·*thya*
chess *ajedrez* ⓜ a·khe·*dreth*
chess board *tablero de ajedrez* ta·*ble*·ro de a·khe·*dreth*
chest *pecho* ⓜ *pe*·cho
chewing gum *chicle* ⓜ *chee*·kle
chicken *pollo* ⓜ *po*·lyo
chicken breast *pechuga* ⓕ pe·*choo*·ga
chickpeas *garbanzos* ⓜ pl gar·*ban*·thos
child *niño/a* ⓜ/ⓕ *nee*·nyo/a
child seat *asiento de seguridad para bebés* a·*syen*·to de se·goo·ree·*da* *pa*·ra be·*bes*
childminding service *guardería* ⓕ gwar·de·*ree*·a
children *hijos* ⓜ pl *ee*·khos
chilli *guindilla* ⓕ geen·*dee*·lya
chilli sauce *salsa de guindilla* *sal*·sa de geen·*dee*·lya
chocolate *chocolate* ⓜ cho·ko·*la*·te
choose *escoger* es·ko·*kher*
Christian *cristiano/a* ⓜ/ⓕ krees·*tya*·no/a
Christian name *nombre de pila* *nom*·bre de *pee*·la
Christmas *Navidad* ⓕ na·vee·*da*
Christmas Eve *Nochebuena* ⓕ no·che·*bwe*·na
church *iglesia* ⓕ ee·*gle*·sya
cider *sidra* ⓕ *see*·dra
cigar *cigarro* ⓜ thee·*ga*·ro
cigarette *cigarrillo* ⓜ thee·ga·*ree*·lyo
cigarette lighter *mechero* ⓜ me·*che*·ro
cigarette machine *máquina de tabaco* *ma*·kee·na de ta·*ba*·ko
cigarette paper *papel de fumar* pa·*pel* de foo·*mar*
cinema *cine* ⓜ *thee*·ne

circus *circo* ⓜ *theer*·ko
citizenship *ciudadanía* ⓕ theew·da·da·*nee*·a
city *ciudad* ⓕ theew·*da*
city centre *centro de la ciudad* *then*·tro de la theew·*da*
city walls *murallas* ⓕ pl moo·*ra*·lyas
civil rights *derechos civiles* ⓜ pl de·*re*·chos thee·*vee*·les
classical *clásico/a* ⓜ/ⓕ *kla*·see·ko/a
clean *limpio/a* ⓜ/ⓕ *leem*·pyo/a
cleaning *limpieza* ⓕ leem·*pye*·tha
client *clienta/e* ⓕ klee·*en*·ta/e
cliff *acantilado* ⓜ a·kan·tee·*la*·do
climb *subir* soo·*beer*
cloak *capote* ⓜ ka·*po*·te
cloakroom *guardarropa* ⓜ gwar·da·*ro*·pa
clock *reloj* ⓜ re·*lokh*
close *cerrar* the·*rar*
closed *cerrado/a* ⓜ/ⓕ the·*ra*·do/a
clothes line *cuerda para tender la ropa* *kwer*·da *pa*·ra ten·*der* la *ro*·pa
clothing *ropa* ⓕ *ro*·pa
clothing store *tienda de ropa* *tyen*·da de *ro*·pa
cloud *nube* ⓕ *noo*·be
cloudy *nublado* noo·*bla*·do
clove (garlic) *diente (de ajo)* *dyen*·te (de *a*·kho)
cloves *clavos* ⓜ pl *kla*·vos
clutch *embrague* ⓕ em·*bra*·ge
coach *entrenador/entrenadora* ⓜ/ⓕ en·tre·na·*dor*/en·tre·na·*do*·ra
coast *costa* ⓕ *kos*·ta
cocaine *cocaína* ⓕ ko·ka·ee·na
cockroach *cucaracha* ⓕ koo·ka·*ra*·cha
cocoa *cacao* ⓜ ka·*kow*
coconut *coco* ⓜ *ko*·ko
codeine *codeína* ⓕ ko·de·ee·na
coffee *café* ⓜ ka·fe
coins *monedas* ⓕ pl mo·*ne*·das
cold *frío/a* ⓜ/ⓕ *free*·o/a
cold (illness) *resfriado* ⓜ res·free·a·do
colleague *colega* ⓜ&ⓕ ko·*le*·ga

collect call *llamada* ① *a cobro revertido* lya·ma·da a ko·bro re·ver·tee·do
college *residencia* ① *de estudiantes* re·see·den·thya de es·too·dyan·tes
colour *color* ⓜ ko·lor
colour (film) *película* ① *en color* pe·lee·koo·la en ko·lor
comb *peine* ⓜ pey·ne
come *venir* ve·neer
come (arrive) *llegar* lye·gar
comedy *comedia* ① ko·me·dya
comfortable *cómodo/a* ⓜ/① ko·mo·do/a
communion *comunión* ① ko·moo·nyon
communist *comunista* ⓜ&① ko·moo·nees·ta
companion *compañero/a* ⓜ/① kom·pa·nye·ro/a
company *compañía* ① kom·pa·nyee·a
compass *brújula* ① broo·khoo·la
complain *quejarse* ke·khar·se
computer *ordenador* ⓜ or·de·na·dor
computer game *juegos* ⓜ pl *de ordenador* khwe·gos de or·de·na·dor
concert *concierto* ⓜ kon·thyer·to
conditioner *acondicionador* ⓜ a·kon·dee·thyo·na·dor
condoms *condones* ⓜ pl kon·do·nes
confession *confesión* ① kon·fe·syon
confirm *confirmar* kon·feer·mar
connection *conexión* ① ko·ne·ksyon
conservative *conservador/ conservadora* ⓜ/① kon·ser·va·dor/ kon·ser·va·do·ra
constipation *estreñimiento* ⓜ es·tre·nyee·myen·to
consulate *consulado* ⓜ kon·soo·la·do
contact lenses *lentes* ⓜ pl *de contacto* len·tes de kon·tak·to
contraceptives *anticonceptivos* ⓜ pl an·tee·kon·thep·tee·vos
contract *contrato* ⓜ kon·tra·to
convenience store *negocio* ⓜ *de artículos básicos* ne·go·thyo de ar·tee·koo·los ba·see·kos

convent *convento* ⓜ kon·ven·to
cook *cocinero* ⓜ ko·thee·ne·ro
cook *cocinar* ko·thee·nar
cookie *galleta* ① ga·lye·ta
corn *maíz* ⓜ ma·eeth
corn flakes *copos* ⓜ pl *de maíz* ko·pos de ma·eeth
corner *esquina* ① es·kee·na
corrupt *corrupto/a* ⓜ/① ko·roop·to/a
cost *costar* kos·tar
cottage cheese *requesón* ⓜ re·ke·son
cotton *algodón* ⓜ al·go·don
cotton balls *bolas* ① pl *de algodón* bo·las de al·go·don
cough *tos* ① tos
cough medicine *jarabe* ⓜ kha·ra·be
count *contar* kon·tar
counter *mostrador* ⓜ mos·tra·dor
country *país* ⓜ pa·ees
countryside *campo* ⓜ kam·po
coupon *cupón* ⓜ koo·pon
courgette *calabacín* ⓜ ka·la·ba·theen
court (tennis) *pista* ① pees·ta
cous cous *cus cus* ⓜ koos koos
cover charge *precio* ⓜ *del cubierto* pre·thyo del koo·byer·to
cow *vaca* ① va·ka
crab *cangrejo* ⓜ kan·gre·kho
crackers *galletas* ① pl *saladas* ga·lye·tas sa·la·das
crafts *artesanía* ① ar·te·sa·nee·a
crash *choque* ⓜ cho·ke
crazy *loco/a* ⓜ/① lo·ko/a
cream (food) *crema* kre·ma
cream (moisturising) *crema* ① *hidratante* kre·ma e·dra·tan·te
cream cheese *queso* ⓜ *crema* ke·so kre·ma
creche *guardería* ① gwar·de·ree·a
credit card *tarjeta* ① *de crédito* tar·khe·ta de kre·dee·to
cricket *críquet* ⓜ kree·ket
crop *cosecha* ① ko·se·cha
crowded *abarrotado/a* ⓜ/① a·ba·ro·ta·do/a

cucumber *pepino* ⓜ pe·*pee*·no

cuddle *abrazo* ⓜ a·*bra*·tho

cup *taza* ⓕ *ta*·tha

cupboard *armario* ⓜ ar·*ma*·ryo

currency exchange *cambio* ⓜ *(de dinero)* *kam*·byo (de dee·*ne*·ro)

current (electricity) *corriente* ⓕ ko·*ryen*·te

current affairs *informativo* ⓜ een·for·ma·*tee*·vo

curry *curry* ⓜ *koo*·ree

curry powder *curry* ⓜ *en polvo* *koo*·ree en *pol*·vo

customs *aduana* ⓕ a·*dwa*·na

cut *cortar* kor·*tar*

cutlery *cubiertos* ⓜ pl koo·*byer*·tos

CV *historial* ⓜ *profesional* ees·to·*ryal* pro·fe·syo·*nal*

cycle *andar en bicicleta* an·*dar* en bee·thee·*kle*·ta

cycling *ciclismo* ⓜ thee·*klees*·mo

cyclist *ciclista* ⓜ&ⓕ thee·*klees*·ta

cystitis *cistitis* ⓕ thees·*tee*·tees

D

dad *papá* ⓜ pa·*pa*

daily *diariamente* dya·rya·*men*·te

dance *bailar* bai·*lar*

dancing *bailar* ⓜ bai·*lar*

dangerous *peligroso/a* ⓜ/ⓕ pe·lee·*gro*·so/a

dark *oscuro/a* ⓜ/ⓕ os·*koo*·ro/a

date *citarse* thee·*tar*·se

date (a person) *salir con* sa·*leer* kon

date (time) *fecha* ⓕ *fe*·cha

date of birth *fecha* ⓕ *de nacimiento* *fe*·cha de na·thee·*myen*·to

daughter *hija* ⓕ *ee*·kha

dawn *alba* ⓕ *al*·ba

day *día* ⓜ *dee*·a

day after tomorrow *pasado mañana* pa·*sa*·do ma·*nya*·na

day before yesterday *anteayer* an·te·a·*yer*

dead *muerto/a* ⓜ/ⓕ *mwer*·to/a

deaf *sordo/a* ⓜ/ⓕ *sor*·do/a

deal (cards) *repartir* re·par·*teer*

decide *decidir* de·thee·*deer*

deep *profundo/a* ⓜ/ⓕ pro·*foon*·do/a

deforestation *deforestación* ⓕ de·fo·res·ta·*thyon*

degree *título* ⓜ *tee*·too·lo

delay *demora* ⓕ de·*mo*·ra

delirious *delirante* de·lee·*ran*·te

deliver *entregar* en·tre·*gar*

democracy *democracia* ⓕ de·mo·*kra*·thya

demonstration *manifestación* ⓕ ma·nee·fes·ta·*thyon*

dental floss *hilo* ⓜ *dental* ee·lo den·*tal*

dentist *dentista* ⓜ&ⓕ den·*tees*·ta

deny *negar* ne·*gar*

deodorant *desodorante* ⓜ de·so·do·*ran*·te

depart *salir de* sa·*leer* de

department store *grande almacen* ⓜ *gran*·de al·ma·*then*

departure *salida* ⓕ sa·*lee*·da

deposit *depósito* ⓜ de·po·*see*·to

descendant *descendiente* ⓜ des·then·*dyen*·te

desert *desierto* ⓜ de·*syer*·to

design *diseño* ⓜ dee·*se*·nyo

destination *destino* ⓜ des·*tee*·no

destroy *destruir* des·troo·*eer*

detail *detalle* ⓜ de·*ta*·lye

diabetes *diabetes* ⓕ dee·a·*be*·tes

diaper *pañal* ⓜ pa·*nyal*

diaphragm *diafragma* ⓜ dee·a·*frag*·ma

diarrhoea *diarrea* ⓕ dee·a·*re*·a

diary *agenda* ⓕ a·*khen*·da

dice (die) *dados* ⓜ pl *da*·dos

dictionary *diccionario* ⓜ deek·thyo·*na*·ryo

die *morir* mo·*reer*

diet *régimen* ⓜ *re*·khee·men

different *diferente* ⓜ/ⓕ dee·fe·*ren*·te

difficult *difícil* ⓜ/ⓕ dee·*fee*·theel

dining car *vagón* ⓜ *restaurante* va·*gon* res·tow·*ran*·te

dinner *cena* ① the·na
direct *directo/a* ⓜ/① dee·rek·to/a
direct-dial *marcar directo* mar·kar
  dee·rek·to
director *director/directora* ⓜ/①
  dee·rek·tor/dee·rek·to·ra
dirty *sucio/a* ⓜ/① soo·thyo/a
disabled *minusválido/a* ⓜ/①
  mee·noos·va·lee·do/a
disco *discoteca* ① dees·ko·te·ka
discount *descuento* ⓜ des·kwen·to
discover *descubrir* des·koo·breer
discrimination *discriminación* ①
  dees·kree·mee·na·thyon
disease *enfermedad* ① en·fer·me·da
disk *disco* ⓜ dees·ko
dive *bucear* boo·the·ar
diving *submarinismo* ⓜ
  soob·ma·ree·nees·mo
diving equipment *equipo* ⓜ
  de inmersión ⓜ e·kee·po de
  ee·mer·syon
dizzy *mareado/a* ⓜ/① ma·re·a·do/a
do *hacer* a·ther
doctor *doctor/doctora* ⓜ/① dok·tor/
  dok·to·ra
documentary *documental* ⓜ
  do·koo·men·tal
dog *perro/a* ⓜ/① pe·ro/a
dole *paro* ⓜ pa·ro
doll *muñeca* ① moo·nye·ka
dollar *dólar* ⓜ do·lar
domestic flight *vuelo* ⓜ *doméstico*
  vwe·lo do·mes·tee·ko
donkey *burro* ⓜ boo·ro
door *puerta* ① pwer·ta
double *doble* ⓜ/① do·ble
double bed *cama* ① *de matrimonio*
  ka·ma de ma·tree·mo·nyo
double room *habitación* ① *doble*
  a·bee·ta·thyon do·ble
down *abajo* a·ba·kho
downhill *cuesta abajo* kwes·ta a·ba·kho
dozen *docena* ① do·the·na

drama *drama* ⓜ dra·ma
draw *dibujar* dee·boo·khar
dream *soñar* so·nyar
dress *vestido* ⓜ ves·lee·do
dried fruit *fruto* ⓜ *seco* froo·to se·ko
drink *bebida* ① be·bee·da
drink *beber* be·ber
drive *conducir* kon·doo·theer
drivers licence *carnet* ⓜ *de conducir*
  kar·ne de kon·doo·theer
drug *droga* ① dro·ga
drug addiction *drogadicción* ①
  dro·ga·deek·thyon
drug dealer *traficante* ⓜ *de drogas*
  tra·fee·kan·te de dro·gas
drums *batería* ① ba·te·ree·a
drumstick (chicken) *muslo* moos·lo
drunk *borracho/a* ⓜ/① bo·ra·cho/a
dry *secar* se·kar
duck *pato* ⓜ pa·to
dummy (pacifier) *chupete* choo·pe·te

E

each *cada* ka·da
ear *oreja* ① o·re·kha
early *temprano* tem·pra·no
earn *ganar* ga·nar
earplugs *tapones* ⓜ pl *para los oídos*
  la·po·nes pa·ra los o·ee·dos
earrings *pendientes* ⓜ pl pen·dyen·tes
Earth *Tierra* ① tye·ra
earthquake *terremoto* ⓜ te·re·mo·to
east *este* es·te
Easter *Pascua* ① pas·kwa
easy *fácil* fa·theel
eat *comer* ko·mer
economy class *clase* ① *turística* kla·se
  too·rees·tee·ka
eczema *eczema* ① ek·the·ma
editor *editor/editora* ⓜ/① e·dee·tor/
  e·dee·to·ra
education *educación* ① e·doo·ka·thyon
eggplant *berenjenas* ① pl
  be·ren·khe·nas

egg *huevo* Ⓜ we·vo
elections *elecciones* Ⓕ pl
e·lek·thyo·nes
electrical store *tienda* Ⓕ *de productos eléctricos* tyen·da de pro·dook·tos
e·lek·tree·kos
electricity *electricidad* Ⓕ
e·lek·tree·thee·da
elevator *ascensor* Ⓜ as·then·sor
embarrassed *avergonzado/a* Ⓜ/Ⓕ
a·ver·gon·tha·do/a
embassy *embajada* Ⓕ em·ba·kha·da
emergency *emergencia* Ⓕ
e·mer·khen·thya
emotional *emocional* e·mo·thyo·nal
employee *empleado/a* Ⓜ/Ⓕ
em·ple·a·do/a
employer *jefe/a* Ⓜ/Ⓕ khe·fe/a
empty *vacío/a* Ⓜ/Ⓕ va·thee·o/a
end *fin* Ⓜ feen
end *acabar* a·ka·bar
endangered species *especies* Ⓕ pl *en peligro de extinción* es·pe·thyes en
pe·lee·gro de eks·teen·thyon
engagement *compromiso* Ⓜ
kom·pro·mee·so
engine *motor* Ⓜ mo·tor
engineer *ingeniero/a* Ⓜ/Ⓕ
een·khe·nye·ro/a
engineering *ingeniería* Ⓕ
een·khe·nye·ree·a
England *Inglaterra* Ⓕ een·gla·te·ra
English *inglés* Ⓜ een·gles
enjoy (oneself) *divertirse* dee·ver·teer·se
enough *suficiente* Ⓜ/Ⓕ
soo·fee·thyen·te
enter *entrar* en·trar
entertainment guide *guía* Ⓕ *del ocio*
gee·a del o·thyo
envelope *sobre* Ⓜ so·bre
environment *medio* Ⓜ *ambiente*
me·dyo am·byen·te
epilepsy *epilepsia* Ⓕ e·pee·lep·sya
equal opportunity *igualdad* Ⓕ *de oportunidades* ee·gwal·da de
o·por·too·nee·da·des

equality *igualdad* Ⓕ ee·gwal·da
equipment *equipo* Ⓜ e·kee·po
escalator *escaleras* Ⓕ pl *mecánicas*
es·ka·le·ras me·ka·nee·kas
euro *euro* Ⓜ e·oo·ro
Europe *Europa* Ⓕ e·oo·ro·pa
euthanasia *eutanasia* Ⓕ e·oo·ta·na·sya
evening *noche* Ⓕ no·che
everything *todo* to·do
example *ejemplo* Ⓜ e·khem·plo
excellent *excelente* Ⓜ/Ⓕ eks·the·len·te
exchange *cambio* Ⓜ kam·byo
exchange (money) *cambiar* kam·byar
exchange rate *tipo* Ⓜ *de cambio*
tee·po de kam·byo
exchange (give gifts) *regalar* re·ga·lar
excluded *no incluido* no een·kloo·ee·do
exhaust *tubo* Ⓜ *de escape* too·bo de
es·ka·pe
exhibit *exponer* eks·po·ner
exhibition *exposición* Ⓕ
eks·po·see·thyon
exit *salida* Ⓕ sa·lee·da
expensive *caro/a* Ⓜ/Ⓕ ka·ro/a
experience *experiencia* Ⓕ
eks·pe·ryen·thya
express *expreso/a* Ⓜ/Ⓕ eks·pre·so/a
express mail *correo* Ⓜ *urgente* ko·re·o
oor·khen·te
extension (visa) *prolongación* Ⓕ
pro·lon·ga·thyon
eye *ojo* Ⓜ o·kho
eye drops *gotas* Ⓕ pl *para los ojos*
go·tas pa·ra los o·khos

F

fabric *tela* Ⓕ te·la
face *cara* Ⓕ ka·ra
face cloth *toallita* Ⓕ to·a·lyee·ta
factory *fábrica* Ⓕ fa·bree·ka
factory worker *obrero/a* Ⓜ/Ⓕ o·bre·ro/a
fall *caída* Ⓕ ka·ee·da
family *familia* Ⓕ fa·mee·lya
family name *apellido* Ⓜ a·pe·lyee·do
famous *famoso/a* Ⓜ/Ⓕ fa·mo·so/a

fan (hand held) *abanico* ⓜ a·ba·nee·ko
fan (electric) *ventilador* ⓜ
ven·tee·la·dor
fanbelt *correa* ⓕ *del ventilador* ko·re·a
del ven·tee·la·dor
far *lejos* le·khos
farm *granja* ⓕ gran·kha
farmer *agricultor/agricultora* ⓜ/ⓕ
a·gree·kool·tor/a·gree·kool·to·ra
fast *rápido/a* ⓜ/ⓕ ra·pee·do/a
fat *gordo/a* ⓜ/ⓕ gor·do/a
father *padre* ⓜ pa·dre
father-in-law *suegro* ⓜ swe·gro
fault *falta* ⓕ fal·ta
faulty *defectuoso/a* ⓜ/ⓕ
de·fek·too·o·so/a
feed *dar de comer* dar de ko·mer
feel *sentir* sen·teer
feelings *sentimientos* ⓜ pl
sen·tee·myen·tos
fence *cerca* ⓕ ther·ka
fencing *esgrima* ⓕ es·gree·ma
festival *festival* ⓜ fes·tee·val
fever *fiebre* ⓕ fye·bre
few *pocos* po·kos
fiance *prometido* ⓜ pro·me·tee·do
fiancee *prometida* ⓕ pro·me·tee·da
fiction *ficción* ⓕ feek·thyon
field *campo* ⓜ kam·po
fig *higo* ⓜ ee·go
fight *pelea* ⓕ pe·le·a
fight against *luchar contra* loo·char
kon·tra
fill *llenar* lye·nar
fillet *filete* ⓜ fee·le·te
film *película* ⓕ pe·lee·koo·la
film speed *sensibilidad* ⓕ
sen·see·bee·lee·da
filtered *con filtro* kon feel·tro
find *encontrar* en·kon·trar
fine *multa* ⓕ mool·ta
finger *dedo* ⓜ de·do
finish *terminar* ter·mee·nar
fire *fuego* ⓜ fwe·go
firewood *leña* ⓕ le·nya
first *primero/a* ⓜ/ⓕ pree·me·ro/a

first-class *de primera clase* de
pree·me·ra kla·se
first-aid kit *maletín* ⓜ *de primeros
auxilios* ma·le·teen de pree·me·ros
ow·ksee·lyos
fish *pez* ⓜ peth
fish (as food) *pescado* ⓜ pes·ka·do
fish shop *pescadería* ⓕ pes·ka·de·ree·a
fishing *pesca* ⓕ pes·ka
flag *bandera* ⓕ ban·de·ra
flannel *franela* ⓕ fra·ne·la
flashlight *linterna* ⓕ leen·ter·na
flat *llano/a* ⓜ/ⓕ lya·no/a
flea *pulga* ⓕ pool·ga
flooding *inundación* ⓕ ee·noon·da·thyon
floor *suelo* ⓜ swe·lo
florist *florista* ⓜ&ⓕ flo·rees·ta
flour *harina* ⓕ a·ree·na
flower *flor* ⓕ flor
flower seller *vendedor/vendedora* ⓜ/ⓕ
de flores ven·de·dor/
ven·de·do·ra de flo·res
fly *volar* vo·lar
foggy *brumoso/a* ⓜ/ⓕ broo·mo·so/a
follow *seguir* se·geer
food *comida* ⓕ ko·mee·da
food supplies *víveres* ⓜ pl vee·ve·res
foot *pie* ⓜ pye
football *fútbol* ⓜ foot·bol
footpath *acera* ⓕ a·the·ra
foreign *extranjero/a* ⓜ/ⓕ
eks·tran·khe·ro/a
forest *bosque* ⓜ bos·ke
forever *para siempre* pa·ra syem·pre
forget *olvidar* ol·vee·dar
forgive *perdonar* per·do·nar
fork *tenedor* ⓜ te·ne·dor
fortnight *quincena* ⓕ keen·the·na
foul *sucio/a* ⓜ/ⓕ soo·thee·o/a
foyer *vestíbulo* ⓜ ves·tee·boo·lo
fragile *frágil* fra·kheel
free (not bound) *libre* lee·bre
free (of charge) *gratis* gra·tees
freeze *helarse* e·lar·se
friend *amigo/a* ⓜ/ⓕ a·mee·go/a

frost *escarcha* ① es·*kar*·cha

frozen foods *productos congelados* ⓜ pl pro·*dook*·tos kon·khe·*la*·dos

fruit *fruta* ① *froo*·ta

fruit picking *recolección* ① de fruta re·ko·lek·thyon de froo·ta

fry *freír* fre·*eer*

frying pan *sartén* ① sar·*ten*

fuck *follar* fo·*lyar*

full *lleno/a* ⓜ/① lye·no/a

full-time *a tiempo completo* a tyem·po kom·*ple*·to

fun *diversión* ① dee·ver·*syon*

funeral *funeral* ⓜ foo·ne·*ral*

funny *gracioso/a* ⓜ/① gra·*thyo*·so/a

furniture *muebles* ⓜ pl mwe·bles

future *futuro* ⓜ foo·*too*·ro

G

gay *gay* gai

general *general* khe·ne·*ral*

Germany *Alemania* ① a·le·*ma*·nya

gift *regalo* ⓜ re·*ga*·lo

gig *bolo* ⓜ *bo*·lo

gin *ginebra* ① khee·ne·bra

ginger *jengibre* ⓜ khen·*khee*·bre

girl *chica* ① *chee*·ka

girlfriend *novia* ① *no*·vya

give *dar* dar

glandular fever *fiebre* ① *glandular* fye·bre glan·doo·*lar*

glass (material) *vidrio* ⓜ vee·dryo

glass (drinking) *vaso* ⓜ *va*·so

glasses *gafas* ① pl *ga*·fas

gloves *guantes* ⓜ pl *gwan*·tes

go *ir* eer

go out with *salir con* sa·*leer* kon

go shopping *ir de compras* eer de *kom*·pras

goal *gol* ⓜ gol

goalkeeper *portero/a* ⓜ/① por·*te*·ro/a

goat *cabra* ① *ka*·bra

goat's cheese *queso* ⓜ de *cabra* ke·so de *ka*·bra

god *Dios* ⓜ dyos

goggles *gafas* ① pl de submarinismo *ga*·fas de soob·ma·ree·nees·mo

golf ball *pelota* ① de golf pe·*lo*·ta de golf

golf course *campo* ⓜ de golf kam·po de golf

good *bueno/a* ⓜ/① bwe·no/a

government *gobierno* ⓜ go·*byer*·no

gram *gramo* ⓜ *gra*·mo

grandchild *nieto/a* ⓜ/① nye·to/a

grandfather *abuelo* ⓜ a·*bwe*·lo

grandmother *abuela* ① a·*bwe*·la

grapefruit *pomelo* ⓜ po·*me*·lo

grapes *uvas* ① pl *oo*·vas

graphic art *arte* ⓜ *gráfico* ar·te *gra*·fee·ko

grass *hierba* ① *yer*·ba

grave *tumba* ① *toom*·ba

gray *gris* grees

great *fantástico/a* ⓜ/① fan·*tas*·tee·ko/a

green *verde* *ver*·de

greengrocery (shop) *verdulería* ① ver·doo·le·*ree*·a

grocer (shopkeeper) *verdulero/a* ⓜ/① ver·doo·*le*·ro/a

grey *gris* grees

grocery *tienda* ① de comestibles tyen·da de ko·mes·tee·bles

grow *crecer* kre·*ther*

g-string *tanga* ① *tan*·ga

guess *adivinar* a·dee·vee·*nar*

guide (audio) *guía* ① audio gee·a ow·dyo

guide (person) *guía* ⓜ&① gee·a

guide dog *perro lazarillo* ⓜ pe·ro la·tha·*ree*·lyo

guidebook *guía* ① gee·a

guided tour *recorrido* ⓜ *guiado* re·ko·ree·do gee·a·do

guilty *culpable* kool·*pa*·ble

guitar *guitarra* ① gee·*ta*·ra

gum *chicle* ⓜ *chee*·kle

gymnastics *gimnasia* ① *rítmica* kheem·*na*·sya *reet*·mee·ka

gynaecologist *ginecólogo* ⓜ khee·ne·*ko*·lo·go

H

hair *pelo* ⓜ pe·lo
hairbrush *cepillo* ⓜ the·pee·lyo
hairdresser *peluquero/a* ⓜ/①
  pe·loo·ke·ro/a
halal *halal* a·lal
half *medio/a* ⓜ/① me·dyo/a
half a litre *medio litro* ⓜ me·dyo lee·tro
hallucinate *alucinar* a·loo·thee·nar
ham *jamón* ⓜ kha·mon
hammer *martillo* ⓜ mar·tee·lyo
hammock *hamaca* ① a·ma·ka
hand *mano* ① ma·no
handbag *bolso* ⓜ bol·so
handicrafts *artesanía* ① ar·te·sa·nee·a
handlebar *manillar* ⓜ ma·nee·lyar
handmade *hecho a mano* e·cho a ma·no
handsome *hermoso* ⓜ er·mo·so
happy *feliz* fe·leeth
harassment *acoso* ⓜ al a·ko·so
harbour *puerto* ⓜ pwer·to
hard *duro/a* ⓜ/① doo·ro/a
hardware store *ferretería* ① fe·re·te·ree·a
hash *hachís* ⓜ a·chees
hat *sombrero* ⓜ som·bre·ro
have *tener* te·ner
have a cold *estar constipado/a* ⓜ/①
  es·tar kons·tee·pa·do
have fun *divertirse* dee·ver·teer·se
hay fever *alergia* ① al polen a·ler·khya
  al po·len
he *él* el
head *cabeza* ① ka·be·tha
headache *dolor* ⓜ *de cabeza* do·lor de
  ka·be·tha
headlights *faros* ⓜ pl fa·ros
health *salud* ① sa·loo
hear *oír* o·eer
hearing aid *audífono* ⓜ ow·dee·fo·no
heart *corazón* ⓜ ko·ra·thon
heart condition *condición* ① *cardiaca*
  kon·dee·thyon kar·dee·a·ka
heat *calor* ⓜ ka·lor
heater *estufa* ① es·too·fa
heavy *pesado/a* ⓜ/① pe·sa·do/a

helmet *casco* ⓜ kas·ko
help *ayudar* a·yoo·dar
hepatitis *hepatitis* ① e·pa·tee·tees
her *su* soo
herbalist *herbolario/a* ⓜ/①
  er·bo·la·ree·o/a
herbs *hierbas* ① pl yer·bas
here *aquí* a·kee
heroin *heroína* ① e·ro·ee·na
herring *arenque* ⓜ a·ren·ke
high *alto/a* ⓜ/① al·to/a
high school *instituto* ⓜ eens·tee·too·to
hike *ir de excursión*
  eer de eks·koor·syon
hiking *excursionismo* ⓜ
  eks·koor·syo·nees·mo
hiking boots *botas* ① pl *de montaña*
  bo·tas de mon·ta·nya
hiking routes *caminos* ⓜ pl *rurales*
  ka·mee·nos roo·ra·les
hill *colina* ① ko·lee·na
Hindu *hindú* een·doo
hire *alquilar* al·kee·lar
his *su* soo
historical *histórico/a* ⓜ/①
  ees·to·ree·ko/a
hitchhike *hacer dedo* a·ther de·do
HIV positive *seropositivo/a* ⓜ/①
  se·ro·po·see·tee·vo/a
hockey *hockey* ⓜ kho·kee
holiday *día festivo* ⓜ dee·a fes·tee·vo
holidays *vacaciones* ① pl
  va·ka·thyo·nes
Holy Week *Semana* ① *Santa* se ma na
  san·ta
homeless *sin hogar* seen o·gar
homemaker *ama* ① *de casa*
  a·ma de ka·sa
homosexual *homosexual* ⓜ&①
  o·mo·se·kswal
honey *miel* ① myel
honeymoon *luna* ① *de miel* loo·na
  de myel
horoscope *horóscopo* ⓜ o·ros·ko·po
horse *caballo* ⓜ ka·ba·lyo

horse riding *equitación* ① e·kee·ta·*thyon*
horseradish *rábano* ⓜ *picante* ra·ba·no pee·*kan*·te
hospital *hospital* ⓜ os·pee·*tal*
hospitality *hosteleria* ① os·te·le·*ree*·a
hot *caliente* ka·*lyen*·te
hot water *agua caliente* ⓜ a·gwa ka·*lyen*·te
hotel *hotel* ⓜ o·*tel*
house *casa* ① *ka*·sa
housework *trabajo* ⓜ *de casa* tra·*ba*·kho de *ka*·sa
how *cómo* *ko*·mo
how much *cuánto* kwan·to
hug *abrazo* ⓜ a·*bra*·tho
huge *enorme* e·*nor*·me
human rights *derechos* ⓜ pl *humanos* de·*re*·chos oo·*ma*·nos
humanities *humanidades* ① pl oo·ma·nee·*da*·des
hungry *hambriento/a* ⓜ/① am·*bryen*·to/a
hungry *tener hambre* te·*ner* am·bre
hunting *caza* ① *ka*·tha
hurt *dañar* da·*nyar*
husband *marido* ⓜ ma·*ree*·do

I

I *yo* yo
ice *hielo* ⓜ *ye*·lo
ice axe *piolet* ⓜ pyo·*le*
ice cream *helado* ⓜ e·*la*·do
ice cream parlour *heladería* ① e·la·de·*ree*·a
ice hockey *hockey* ⓜ *sobre hielo* kho·kee so·bre *ye*·lo
identification *identificación* ① ee·den·tee·fee·ka·*thyon*
identification card *carnet* ⓜ *de identidad* kar·*net* de ee·den·tee·*da*
idiot *idiota* ⓜ&① ee·*dyo*·ta
if *si* see
ill *enfermo/a* ⓜ/① en·*fer*·mo/a
immigration *inmigración* ① een·mee·gra·*thyon*

important *importante* eem·por·*tan*·te
in a hurry *de prisa* de *pree*·sa
in front of *enfrente de* en·*fren*·te de
included *incluido* een·*kloo*·ee·do
income tax *impuesto* ⓜ *sobre la renta* eem·*pwes*·to so·bre la *ren*·ta
India *India* ① *een*·dya
indicator *indicador* ⓜ een·dee·ka·*dor*
indigestion *indigestion* ① een·dee·*khes*·tyon
industry *industria* ① een·*doos*·trya
infection *infección* ① een·fek·*thyon*
inflammation *inflamación* ① een·fla·ma·*thyon*
influenza *gripe* ① *gree*·pe
ingredient *ingrediente* ⓜ een·gre·*dyen*·te
inject *inyectarse* een·yek·*tar*·se
injection *inyección* ① een·yek·*thyon*
injury *herida* ① e·*ree*·da
innocent *inocente* ee·no·*then*·te
inside *adentro* a·*den*·tro
instructor *profesor/profesora* ⓜ/① pro·fe·*sor*/pro·fe·*sor*·ra
insurance *seguro* ⓜ se·*goo*·ro
interesting *interesante* een·te·re·*san*·te
intermission *descanso* ⓜ des·*kan*·so
international *internacional* een·ter·na·thyo·*nal*
Internet *Internet* een·ter·net
Internet cafe *cibercafé* thee·ber·ka·*fe*
interpreter *intérprete* ⓜ&① een·*ter*·pre·te
intersection *cruce* ⓜ *croo*·the
interview *entrevista* ① en·tre·*vees*·ta
invite *invitar* een·vee·*tar*
Ireland *Irlanda* ① plan·cha
iron *plancha* ① *plan*·cha
island *isla* ① *ees*·la
IT *informática* ① een·for·ma·*tee*·ka
itch *picazón* ① pee·ka·*thon*
itemised *detallado/a* ⓜ/① de·ta·*lya*·do/a
itinerary *itinerario* ① ee·tee·ne·*ra*·ryo
IUD *DIU* ⓜ de ee oo

J

jacket *chaqueta* ① cha·ke·ta
jail *cárcel* ① kar·thel
jam *mermelada* ① mer·me·la·da
Japan *Japón* ⑩ kha·pon
jar *jarra* ① kha·ra
jaw *mandíbula* ① man·dee·boo·la
jealous *celoso/a* ⑩/① the·lo·so/a
jeans *vaqueros* ⑩ pl va·ke·ros
jeep *yip* ⑩ yeep
jet lag *jet lag* ⑩ dyet lag
jewellery shop *joyería* ① kho·ye·ree·a
Jewish *judío/a* ⑩/① khoo·dee·o/a
job *trabajo* ⑩ tra·ba·kho
jockey *jockey* ⑩ dyo·kee
jogging *footing* ⑩ foo·teen
joke *broma* ① bro·ma
joke *bromear* bro·me·ar
journalist *periodista* ⑩&①
pe·ryo·dees·ta
judge *juez* ⑩&① khweth
juice *jugo* ⑩ khoo·go • *zumo* ⑩
thoo·mo
jump *saltar* sal·tar
jumper (sweater) *jersey* ⑩ kher·say
jumper leads *cables* ⑩ pl *de arranque*
ka·bles de a·ran·ke

K

ketchup *salsa* ① *de tomate* sal·sa de
to·ma·te
key *llave* ① lya·ve
keyboard *teclado* ⑩ te·kla·do
kick *dar una patada* dar oo·na pa·ta·da
kick (a goal) *meter (un gol)* me·ter
(oon gol)
kill *matar* ma·tar
kilogram *kilogramo* ⑩ kee·lo·gram·o
kilometre *kilómetro* ⑩ kee·lo·me·tro
kind *amable* a·ma·ble
kindergarten *escuela* ① *de párvulos*
es·kwe·la de par·voo·los
king *rey* ⑩ rey

kiss *beso* ⑩ be·so
kiss *besar* be·sar
kitchen *cocina* ① ko·thee·na
kitten *gatito/a* ⑩/① ga·tee·to/a
kiwifruit *kiwi* ⑩ kee·wee
knapsack *mochila* ① mo·chee·la
knee *rodilla* ① ro·dee·lya
knife *cuchillo* ⑩ koo·chee·lyo
know (someone) *conocer* ko·no·ther
know (something) *saber* sa·ber
Kosher *kosher* ko·sher

L

labourer *obrero/a* ⑩/① o·bre·ro/a
lace *encaje* ⑩ en·ka·khe
lager *cerveza* ① *rubia* ther·ve·tha
roo·bya
lake *lago* ⑩ la·go
lamb *cordero* ⑩ kor·de·ro
land *tierra* ① tye·ra
landlady *propietaria* ① pro·pye·ta·rya
landlord *propietario* ⑩ pro·pye·ta·ryo
languages *idiomas* ⑩ pl ee·dyo·mas
laptop *ordenador* ⑩ *portátil*
or·de·na·dor por·ta·teel
lard *manteca* ① man·te·ka
large *grande* gran·de
late *tarde* tar·de
laugh *reírse* re·eer·se
laundrette *lavandería* ① la·van·de·ree·a
laundry *lavadero* ⑩ la·va·de·ro
law *ley* ① ley
lawyer *abogado/a* ⑩/① a·bo·ga·do/a
leader *líder* ⑩&① lee·der
leaf *hoja* ① o·kha
learn *aprender* a·pren·der
leather *cuero* ⑩ kwe·ro
leave *dejar* de·khar
lecturer *profesor/profesora* ⑩/①
pro·fe·sor/pro·fe·so·ra
ledge *saliente* ⑩ sa·lyen·te
leek *puerro* ⑩ pwe·ro
left *izquierda* ① eeth·kyer·da

left (behind/over) *quedar* ke·*dar*
left luggage *consigna* ① kon·*seeg*·na
left-wing *de izquierda* de eeth·*kyer*·da
leg *pierna* ① *pyer*·na
legal *legal* le·*gal*
legislation *legislación* ①
  le·khees·la·*thyon*
lemon *limón* ① lee·*mon*
lemonade *limonada* ① lee·mo·na·da
lens *objetivo* ⓜ ob·khe·*tee*·vo
Lent *Cuaresma* ① kwa·*res*·ma
lentils *lentejas* ① pl len·*te*·khas
lesbian *lesbiana* ① les·bee·*a*·na
less *menos* *me*·nos
letter *carta* ① *kar*·ta
lettuce *lechuga* ① le·*choo*·ga
liar *mentiroso/a* ⓜ/① men·tee·*ro*·so/a
library *biblioteca* ① bee·blyo·*te*·ka
lice *piojos* ⓜ pl *pyo*·khos
license plate number *matrícula* ①
  ma·*tree*·koo·la
lie (not stand) *tumbarse* toom·*bar*·se
life *vida* ① *vee*·da
lifejacket *chaleco* ⓜ *salvavidas*
  cha·*le*·ko sal·va·*vee*·das
lift *ascensor* ⓜ as·then·*sor*
light (weight) *leve* *le*·ve
light *luz* ① looth
light bulb *bombilla* ① bom·*bee*·lya
light meter *fotómetro* ⓜ fo·*to*·me·tro
lighter *encendedor* ⓜ en·then·de·*dor*
like *gustar(le)* goos·*tar*(le)
lime *lima* ① *lee*·ma
line *línea* ① *lee*·ne·a
lip balm *bálsamo* ⓜ *de labios*
  bal·sa·mo de *la*·byos
lips *labios* ⓜ pl *la*·byos
lipstick *pintalabios* ⓜ peen·ta *la*·byos
liquor store *bodega* ① bo·*de*·ga
listen *escuchar* es·koo·*char*
live (life) *vivir* vee·*veer*
live (somewhere) *ocupar* o·koo·*par*
liver *hígado* ⓜ *ee*·ga·do
lizard *lagartija* ① la·gar·*tee*·kha

local *de cercanías* de ther·ka·*nee*·as
lock *cerradura* ① the·ra·*doo*·ra
lock *cerrar* the·*rar*
locked *cerrado/a* ⓜ/① *con llave*
  the·ra·do/a kon *lya*·ve
lollies *caramelos* ⓜ pl ka·ra·*me*·los
long *largo/a* ⓜ/① *lar*·go/a
long-distance *a larga distancia* a *lar*·ga
  dees·*tan*·thya
look *mirar* mee·*rar*
look after *cuidar* kwee·*dar*
look for *buscar* boos·*kar*
lookout *mirador* ⓜ mee·ra·*dor*
lose *perder* per·*der*
lost *perdido/a* ⓜ/① per·*dee*·do/a
lost property office *oficina* ① *de*
  objetos perdidos o·fee·*thee*·na de
  ob·*khe*·tos per·*dee*·dos
loud *ruidoso/a* ⓜ/① rwee·*do*·so/a
love *querer* ke·*rer*
lover *amante* ⓜ&① a·*man*·te
low *bajo/a* ⓜ/① *ba*·kho/a
lubricant *lubricante* ⓜ loo·bree·*kan*·te
luck *suerte* ① *swer*·te
lucky *afortunado/a* ⓜ/①
  a·for·too·na·do/a
luggage *equipaje* ⓜ e·kee·*pa*·khe
luggage lockers *consigna* ①
  automática kon·*seeg*·na
  ow·to·ma·tee·ka
luggage tag *etiqueta* ① *de equipaje*
  e·tee·*ke*·ta de e·kee·*pa*·khe
lump *bulto* ⓜ *bool*·to
lunch *almuerzo* ⓜ al·*mwer*·tho
lungs *pulmones* ⓜ pl pool·*mo*·nes
luxury *lujo* ⓜ *loo*·kho

M

machine *máquina* ① *ma*·kee·na
made of (cotton) *hecho a de (algodón)*
  e·cho a de (al·go·*don*)
magazine *revista* ① re·*vees*·ta
magician *mago/a* ⓜ/① *ma*·go/a
mail *correo* ⓜ ko·*re*·o

mailbox *buzón* ⓜ boo·thon

main *principal* preen·thee·*pal*

make *hacer* a·ther

make fun of *burlarse de* boor·lar·se de

make-up *maquillaje* ⓜ ma·kee·lya·khe

mammogram *mamograma* ⓜ
ma·mo·gra·ma

man *hombre* ⓜ om·bre

manager *gerente* ⓜ&ⓕ khe·ren·te

mandarin *mandarina* ⓕ man·da·ree·na

mango *mango* ⓜ man·go

manual worker *obrero/a* ⓜ/ⓕ o·bre·ro/a

many *muchas/os* ⓜ/ⓕ pl moo·chas/os

map *mapa* ⓦ ma·pa

margarine *margarina* ⓕ mar·ga·ree·na

marijuana *marihuana* ⓕ ma·ree·wa·na

marital status *estado* ⓜ *civil* es·ta·do
thee·veel

market *mercado* ⓜ mer·ka·do

marmalade *mermelada* ⓕ
mer·me·la·da

marriage *matrimonio* ⓜ ma·tree·mo·nyo

marry *casarse* ka·sar·se

martial arts *artes* ⓜ pl *marciales* ar·tes
mar·thya·les

mass *misa* ⓕ mee·sa

massage *masaje* ⓜ ma·sa·khe

masseur/masseuse *masajista* ⓜ&ⓕ
ma·sa·khees·ta

mat *esterilla* ⓕ es·te·ree·lya

match *partido* ⓜ par·tee·do

matches *cerillas* ⓕ pl the·ree·lyas

mattress *colchón* ⓜ kol·chon

maybe *quizás* kee·thas

mayonnaise *mayonesa* ⓕ ma·yo·ne·sa

mayor *alcalde* ⓜ&ⓕ al·kal·de

measles *sarampión* ⓜ sa·ram·pyon

meat *carne* ⓕ kar·ne

mechanic *mecánico/a* ⓜ/ⓕ
me·ka·nee·ko

media *medios* ⓜ pl *de comunicación*
me·dyos de ko·moo·nee·ka·thyon

medicine *medicina* ⓕ me·dee·thee·na

meet *encontrar* en·kon·trar

melon *melón* ⓜ me·lon

member *miembro* ⓜ myem·bro

menstruation *menstruación* ⓕ
mens·trwa·thyon

menu *menú* ⓦ me·noo

message *mensaje* ⓜ men·sa·khe

metal *metal* ⓜ me·tal

metre *metro* ⓜ me·tro

metro station *estación* ⓕ *de metro*
es·ta·thyon de me·tro

microwave *microondas* ⓜ
mee·kro·on·das

midnight *medianoche* ⓕ me·dya·no·che

migraine *migraña* ⓕ mee·gra·nya

military service *servicio* ⓜ *militar*
ser·vee·thyo mee·lee·tar

milk *leche* ⓕ le·che

millimetre *milímetro* ⓜ mee·lee·me·tro

million *millón* ⓜ mee·lyon

mince (meat) *carne* ⓕ *molida* kar·ne
mo·lee·da

mind (object) *cuidar* kwee·dar

mineral water *agua* ⓜ *mineral* a·gwa
mee·ne·ral

mints *pastillas* ⓕ pl *de menta*
pas·tee·lyas de men·ta

minute *minuto* ⓜ mee·noo·to

mirror *espejo* ⓜ es·pe·kho

miscarriage *aborto* ⓜ *natural* a·bor·to
na·too·ral

miss (feel sad) *echar de menos* e·char
de me·nos

mistake *error* ⓜ e·ror

mix *mezclar* meth·klar

mobile phone *teléfono* ⓜ *móvil*
te·le·fo·no mo·veel

modem *módem* ⓜ mo·dem

moisturiser *crema* ⓕ *hidratante* kre·ma
ee·dra·tan·te

monastery *monasterio* ⓜ mo·nas·te·ryo

money *dinero* ⓜ dee·ne·ro

month *mes* ⓜ mes

monument *monumento* ⓜ
mo·noo·men·to

(full) moon *luna* ① *(llena)* loo·na (lye·na)
morning (6am - 1pm) *mañana* ① ma·nya·na
morning sickness *náuseas* ① pl *del embarazo* now·se·as del em·ba·ra·tho
mosque *mezquita* ① meth·kee·ta
mosquito *mosquito* ⓜ mos·kee·to
mosquito coil *rollo* ⓜ *repelente contra mosquitos* ro·lyo re·pe·len·te kon·tra mos·kee·tos
mosquito net *mosquitera* ① mos·kee·te·ra
mother *madre* ① ma·dre
mother-in-law *suegra* ① swe·gra
motorboat *motora* ① mo·to·ra
motorcycle *motocicleta* ① mo·to·thee·kle·ta
motorway *autovía* ① ow·to·vee·a
mountain *montaña* ① mon·ta·nya
mountain bike *bicicleta* ① *de montaña* bee·thee·kle·ta de mon·ta·nya
mountain path *sendero* ⓜ sen·de·ro
mountain range *cordillera* ① kor·dee·lye·ra
mountaineering *alpinismo* ⓜ al·pee·nees·mo
mouse *ratón* ⓜ ra·ton
mouth *boca* ① bo·ka
movie *película* ① pe·lee·koo·la
mud *lodo* ⓜ lo·do
muesli *muesli* ⓜ mwes·lee
mum *mamá* ① ma·ma
muscle *músculo* ⓜ moos·koo·lo
museum *museo* ⓜ moo·se·o
mushroom ⓜ *champiñón* cham·pee·nyon
music *música* ① moo·see·ka
musician *músico/a* ⓜ/① moo·see·ko/a
Muslim *musulmán/musulmána* ⓜ/① moo·sool·man/moo·sool·ma·na
mussels *mejillones* ⓜ pl me·khee·lyo·nes
mustard *mostaza* ① mos·ta·tha
mute *mudo/a* ⓜ/① moo·do/a
my *mi* mee

N

nail clippers *cortauñas* ⓜ pl kor·ta·oo·nyas
name *nombre* ⓜ nom·bre
napkin *servilleta* ① ser·vee·lye·ta
nappy *pañal* ⓜ pa·nyal
nappy rash *irritación* ① *de pañal* ee·ree·ta·thyon de pa·nyal
national park *parque* ⓜ *nacional* par·ke na·thyo·nal
nationality *nacionalidad* ① na·thyo·na·lee·da
nature *naturaleza* ① na·too·ra·le·tha
naturopathy *naturopatia* ① na·too·ro·pa·tya
nausea *náusea* ① now·se·a
near *cerca* ther·ka
nearby *cerca* ther·ka
nearest *más cercano/a* ⓜ/① mas ther·ka·no/a
necessary *necesario/a* ⓜ/① ne·the·sa·ryo/a
neck *cuello* ⓜ kwe·lyo
necklace *collar* ⓜ ko·lyar
need *necesitar* ne·the·see·tar
needle (sewing) *aguja* ① a·goo·kha
needle (syringe) *jeringa* ① khe·reen·ga
neither *tampoco* tam·po·ko
net *red* ① red
Netherlands *Holanda* ① o·lan·da
never *nunca* noon·ka
new *nuevo/a* ⓜ/① nwe·vo/a
New Year *Año Nuevo* ⓜ a·nyo nwe·vo
New Year's Eve *Nochevieja* ① no·che·vye·kha
New Zealand *Nueva Zelanda* ① nwe·va the·lan·da
news *noticias* ① pl no·tee·thyas
news stand *quiosco* ⓜ kyos·ko
newsagency *quiosco* ⓜ kyos·ko
newspaper *periódico* ⓜ pe·ryo·dee·ko
next (month) *el próximo (mes)* el prok·see·mo (mes)
next to *al lado de* al la·do de

nice *simpático/a* ⓜ/ⓕ seem·pa·tee·ko/a

nickname *apodo* ⓜ a·po·do

night *noche* ⓕ no·che

no *no* no

noisy *ruidoso/a* ⓜ/ⓕ rwee·do·so/a

none *nada* na·da

non-smoking *no fumadores* no foo·ma·do·res

noodles *fideos* ⓜ pl fee·de·os

noon *mediodía* ⓜ me·dyo·dee·a

north *norte* ⓜ nor·te

nose *nariz* ⓕ na·reeth

notebook *cuaderno* ⓜ kwa·der·no

nothing *nada* na·da

now *ahora* a·o·ra

nuclear energy *energía* ⓕ *nuclear* e·ner·khee·a noo·kle·ar

nuclear testing *pruebas* ⓕ pl *nucleares* prwe·bas noo·kle·a·res

nuclear waste *desperdicios* ⓜ pl *nucleares* des·per·dee·thyos noo·kle·a·res

number *número* ⓜ noo·me·ro

nun *monja* ⓕ mon·kha

nurse *enfermero/a* ⓜ/ⓕ en·fer·me·ro/a

nuts *nueces* ⓕ pl nwe·thes

nuts (raw) *nueces* ⓕ pl (*crudas*) nwe·thes (kroo·das)

nuts (roasted) *nueces* ⓕ pl (*tostadas*) nwe·thes (tos·ta·das)

O

oats *avena* ⓕ a·ve·na

ocean *océano* ⓜ o·the·a·no

off (food) *pasado/a* ⓜ/ⓕ pa·sa·do/a

office *oficina* ⓕ o·fee·thee·na

office worker *oficinista* ⓜ&ⓕ o·fee·thee·nees·ta

offside *fuera de juego* fwe·ra de khwe·go

often *a menudo* a me·noo·do

oil *aceite* ⓜ a·they·te

old *viejo/a* ⓜ/ⓕ vye·kho/a

olive oil *aceite* ⓜ *de oliva* a·they·te de o·lee·va

Olympic Games *juegos* ⓜ pl *olímpicos* khwe·gos o·leem·pee·kos

on *en* en

once *vez* ⓕ veth

one way ticket *billete* ⓜ *sencillo* bee·lye·te sen·thee·lyo

onion *cebolla* ⓕ the·bo·lya

only *sólo* so·lo

open *abierto/a* ⓜ/ⓕ a·byer·to/a

open *abrir* a·breer

opening hours *horas* ⓕ pl *de abrir* o·ras de a·breer

opera *ópera* ⓕ o·pe·ra

opera house *teatro* ⓜ *de la ópera* te·a·tro de la o·pe·ra

operation *operación* ⓕ o·pe·ra·thyon

operator *operador/operadora* ⓜ/ⓕ o·pe·ra·dor/o·pe·ra·do·ra

opinion *opinión* ⓕ o·pee·nyon

opposite *frente a* fren·te a

or *o* o

orange (fruit) *naranja* ⓕ na·ran·kha

orange (colour) *naranja* na·ran·kha

orange juice *zumo* ⓜ *de naranja* thoo·mo de na·ran·kha

orchestra *orquesta* ⓕ or·kes·ta

order *orden* ⓜ or·den

order *ordenar* or·de·nar

ordinary *corriente* ko·ryen·te

orgasm *orgasmo* ⓜ or·gas·mo

original *original* o·ree·khee·nal

other *otro/a* ⓜ/ⓕ o·tro/a

our *nuestro/a* ⓜ/ⓕ nwes·tro/a

outside *exterior* ⓜ eks·te·ryor

ovarian cyst *quiste* ⓜ *ovárico* kees·te o·va·ree·ko

oven *horno* ⓜ or·no

overcoat *abrigo* ⓜ a·bree·go

overdose *sobredosis* ⓕ so·bre·do·sees

owe *deber* de·ver

owner *dueño/a* ⓜ/ⓕ dwe·nyo/a

oxygen *oxígeno* ⓜ o·ksee·khe·no

oyster *ostra* ⓕ os·tra

ozone layer *capa* ⓕ *de ozono* ka·pa de o·tho·no

P

pacemaker *marcapasos* ⓜ mar·ka·*pa*·sos
pacifier *chupete* ⓜ choo·*pe*·te
package *paquete* ⓜ pa·*ke*·te
packet *paquete* ⓜ pa·*ke*·te
padlock *candado* ⓜ kan·*da*·do
page *página* ⓕ *pa*·khee·na
pain *dolor* ⓜ do·*lor*
painful *doloroso/a* ⓜ/ⓕ do·lo·*ro*·so/a
painkillers *analgésicos* ⓜ pl
  a·nal·*khe*·see·kos
paint *pintar* peen·*tar*
painter *pintor/pintora* ⓜ/ⓕ peen·*tor*/
  peen·*to*·ra
painting *pintura* ⓕ peen·*too*·ra
pair (couple) *pareja* ⓕ pa·*re*·kha
palace *palacio* ⓜ pa·*la*·thyo
pan *cazuela* ⓕ ka·*thwe*·la
pants *pantalones* ⓜ pl pan·ta·*lo*·nes
panty liners *salvaeslips* ⓜ pl
  sal·va·e·*sleeps*
pantyhose *medias* ⓕ pl *me*·dyas
pap smear *citología* ⓕ thee·to·lo·*khee*·a
paper *papel* ⓜ pa·*pel*
paperwork *trabajo* ⓜ *administrativo*
  tra·*ba*·kho ad·mee·nees·tra·*tee*·vo
paraplegic *parapléjico/a* ⓜ/ⓕ
  pa·ra·*ple*·khee·ko/a
parasailing *esquí* ⓜ *acuático con*
  paracaídas es·*kee* a·*kwa*·tee·ko kon
  pa·ra·ka·*ee*·das
parcel *paquete* ⓜ pa·*ke*·te
parents *padres* ⓜ pl *pa*·dres
park *parque* ⓜ *par*·ke
park (car) *estacionar* es·ta·thyo·*nar*
parliament *parlamento* ⓜ
  par·la·*men*·to
parsley *perejil* ⓜ pe·re·*kheel*
part *parte* ⓕ *par*·te
part-time *a tiempo parcial* a *tyem*·po
  par·*thyal*
party *fiesta* ⓕ *fyes*·ta
party (political) *partido* ⓜ par·*tee*·do
pass *pase* ⓜ *pa*·se

passenger *pasajero/a* ⓜ/ⓕ
  pa·sa·*khe*·ro
passport *pasaporte* ⓜ pa·sa·*por*·te
passport number *número* ⓜ *de pasaporte*
  noo·me·ro de pa·sa·*por*·te
past *pasado* ⓜ pa·*sa*·do
pasta *pasta* ⓕ *pas*·ta
pate (food) *paté* ⓜ pa·*te*
path *sendero* ⓜ sen·*de*·ro
pay *pagar* pa·*gar*
payment *pago* ⓜ *pa*·go
peace *paz* ⓕ path
peach *melocotón* ⓜ me·lo·ko·*ton*
peak *cumbre* ⓕ *koom*·bre
peanuts *cacahuetes* ⓜ pl ka·ka·*we*·tes
pear *pera* ⓕ *pe*·ra
peas *guisantes* ⓜ pl gee·*san*·tes
pedal *pedal* ⓜ pe·*dal*
pedestrian *peatón* ⓜ&ⓕ pe·a·*ton*
pedestrian crossing *paso* ⓜ *de cebra*
  pa·so de *the*·bra
pen *bolígrafo* ⓜ bo·*lee*·gra·fo
pencil *lápiz* ⓜ *la*·peeth
penis *pene* ⓜ *pe*·ne
penknife *navaja* ⓕ na·*va*·kha
pensioner *pensionista* ⓜ&ⓕ
  pen·syo·*nees*·ta
people *gente* ⓕ *khen*·te
pepper (vegetable) *pimiento* ⓜ
  pee·*myen*·to
pepper (spice) *pimienta* ⓕ
  pee·*myen*·ta
per (day) *por (dia)* por (*dee*·a)
percent *por ciento* por *thyen*·to
performance *actuación* ⓕ ak·twa·*thyon*
perfume *perfume* ⓜ per·*foo*·me
period pain *dolor* ⓜ *menstrual* do·*lor*
  mens·*trwal*
permission *permiso* ⓜ per·*mee*·so
permit *permiso* ⓜ per·*mee*·so
permit *permitir* per·mee·*teer*
person *persona* ⓕ per·*so*·na
perspire *sudar* soo·*dar*
petition *petición* ⓕ pe·tee·*thyon*
petrol *gasolina* ⓕ ga·so·*lee*·na

pharmacy farmacia ① far·ma·thya

phone book guía ① telefónica
gee·a te·le·fo·nee·ka

phone box cabina ① telefónica
ka bee·ka te·le·fo·nee·ka

phone card tarjeta ① de teléfono
tar·khe·ta de te·le·fo·no

photo foto ① fo·to

photographer fotógrafo/a ⑩/①
fo·to·gra·fo/a

photography fotografía ①
fo·to·gra·fee·a

phrasebook libro ⑩ de frases lee·bro
de fra·ses

pick up ligar lee·gar

pickaxe piqueta ① pee·ke·ta

pickles encurtidos ⑩ pl en·koor·tee·dos

picnic comida ① en el campo
ko·mee·da en el kam·po

pie pastel ⑩ pas·tel

piece pedazo ⑩ pe·da·tho

pig cerdo ⑩ ther·do

pill pastilla ① pas·tee·lya

pillow almohada ① al·mwa·da

pillowcase funda ① de almohada
foon·da de al·mwa·da

pineapple piña ① pee·nya

pink rosa ro·sa

pistachio pistacho ⑩ pees·ta·cho

place lugar ⑩ loo·gar

place of birth lugar ⑩ de nacimiento
loo·gar de na·thee·myen·to

plane avión ⑩ a·vyon

planet planeta ⑩ pla·ne·ta

plant planta ① plan·ta

plant sembrar sem·brar

plastic plástico ⑩ plas·tee·ko

plate plato ⑩ pla·to

plateau meseta ① me·se·ta

platform plataforma ① pla·ta·for·ma

play obra ① o·bra

play (musical instrument) tocar to·kar

play (sport/games) jugar khoo·gar

plug tapar ta·par

plum ciruela thee·rwe·la

pocket bolsillo ⑩ bol·see·lyo

poetry poesía ① po·e·see·a

point apuntar a·poon·tar

point (tip) punto ⑩ poon·to

poisonous venenoso/a ⑩/①
ve·ne·no·so/a

poker póquer ⑩ po·ker

police policía ① po·lee·thee·a

police station comisaría ①
ko·mee·sa·ree·a

policy política ① po·lee·tee·ka

policy (insurance) póliza ① po·lee·tha

politician político ⑩ po·lee·tee·ko

politics política ① po·lee·tee·ka

pollen polen ⑩ po·len

polls sondeos ⑩ pl son de os

pollution contaminación ①
kon·ta·mee·na·thyon

pool (swimming) piscina ①
pees·thee·na

poor pobre po·bre

popular popular po·poo·lar

pork cerdo ⑩ ther·do

pork sausage chorizo ⑩ cho·ree·tho

port puerto ⑩ pwer·to

port (wine) oporto ⑩ o·por·to

possible posible po·see·ble

post code código postal ⑩ ko·dee·go
pos tal

post office correos ⑩ ko·re·os

postage franqueo ⑩ fran·ke·o

postcard postal ① pos·tal

poster póster ⑩ pos·ter

pot (kitchen) cazuela ① ka·thwe·la

pot (plant) tiesto ⑩ tyes·to

potato patata ① pa·ta·ta

pottery alfarería ① al·fa·re·ree·a

pound (money) libra ① lee·bra

poverty pobreza ① po·bre·tha

power poder ⑩ po·der

prawns gambas ① pl gam·bas

prayer oración ① o·ra·thyon

prayer book devocionario ⑩
de·vo·thyo·na·ryo

prefer *preferir* pre·fe·reer

pregnancy test *prueba* ① *del embarazo* prwe·ba del em·ba·ra·tho

pregnant *embarazada* ① em·ba·ra·tha·da

premenstrual tension *tensión* ① *premenstrual* ten·syon pre·mens·trwal

prepare *preparar* pre·pa·rar

president *presidente/a* ⓜ/① pre·see·den·te/a

pressure *presión* ① pre·syon

pretty *bonito/a* ⓜ/① bo·nee·to/a

prevent *prevenir* pre·ve·neer

price *precio* ⓜ pre·thyo

priest *sacerdote* ⓜ sa·ther·do·te

prime minister *primer ministro/ primera ministra* ⓜ/① pree·mer mee·nees·tro/pree·me·ra mee·nees·tra

prison *cárcel* ① kar·thel

prisoner *prisionero/a* ⓜ/① pree·syon·ne·ro/a

private *privado/a* ⓜ/① pree·va·do/a

private hospital *clínica* ① klee·nee·ka

produce *producir* pro·doo·theer

profit *beneficio* ⓜ be·ne·fee·thyo

programme *programa* ⓜ pro·gra·ma

projector *proyector* ⓜ pro·yek·tor

promise *promesa* ① pro·me·sa

protect *proteger* pro·te·kher

protected (species) *protegido/a* ⓜ/① pro·te·khee·do/a

protest *protesta* ① pro·tes·ta

protest *protestar* pro·tes·tar

provisions *provisiones* ① pl pro·bee·syo·nes

prune *ciruela* ① *pasa* thee·rwe·la pa·sa

pub *pub* ⓜ poob

public telephone *teléfono* ⓜ *público* te·le·fo·no poo·blee·ko

public toilet *servicios* ⓜ pl ser·vee·thyos

pull *tirar* tee·rar

pump *bomba* ① bom·ba

pumpkin *calabaza* ① ka·la·ba·tha

puncture *pinchar* peen·char

punish *castigar* kas·tee·gar

puppy *cachorro* ⓜ ka·cho·ro

pure *puro/a* ⓜ/① poo·ro/a

purple *lila* lee·la

push *empujar* em·poo·khar

put *poner* po·ner

Q

qualifications *cualificaciones* ① pl kwa·lee·fee·ka·thyo·nes

quality *calidad* ① ka·lee·da

quarantine *cuarentena* ① kwa·ren·te·na

quarrel *pelea* ① pe·le·a

quarter *cuarto* ⓜ kwar·to

queen *reina* ① rey·na

question *pregunta* ① pre·goon·ta

question *cuestionar* kwes·tyo·nar

queue *cola* ① ko·la

quick *rápido/a* ⓜ/① ra·pee·do/a

quiet *tranquilo/a* ⓜ/① tran·kee·lo/a

quiet *tranquilidad* ① tran·kee·lee·da

quit *dejar* de·khar

R

rabbit *conejo* ⓜ ko·ne·kho

race (people) *raza* ① ra·tha

race (sport) *carrera* ① ka·re·ra

racetrack (bicycles) *velódromo* ⓜ ve·lo·dro·mo

racetrack (cars) *circuito* ⓜ *de carreras* theer·kwee·to de ka·re·ras

racetrack (horses) *hipódromo* ⓜ ee·po·dro·mo

racetrack (runners) *pista* ① pees·ta

racing bike *bicicleta* ① *de carreras* bee·thee·kle·ta de ka·re·ras

racquet *raqueta* ① ra·ke·ta

radiator *radiador* ⓜ ra·dya·dor

radish *rábano* ⓜ ra·ba·no

railway station *estación* ① *de tren* es·ta·thyon de tren

rain *lluvia* ① lyoo·vya

raincoat *impermeable* ⓜ
  eem·per·me·a·ble
raisin *uva* ⓕ *pasa* oo·va pa·sa
rally *concentración* ⓕ
  kon·then·tra·*thyon*
rape *violar* vyo·*lar*
rare *raro/a* ⓜ/ⓕ ra·ro/a
rash *irritación* ⓕ ee·ree·ta·*thyon*
raspberry *frambuesa* ⓕ fram·*bwe*·sa
rat *rata* ⓕ ra·ta
rate of pay *salario* ⓜ sa·*la*·ryo
raw *crudo/a* ⓜ/ⓕ *kroo*·do/a
razor *afeiladora* ⓕ a·fey·ta·*do*·ra
razor blades *cuchillas* ⓕ pl *de afeitar*
  koo·*chee*·lyas de a·fey·*tar*
read *leer* le·*er*
ready *listo/a* ⓜ/ⓕ *lees*·to/a
real estate agent *agente inmobiliario* ⓜ
  a·*khen*·te een·mo·bee·*lya*·ryo
realise *darse cuenta de* *dar*·se kwen·ta de
realistic *realista* re·a·*lees*·ta
reason *razón* ⓕ ra·*thon*
receipt *recibo* ⓜ re·*thee*·bo
receive *recibir* re·thee·*beer*
recently *recientemente* re·thyen·te·*men*·te
recognise *reconocer* re·ko·no·*ther*
recommend *recomendar* re·ko·men·*dar*
recording *grabación* ⓕ gra·ba·*thyon*
recyclable *reciclable* ro·thee·*kla*·ble
recycle *reciclar* re·thee·*klar*
red *rojo/a* ⓜ/ⓕ ro·kho/a
referee *árbitro* ⓜ *ar*·bee·tro
reference *referencias* ⓕ pl
  re·fe·*ren*·thyas
refrigerator *nevera* ⓕ ne·*ve*·ra •
  frigorífico ⓜ free·ge·*ree*·fee·ko
refugee *refugiado/a* ⓜ/ⓕ
  re·foo·*khya*·do/a
refund *reembolso* ⓜ re·em·*bol*·so
refund *reembolsar* re·em·bol·*sar*
refuse *negar* ne·*gar*
registered mail *correo* ⓜ *certificado*
  ko·*re*·o ther·tee·fee·*ka*·do
regret *lamentar* la·men·*tar*

relationship *relación* ⓕ re·la·*thyon*
relax *relajarse* re·la·*khar*·se
relic *reliquia* ⓕ re·*lee*·kya
religion *religión* ⓕ re·lee·*khyon*
religious *religioso/a* ⓜ/ⓕ
  re·lee·*khyo*·so/a
remember *recordar* re·kor·*dar*
remote *remoto/a* ⓜ/ⓕ re·*mo*·to/a
remote control *mando* ⓜ *a distancia*
  man·do a dees·*tan*·thya
rent *alquiler* ⓜ al·kee·*ler*
rent *alquilar* al·kee·*lar*
repair *reparar* re·pa·*rar*
repeat *repetir* re·pe·*teer*
republic *república* ⓕ re·*poo*·blee·ka
reservation *reserva* ⓕ re·*ser*·va
reserve *reservar* re·ser·*var*
rest *descansar* des·kan·*sar*
restaurant *restaurante* ⓜ res·tow·*ran*·te
resumé *curriculum* ⓜ
  koo·*ree*·koo·loom
retired *jubilado/a* ⓜ/ⓕ khoo·bee·*la*·do/a
return *volver* vol·*ver*
return ticket *billete* ⓜ *de ida y vuelta*
  bee·*lye*·te de ee·da ee *vwel*·ta
review *crítica* ⓕ *kree*·tee·ka
rhythm *ritmo* ⓜ *reet*·mo
rice *arroz* ⓜ a·*roth*
rich *rico/a* ⓜ/ⓕ *ree*·ko/a
ride *paseo* ⓜ pa·*se*·o
ride *montar* mon·*tar*
right (correct) *correcto/a* ⓜ/ⓕ
  ko *rek*·to/a
right (not left) *derecha* de·*re*·cha
right-wing *derechista* de·re·*chees*·ta
ring *llamada* ⓕ lya·*ma*·da
ring *llamar por telefono* lya·*mar* por
  te·*le*·fo·no
rip-off *estafa* ⓕ es·*ta*·fa
risk *riesgo* ⓜ *ryes*·go
river *río* ⓜ *ree*·o
road *carretera* ⓕ ka·re·*te*·ra
rob *robar* ro·*bar*
rock (stone) *roca* ⓕ *ro*·ka

rock (music) *rock* ⓜ rok
rock climbing *escalada* ⓕ es·ka·la·da
rock group *grupo* ⓜ *de rock* groo·po de rok
rollerblading *patinar* pa·tee·nar
romantic *romántico/a* ⓜ/ⓕ ro·man·tee·ko/a
room *habitación* ⓕ a·bee·ta·thyon
room number *número* ⓜ *de la habitación* noo·me·ro de la a·bee·ta·thyon
rope *cuerda* ⓕ kwer·da
round *redondo/a* ⓜ/ⓕ re·don·do/a
roundabout *glorieta* ⓕ glo·rye·ta
route *ruta* ⓕ roo·ta
rowing *remo* ⓜ re·mo
rubbish *basura* ⓕ ba·soo·ra
rug *alfombra* ⓕ al·fom·bra
rugby *rugby* ⓜ roog·bee
ruins *ruinas* ⓕ pl rwee·nas
rules *reglas* ⓕ pl re·glas
rum *ron* ron
run *correr* ko·rer
run out of *quedarse sin* ke·dar·se seen

S

sad *triste* trees·te
saddle *sillín* ⓜ see·lyeen
safe *seguro/a* ⓜ/ⓕ se·goo·ro/a
safe *caja* ⓕ *fuerte* ka·kha fwer·te
safe sex *sexo* ⓜ *seguro* se·kso se·goo·ro
saint *santo/a* ⓜ/ⓕ san·to/a
salad *ensalada* ⓕ en·sa·la·da
salami (Spanish sausage) *chorizo* cho·ree·tho
salary *salario* ⓜ sa·la·ryo
sales tax *IVA* ⓜ ee·va
salmon *salmón* ⓜ sal·mon
salt *sal* ⓕ sal
same *igual* ee·gwal
sand *arena* ⓕ a·re·na
sandals *sandalias* ⓕ pl san·da·lyas
sanitary napkins *compresas* ⓕ pl kom·pre·sas

sauna *sauna* ⓕ sow·na
sausage *salchicha* ⓕ sal·chee·cha
save *salvar* sal·var
save (money) *ahorrar* a·o·rar
say *decir* de·theer
scale/climb *trepar* tre·par
scarf *bufanda* ⓕ boo·fan·da
school *escuela* ⓕ es·kwe·la
science *ciencias* ⓕ pl thyen·thyas
scientist *científico/a* ⓜ/ⓕ thyen·tee·fee·ko/a
scissors *tijeras* ⓕ pl tee·khe·ras
score *marcar* mar·kar
scoreboard *marcador* ⓜ mar·ka·dor
Scotland *Escocia* ⓕ es·ko·thya
screen *pantalla* ⓕ pan·ta·lya
script *guión* ⓜ gee·on
sculpture *escultura* ⓕ es·kool·too·ra
sea *mar* ⓜ mar
seasick *mareado/a* ⓜ/ⓕ ma·re·a·do/a
seaside *costa* ⓕ kos·ta
season *estación* ⓕ es·ta·thyon
season (in sport) *temporada* ⓕ tem·po·ra·da
seat *asiento* ⓜ a·syen·to
seatbelt *cinturón* ⓜ *de seguridad* theen·too·ron de se·goo·ree·da
second *segundo/a* ⓜ/ⓕ se·goon·do/a
second *segundo* ⓜ se·goon·do
second-hand *de segunda mano* de se·goon·da ma·no
secretary *secretario/a* ⓜ/ⓕ se·kre·ta·ryo/a
see *ver* ver
selfish *egoísta* e·go·ees·ta
self-service *autoservicio* ⓜ ow·to·ser·vee·thyo
sell *vender* ven·der
send *enviar* en·vee·ar
sensible *prudente* proo·den·te
sensual *sensual* sen·swal
separate *separado/a* ⓜ/ⓕ se·pa·ra·do/a
separate *separar* se·pa·rar
series *serie* ⓕ se·rye

serious *serio/a* ⓜ/ⓕ *se·ryo·a*
service station *gasolinera* ⓕ ga·so·lee·*ne*·ra
service charge *carga* ⓕ *kar*·ga
several *varias/os* ⓜ/ⓕ *va*·ryas·os
sew *coser* ko·*ser*
sex *sexo* ⓜ *se*·kso
sexism *machismo* ⓜ ma·*chees*·mo
sexy *sexy* *se*·ksee
shadow *sombra* ⓕ *som*·bra
shampoo *champú* ⓜ cham·*poo*
shape *forma* ⓕ *for*·ma
share (a dorm) *compartir (un dormitorio)* kom·par·*teer* (oon dor·mee·*to*·ryo)
share (with) *compartir* kom·par·*teer*
shave *afeitarse* a·fey·*tar*·se
shaving cream *espuma* ⓕ *de afeitar* es·*poo*·ma de a·fey·*tar*
she *ella* ⓕ *e*·lya
sheep *oveja* ⓕ o·ve·kha
sheet (bed) *sábana* ⓕ *sa*·ba·na
sheet (of paper) *hoja* ⓕ *o*·kha
shelf *estante* ⓜ es·*tan*·te
ship *barco* ⓜ *bar*·ko
ship *enviar* en·vee·*ar*
shirt *camisa* ⓕ ka·*mee*·sa
shoe shop *zapatería* ⓕ tha·pa·te·*ree*·a
shoes *zapatos* ⓜ pl tha·*pa*·tos
shoot *disparar* dees·pa·*rar*
shop *tienda* ⓕ *tyen*·da
shoplifting *ratería* ⓕ ra·te·*ree*·a
shopping centre *centro* ⓜ *comercial* *then*·tro ko·mer·*thyal*
short (height) *bajo/a* ⓜ/ⓕ *ba*·kho·a
short (length) *corto/a* ⓜ/ⓕ *kor*·to·a
shortage *escasez* ⓕ es·ka·*seth*
shorts *pantalones* ⓜ pl *cortos* pan·ta·*lo*·nes
shoulders *hombros* ⓜ pl *om*·bros
shout *gritar* gree·*tar*
show *espectáculo* ⓜ es·pek·*ta*·koo·lo
show *mostrar* mos·*trar*
show *enseñar* en·se·*nyar*
shower *ducha* ⓕ *doo*·cha

shrine *capilla* ⓕ ka·*pee*·lya
shut *cerrado/a* ⓜ/ⓕ the·*ra*·do·a
shut *cerrar* the·*rar*
shy *tímido/a* ⓜ/ⓕ *tee*·mee·do·a
sick *enfermo/a* ⓜ/ⓤ en·*fer*·mo·a
side *lado* ⓜ *la*·do
sign *señal* ⓕ se·*nyal*
sign *firmar* feer·*mar*
signature *firma* ⓕ *feer*·ma
silk *seda* ⓕ *se*·da
silver *plateado/a* ⓜ/ⓕ pla·te·a·do·a
silver *plata* ⓕ *pla*·ta
similar *similar* see·mee·*lar*
simple *sencillo/a* ⓜ/ⓕ sen·*thee*·lyo·a
since *desde (mayo)* des·de (*ma*·yo)
sing *cantar* kan·*tar*
Singapore *Singapur* ⓜ seen·ga·*poor*
singer *cantante* ⓜ&ⓕ kan·*tan*·te
single *soltero/a* ⓜ/ⓕ sol·*te*·ro·a
single room *habitación* ⓕ *individual* a·bee·ta·*thyon* een·dee·vee·*dwal*
singlet *camiseta* ⓕ ka·mee·*se*·ta
sister *hermana* ⓕ er·*ma*·na
sit *sentarse* sen·*tar*·se
size (clothes) *talla* ⓕ *ta*·lya
skateboarding *monopatinaje* ⓜ mo·no·pa·tee·*na*·khe
ski *esquiar* es·kee·*ar*
skiing *esquí* ⓜ es·*kee*
skimmed milk *leche* ⓕ *desnatada* *le*·che des·na·*ta*·da
skin *piel* ⓕ pyel
skirt *falda* ⓕ *fal*·da
sky *cielo* ⓜ *thye*·lo
skydiving *paracaidismo* ⓜ pa·ra·kai·*dees*·mo
sleep *dormir* dor·*meer*
sleeping bag *saco* ⓜ *de dormir* *sa*·ko de dor·*meer*
sleeping car *coche cama* ⓜ *ko*·che *ka*·ma
sleeping pills *pastillas* ⓕ pl *para dormir* pas·*tee*·lyas *pa*·ra dor·*meer*
(to be) sleepy *tener sueño* te·*ner* *swe*·nyo

slide *diapositiva* ① dya·po·see·*tee*·va
slow *lento/a* ⓜ/① *len*·to/a
slowly *despacio* des·pa·thyo
small *pequeño/a* ⓜ/① pe·ke·nyo/a
smell *olor* ⓜ o·lor
smell *oler* o·ler
smile *sonreír* son·re·eer
smoke *fumar* foo·mar
snack *tentempié* ⓜ ten·tem·*pye*
snail *caracol* ⓜ ka·ra·kol
snake *serpiente* ① ser·*pyen*·te
snorkel *tubos* ⓜ pl *respiratorios*
snorkel *buceo* ⓜ boo·*the*·o
snow *nieve* ① nye·ve
snowboarding *surf* ⓜ *sobre la nieve* soorf *so*·bre la *nye*·ve
soap *jabón* ⓜ kha·*bon*
soap opera *telenovela* ① te·le·no·ve·la
soccer *fútbol* ⓜ *foot*·bol
social welfare *estado* ⓜ *del bienestar* es·*ta*·do del byen·es·*tar*
socialist *socialista* ⓜ&① so·thya·*lees*·ta
socks *calcetines* ⓜ pl kal·the·*tee*·nes
soft drink *refresco* ⓜ re·*fres*·ko
soldier *soldado* ⓜ sol·*da*·do
some *alguno/a* ⓜ/① al·*goon*
someone *alguien* al·gyen
something *algo* al·go
sometimes *de vez en cuando* de veth en *kwan*·do
son *hijo* ⓜ ee·kho
song *canción* ① kan·thyon
soon *pronto* pron·to
sore *dolorido/a* ⓜ/① do·lo·ree·do/a
soup *sopa* ① *so*·pa
sour cream *nata* ① *agria* na·ta a·grya
south *sur* ⓜ soor
souvenir *recuerdo* ⓜ re·*kwer*·do
souvenir shop *tienda* ① *de recuerdos* tyen·da de re·*kwer*·dos
soy milk *leche* ① *de soja* le·che de *so*·kha
soy sauce *salsa* ① *de soja* sal·sa de *so*·kha

space *espacio* ⓜ es·*pa*·thyo
Spain *España* ① es·*pa*·nya
sparkling *espumoso/a* ⓜ/① es·poo·mo·so
speak *hablar* a·blar
special *especial* es·pe·thyal
specialist *especialista* ⓜ&① es·pe·thya·*lees*·ta
speed *velocidad* ① ve·lo·thee·*da*
speeding *exceso* ⓜ *de velocidad* eks·*the*·so de ve·lo·thee·*da*
speedometer *velocímetro* ⓜ ve·lo·*thee*·me·tro
spider *araña* ① a·ra·nya
spinach *espinacas* es·pee·*na*·kas
spoon *cuchara* ① koo·cha·ra
sport *deportes* ⓜ pl de·*por*·tes
sports store *tienda* ① *deportiva* tyen·da de·por·tee·va
sportsperson *deportista* ⓜ&① de·por·*tees*·ta
sprain *torcedura* ① tor·the·*doo*·ra
spring (wire) *muelle* ⓜ *mwe*·lye
spring (season) *primavera* ① pree·ma·ve·ra
square (shape) *cuadrado* ⓜ kwa·*dra*·do
(main) square *plaza* ① *(mayor)* ① pla·tha ma·yor
stadium *estadio* ⓜ es·*ta*·dyo
stage *escenario* ⓜ es·the·*na*·ryo
stairway *escalera* ① es·ka·le·ra
stamp *sello* ⓜ *se*·lyo
standby ticket *billete* ⓜ *de lista de espera* bee·*lye*·te de *lees*·ta de es·*pe*·ra
stars *estrellas* ① pl es·*tre*·lyas
start *comenzar* ko·men·*thar*
station *estación* ① es·ta·thyon
statue *estatua* ① es·*ta*·twa
stay (remain) *quedarse* ke·dar·se
stay (somewhere) *alojarse* a·lo·khar·se
steak (beef) *bistec* ⓜ bees·*tek*
steal *robar* ro·bar
steep *escarpado/a* ⓜ/① es·kar·pa·do/a

step *paso* ⓜ pa·so

stereo *equipo* ⓜ *de música* e·kee·po de moo·see·ka

stingy *tacaño/a* ⓜ/ⓕ ta·ka·nyo/a

stock *caldo* ⓜ kal·do

stockings *medias* ⓕ pl me·dyas

stomach *estómago* ⓜ es·to·ma·go

stomachache *dolor* ⓜ *de estómago* do·lor de es·to·ma·go

stone *piedra* ⓕ pye·dra

stoned *colocado/a* ⓜ/ⓕ ko·lo·ka·do/a

stop *parada* ⓕ pa·ra·da

stop *parar* pa·rar

storm *tormenta* ⓕ tor·men·ta

story *cuento* ⓜ kwen·to

stove *cocina* ⓕ ko·thee·na

straight *recto/a* ⓜ/ⓕ rek·to/a

strange *extraño/a* ⓜ/ⓕ eks·tra·nyo/a

stranger *desconocido/a* ⓜ/ⓕ des·ko·no·thee·do/a

strawberry *fresa* ⓕ fre·sa

stream *arroyo* ⓜ a·ro·yo

street *calle* ⓕ ka·lye

string *cuerda* ⓕ kwer·da

strong *fuerte* fwer·te

stubborn *testarudo/a* ⓜ/ⓕ tes·ta·roo·do/a

student *estudiante* ⓜ&ⓕ es·too·dyan·te

studio *estudio* ⓜ es·too·dyo

stupid *estúpido/a* ⓜ/ⓕ es·too·pec·do/a

style *estilo* ⓜ es·tee·lo

subtitles *subtítulos* ⓜ pl soob·tee·too·los

suburb *barrio* ⓜ ba·ryo

subway *parada* ⓕ *de metro* pa·ra·da de me·tro

suffer *sufrir* soo·freer

sugar *azúcar* ⓜ a·thoo·kar

suitcase *maleta* ⓕ ma·le·ta

summer *verano* ⓜ ve·ra·no

sun *sol* ⓜ sol

sunblock *crema* ⓕ *solar* kre·ma so·lar

sunburn *quemadura* ⓕ *de sol* ke·ma·doo·ra de sol

sun-dried tomato *tomate* ⓜ *secado al sol* to·ma·te se·ka·do al sol

sunflower oil *aceite* ⓜ *de girasol* a·they·te khee·ra·sol

sunglasses *gafas* ⓕ pl *de sol* ga·fas de sol

(to be) sunny *hace sol* a·the sol

sunrise *amanecer* ⓜ a·ma·ne·ther

sunset *puesta* ⓕ *del sol* pwes·ta del sol

supermarket *supermercado* ⓜ soo·per·mer·ka·do

superstition *superstición* ⓕ soo·pers·tee·thyon

supporters *hinchas* ⓜ&ⓕ pl een·chas

surf *hacer surf* a·ther soorf

surface mail *por vía terrestre* por vee·a te·res·tre

surfboard *tabla de surf* ⓕ ta·bla de soorf

surname *apellido* ⓜ a·pe·lyee·do

surprise *sorpresa* ⓕ sor·pre·sa

survive *sobrevivir* so·bre·vee·veer

sweater *jersey* ⓜ kher·sey

sweet *dulce* dool·the

sweets (candy) *dulces* ⓜ pl dool·thes

swim *nadar* na·dar

swimming pool *piscina* ⓕ pees·thee·na

swimsuit *bañador* ⓜ ba·nya·dor

synagogue *sinagoga* ⓕ see·na·go·ga

synthetic *sintético/a* ⓜ/ⓕ seen·te·tee·ko/a

syringe *jeringa* ⓕ khe·reen·ga

T

table *mesa* ⓕ me·sa

table tennis *ping pong* ⓜ peeng pong

tablecloth *mantel* ⓜ man·tel

tail *rabo* ⓜ ra·bo

tailor *sastre* ⓜ sas·tre

take (away) *llevar* lye·var

take (the train) *tomar* to·mar

take (photo) *sacar* sa·kar

take photographs *sacar fotos* sa·kar fo·tos

talk *hablar* a·blar
tall *alto/a* ⓜ/ⓕ al·to/a
tampons *tampones* ⓜ pl tam·po·nes
tanning lotion *bronceador* ⓜ bron·the·a·dor
tap *grifo* ⓜ gree·fo
tasty *sabroso/a* ⓜ/ⓕ sa·bro·so/a
tax *impuestos* ⓜ pl eem·pwes·tos
taxi *taxi* ⓜ tak·see
taxi stand *parada* ⓕ *de taxis* pa·ra·da de tak·sees
tea *té* ⓜ te
teacher *profesor/profesora* ⓜ/ⓕ pro·fe·sor/pro·fe·so·ra
team *equipo* ⓜ e·kee·po
teaspoon *cucharita* ⓕ koo·cha·ree·ta
technique *técnica* ⓕ tek·nee·ka
teeth *dientes* ⓜ pl dyen·tes
telegram *telegrama* ⓜ te·le·gra·ma
telephone *teléfono* ⓜ te·le·fo·no
telephone *llamar (por teléfono)* lya·mar (por te·le·fo·no)
telephone centre *central* ⓕ *telefónica* then·tral te·le·fo·nee·ka
telescope *telescopio* ⓜ te·les·ko·pyo
television *televisión* ⓕ te·le·vee·syon
tell *decir* de·theer
temperature (fever) *fiebre* ⓕ fye·bre
temperature (weather) *temperatura* ⓕ tem·pe·ra·too·ra
temple *templo* ⓜ tem·plo
tennis *tenis* ⓜ te·nees
tennis court *pista* ⓕ *de tenis* pees·ta de te·nees
tent *tienda* ⓕ *(de campaña)* tyen·da (de kam·pa·nya)
tent pegs *piquetas* ⓕ pl pee·ke·tas
terrible *terrible* te·ree·ble
test *prueba* ⓕ prwe·ba
thank *dar gracias* dar gra·thyas
the Pill *píldora* ⓕ peel·do·ra
theatre *teatro* ⓜ te·a·tro
their *su* soo
they *ellos/ellas* ⓜ/ⓕ e·lyos/e·lyas

thief *ladrón/ladrona* ⓜ/ⓕ la·dron/la·dro·na
thin *delgado/a* ⓜ/ⓕ del·ga·do/a
think *pensar* pen·sar
third *tercio* ⓜ ter·thyo
thirst *sed* ⓕ se
this *éste/a* ⓜ/ⓕ es·te/a
this month *este mes* es·te mes
throat *garganta* ⓕ gar·gan·ta
ticket *billete* ⓜ bee·lye·te
ticket collector *revisor/revisora* ⓜ/ⓕ re·vee·sor/re·vee·so·ra
ticket machine *máquina* ⓕ *de billetes* ma·kee·na de bee·lye·tes
ticket office *taquilla* ⓕ ta·kee·lya
tide *marea* ⓕ ma·re·a
tight *apretado/a* ⓜ/ⓕ a·pre·ta·do/a
time *hora* ⓕ o·ra • *tiempo* ⓜ tyem·po
time difference *diferencia* ⓕ *de horas* dee·fe·ren·thya de o·ras
timetable *horario* ⓜ o·ra·ryo
tin *hojalata* ⓕ o·kha·la·ta
tin opener *abrelatas* ⓜ a·bre·la·tas
tiny *pequeñito/a* ⓜ/ⓕ pe·ke·nyee·to/a
tip *propina* ⓕ pro·pee·na
tired *cansado/a* ⓜ/ⓕ kan·sa·do/a
tissues *pañuelos* ⓜ pl *de papel* pa·nywe·los de pa·pel
toast *tostada* ⓕ tos·ta·da
toaster *tostadora* ⓕ tos·ta·do·ra
tobacco *tabaco* ⓜ ta·ba·ko
tobacconist *estanquero* ⓜ es·tan·ke·ro
tobogganing *ir en tobogán* eer en to·bo·gan
today *hoy* oy
toe *dedo* ⓜ *del pie* de·do del pye
tofu *tofú* ⓜ to·foo
together *juntos/as* ⓜ/ⓕ khoon·tos/as
toilet *servicio* ⓜ ser·vee·thyo
toilet paper *papel* ⓜ *higiénico* pa·pel ee·khye·nee·ko
tomato *tomate* ⓜ to·ma·te
tomato sauce *salsa* ⓕ *de tomate* sal·sa de to·ma·te
tomorrow *mañana* ma·nya·na

tomorrow afternoon *mañana por la tarde* ma·nya·na por la tar·de

tomorrow evening *mañana por la noche* ma·nya·na por la no·che

tomorrow morning *mañana por la mañana* ma·nya·na por la ma·nya·na

tone *tono* ⓜ to·no

tonight *esta noche* es·ta no·che

too (expensive) *demasiado (caro/a)* ⓜ/ⓕ de·ma·sya·do (ka·ro/a)

tooth *diente* ⓜ dyen·te

tooth (back) *muela* ⓕ mwe·la

toothache *dolor* ⓜ *de muelas* do·lor de mwe·las

toothbrush *cepillo* ⓜ *de dientes* the·pee·lyo de dyen·tes

toothpaste *pasta* ⓕ *dentífrica* pas·ta den·tee·free·ka

toothpick *palillo* ⓜ pa·lee·lyo

torch *linterna* ⓕ leen·ter·na

touch *tocar* to·kar

tour *excursión* ⓕ eks·koor·syon

tourist *turista* ⓜ&ⓕ too·rees·ta

tourist (slang) *guiri* ⓜ gee·ree

tourist office *oficina* ⓕ *de turismo* o·fee·thee·na de too·rees·mo

towards *hacia* a·thya

towel *toalla* ⓕ to·a·lya

tower *torre* ⓕ to·re

toxic waste *residuos* ⓜ pl *tóxicos* re·see·dwos tok·see·kos

toyshop *juguetería* ⓕ khoo·ge·te·ree·a

track (car racing) *autódromo* ⓜ ow·to·dro·mo

track (footprints) *rastro* ⓜ ras·tro

trade *comercio* ⓜ ko·mer·thyo

traffic *tráfico* ⓜ tra·fee·ko

traffic lights *semáforos* ⓜ pl se·ma·fo·ros

trail *camino* ⓜ ka·mee·no

train *tren* ⓜ tren

train station *estación* ⓕ *de tren* es·ta·thyon de tren

tram *tranvía* ⓜ tran·vee·a

transit lounge *sala* ⓕ *de tránsito* sa·la de tran·see·to

translate *traducir* tra·doo·theer

transport *medios* ⓜ pl *de transporte* me·dyos de trans·por·te

travel *viajar* vya·khar

travel agency *agencia* ⓕ *de viajes* a·khen·thya de vya·khes

travel books *libros* ⓜ pl *de viajes* lee·bros de vya·khes

travel sickness *mareo* ⓜ ma·re·o

travellers cheque *cheques* ⓜ pl *de viajero* che·kes de vya·khe·ro

tree *árbol* ⓜ ar·bol

trip *viaje* ⓜ vya·khe

trousers *pantalones* ⓜ pl pan·ta·lo·nes

truck *camión* ⓜ ka·myon

trust *confianza* ⓕ kon·fee·an·tha

trust *confiar* kon·fee·ar

try *probar* pro·bar

try (to do something) *intentar (hacer algo)* een·ten·tar (a·ther al·go)

T-shirt *camiseta* ⓕ ka·mee·se·ta

tube (tyre) *cámara* ⓕ *de aire* ka·ma·ra de ai·re

tuna *atún* ⓜ a·toon

tune *melodía* ⓕ me·lo·dee·a

turkey *pavo* ⓜ pa·vo

turn *doblar* do·blar

TV *tele* ⓕ te·le

TV series *serie* ⓕ se·rye

tweezers *pinzas* ⓕ pl peen·thas

twice *dos veces* dos ve·thes

twin beds *dos camas* ⓕ pl dos ka·mas

twins *gemelos* ⓜ pl khe·me·los

type *tipo* ⓜ tee·po

type *escribir a máquina* es·kree·beer a ma·kee·na

typical *típico/a* ⓜ/ⓕ tee·pee·ko/a

tyre *neumático* ⓜ ne·oo·ma·tee·ko

U

ultrasound *ecografía* ⓕ e·ko·gra·fee·a

umbrella *paraguas* ⓜ pa·ra·gwas

umpire *árbitro* ⓜ ar·bee·tro

uncomfortable *incómodo/a* ⓜ/ⓕ een·ko·mo·do/a

underpants (men) *calzoncillos* ⓜ pl
kal·thon·*thee*·lyos

underpants (women) *bragas* ① pl
bra·gas

understand *comprender* kom·pren·*der*

underwear *ropa interior* ① *ro*·pa
een·te·ryor

unemployed *en el paro* en el *pa*·ro

unfair *injusto* een·*khoos*·to

uniform *uniforme* ⓜ oo·nee·*for*·me

universe *universo* ⓜ oo·nee·*ver*·so

university *universidad* ①
oo·nee·ver·*see*·da

unleaded *sin plomo* seen *plo*·mo

unsafe *inseguro/a* ⓜ/① een·se·*goo*·ro/a

until (June) *hasta (junio)* as·ta
(*khoo*·nyo)

unusual *extraño/a* ⓜ/① eks·*tra*·nyo/a

up *arriba* a·*ree*·ba

uphill *cuesta arriba* kwes·ta a·*ree*·ba

urgent *urgente* oor·*khen*·te

USA *Los Estados* ⓜ pl *Unidos*
los es·*ta*·dos oo·*nee*·dos

useful *útil* oo·teel

V

vacant *vacante* va·*kan*·te

vacation *vacaciones* ① pl
va·ka·*thyo*·nes

vaccination *vacuna* ① va·*koo*·na

vagina *vagina* ① va·*khee*·na

validate *validar* va·lee·*dar*

valley *valle* ⓜ va·*lye*

valuable *valioso/a* ⓜ/① va·*lyo*·so/a

value *valor* ⓜ va·*lor*

van *caravana* ① ka·ra·*va*·na

veal *ternera* ① ter·*ne*·ra

vegetable *verdura* ① ver·*doo*·ra

vegetables *verduras* ① pl ver·*doo*·ras

vegetarian *vegetariano/a* ⓜ/①
ve·khe·ta·*rya*·no/a

vein *vena* ① *ve*·na

venereal disease *enfermedad* ①
venérea en·fer·me·da ve·*ne*·re·a

venue *local* ⓜ lo·*kal*

very *muy* mooy

video tape *cinta* ① *de vídeo* theen·ta
de *vee*·de·o

view *vista* ① *vees*·ta

village *pueblo* ⓜ *pwe*·blo

vine *vid* ① veed

vinegar *vinagre* ⓜ vee·*na*·gre

vineyard *viñedo* ⓜ vee·*nye*·do

virus *virus* ⓜ *vee*·roos

visa *visado* ⓜ vee·*sa*·do

visit *visitar* vee·see·*tar*

vitamins *vitaminas* ① pl
vee·ta·*mee*·nas

vodka *vodka* ① *vod*·ka

voice *voz* ① voth

volume *volumen* ⓜ vo·*loo*·men

vote *votar* vo·*tar*

wage *sueldo* ⓜ *swel*·do

W

wait *esperar* es·pe·*rar*

waiter *camarero/a* ⓜ/① ka·ma·*re*·ro/a

waiting room *sala* ① *de espera* sa·la
de es·*pe*·ra

walk *caminar* ka·mee·*nar*

wall (inside) *pared* ① pa·*re*

wallet *cartera* ① kar·*te*·ra

want *querer* ke·*rer*

war *guerra* ① *ge*·ra

wardrobe *vestuario* ⓜ ves·*twa*·ryo

warm *templado/a* ⓜ/① tem·*pla*·do/a

warn *advertir* ad·ver·*teer*

wash (oneself) *lavarse* la·*var*·se

wash (something) *lavar* la·*var*

wash cloth *toallita* ① to·a·*lyee*·ta

washing machine *lavadora* ① la·va·*do*·ra

watch *reloj* ⓜ *de pulsera* re·*lokh* de
pool·*se*·ra

watch *mirar* mee·*rar*

water *agua* ① *a*·gwa
— **tap** *del grifo* del *gree*·fo
— **bottle** *cantimplora* ①
kan·teem·*plo*·ra

waterfall *cascada* ① kas·ka·da
watermelon ① *sandía* san·dee·a
waterproof *impermeable* eem·per·me·a·ble
waterskiing *esquí* ⓜ *acuático* es·kee a·kwa·tee·ko
wave *ola* ① o·la
way *camino* ⓜ ka·mee·no
we *nosotros/nosotras* ⓜ/① no·so·tros/no·so·tras
weak *débil* de·beel
wealthy *rico/a* ⓜ/① ree·ko/a
wear *llevar* lye·var
weather *tiempo* ⓜ tyem·po
wedding *boda* ① bo·da
wedding cake *tarta* ① *nupcial* tar·ta noop·thyal
wedding present *regalo* ⓜ *de bodas* re·ga·lo de bo·das
weekend *fin de semana* ⓜ feen de se·ma·na
weigh *pesar* pe·sar
weight *peso* ⓜ pe·so
weights *pesas* ① pl pe·sas
welcome *bienvenida* ① byen·ve·nee·da
welcome *dar la bienvenida* dar la byen·ve·nee·da
welfare *bienestar* ⓜ byen·es·tar
well *bien* byen
well *pozo* ⓜ po·tho
west *oeste* ⓜ o·es·te
wet *mojado/a* ⓜ/① mo·kha·do/a
what *lo que* lo ke
wheel *rueda* ① rwe·da
wheelchair *silla* ① *de ruedas* see·lya de rwe·das
when *cuando* kwan·do
where *donde* don·de
whiskey *güisqui* ⓜ gwees·kee
white *blanco/a* ⓜ/① blan·ko/a
white-water rafting *rafting* ⓜ rahf·teen
who *quien* kyen
why *por qué* por ke
wide *ancho/a* ⓜ/① an·cho/a

wife *esposa* ① es·po·sa
win *ganar* ga·nar
wind *viento* ⓜ vyen·to
window *ventana* ① ven·ta·na
window-shopping *mirar los escaparates* mee·rar los es·ka·pa·ra·tes
windscreen *parabrisas* ⓜ pa·ra·bree·sas
windsurfing *hacer windsurf* a·ther ween·soorf
wine *vino* ⓜ vee·no
wineglass *copa* ① *de vino* co·pa de vee·no
winery *bodega* ① bo·de·ga
wings *alas* ① pl a·las
winner *ganador/ganadora* ⓜ/① ga·na·dor/ga·na·do·ra
winter *invierno* ⓜ een·vyer·no
wire *alambre* ⓜ a·lam·bre
wish *desear* de·se·ar
with *con* kon
within (an hour) *dentro de (una hora)* den·tro de (oo·na o·ra)
without *sin* seen
woman *mujer* ① moo·kher
wonderful *maravilloso/a* ⓜ/① ma·ra·vee·lyo·so/a
wood *madera* ① ma·de·ra
wool *lana* ① la·na
word *palabra* ① pa·la·bra
work *trabajo* ⓜ tra·ba·kho
work *trabajar* tra·ba·khar
work experience *experiencia* ① *laboral* eks·pe·ryen·thya la·bo·ral
work permit *permiso* ⓜ *de trabajo* per·mee·so de tra·ba·kho
workout *entreno* ⓜ en·tre·no
workshop *taller* ⓜ ta·lyer
world *mundo* ⓜ moon·do
World Cup *La Copa* ① *Mundial* la ko·pa moon·dyal
worms *lombrices* ① pl lom·bree·thes
worried *preocupado/a* ⓜ/① pre·o·koo·pa·do/a

worship *adoración* ① a·do·ra·*thyon*
wrist *muñeca* ① moo·*nye*·ka
write *escribir* es·kree·*beer*
writer *escritor/escritora* ⓜ/①
　es·kree·*tor*/es·kree·*to*·ra
wrong *equivocado/a* ⓜ/①
　e·kee·vo·*ka*·do/a

Y

yellow *amarillo/a* ⓜ/① a·ma·*ree*·lyo/a
yes *sí* see
(not) yet *todavía (no)* to·da·*vee*·a (no)
yesterday *ayer* a·*yer*

yoga *yoga* ⓜ *yo*·ga
yogurt *yogur* ⓜ yo·*goor*
you pol sg *Usted* oos·*te*
you inf sg *tú* too
young *joven* kho·ven
your pol sg *su* soo
your inf sg *tu* too
youth hostel *albergue* ⓜ *juvenil*
　al·*ber*·ge khoo·ve·*neel*

Z

zodiac *zodíaco* ⓜ tho·*dee*·a·ko
zoo *zoológico* ⓜ zo·o·*lo*·khee·ko

Nouns in the dictionary have their gender indicated by ⓜ or ⓕ. If it's a plural noun, you'll also see pl. Where a word that could be either a noun or a verb has no gender indicated, it's a verb.

A

abajo a·*ba*·kho *below*

abanico ⓜ a·ba·*nee*·ko *fan (hand held)*

abarrotado a·ba·ro·*ta*·do *crowded*

abeja ⓕ a·*be*·kha *bee*

abierto/a ⓜ/ⓕ a·*byer*·to/a *open*

abogado/a ⓜ/ⓕ a·bo·*ga*·do/a *lawyer*

aborto ⓜ a·*bor*·to *abortion*

abrazo ⓜ a·*bra*·tho *hug*

abrebotellas ⓜ a·bre·bo·*te*·lyas *bottle opener*

abrelatas ⓜ a·bre·*la*·tas *can opener • tin opener*

abrigo ⓜ a·*bree*·go *overcoat*

abrir a·*breer* *open*

abuela ⓕ a·*bwe*·la *grandmother*

abuelo ⓜ a·*bwe*·lo *grandfather*

aburrido/a ⓜ/ⓕ a·boo·*ree*·do/a *bored • boring*

acabar a·ka·*bar* *end*

acampar a·kam·*par* *camp*

acantilado a·kan·tee·*la*·do *cliff*

accidente ⓜ ak·thee·*den*·te *accident*

aceite ⓜ a·*they*·te *oil*

aceptar a·thep·*tar* *accept*

acera ⓕ a·*the*·ra *footpath*

acondicionador ⓜ a·kon·dee·thyo·na·*dor* *conditioner*

acoso a·*ko*·so *harassment*

activista ⓜ&ⓕ ak·tee·*vees*·ta *activist*

actuación ⓕ ak·twa·*thyon* *performance*

acupuntura ⓕ a·koo·poon·*too*·ra *acupuncture*

adaptador ⓜ a·dap·ta·*dor* *adaptor*

adentro a·*den*·tro *inside*

adivinar a·dee·vee·*nar* *guess*

administración ⓕ ad·mee·nees·tra·*thyon* *administration*

admitir ad·mee·*teer* *admit*

adoración ⓕ a·do·ra·*thyon* *worship*

aduana ⓕ a·*dwa*·na *customs*

adulto/a ⓜ/ⓕ a·*dool*·to/a *adult*

aeróbic ⓜ ay·ro·beek *aerobics*

aerolínea ⓕ ay·ro·*lee*·nya *airline*

aeropuerto ⓜ ay·ro·*pwer*·to *airport*

afeitadora ⓕ a·fey·ta·*do*·ra *razor*

afeitarse a·fey·*tar*·se *shave*

afortunado/a ⓜ/ⓕ a·for·too·na·do/a *lucky*

África ⓕ a·*free*·ka *Africa*

agencia de viajes ⓕ a·*khen*·thya de *vya*·khes *travel agency*

agenda ⓕ a·*khen*·da *diary*

agente inmobiliario ⓜ a·*khen*·te een·mo·bee·*lya*·ryo *real estate agent*

agresivo/a ⓜ/ⓕ a·gre·*see*·vo/a *aggressive*

agricultor(a) ⓜ/ⓕ a·gree·kool·*tor*/a·gree·kool·*to*·ra *farmer*

agricultura ⓕ a·gree·kool·*too*·ra *agriculture*

agua ⓕ a·*gwa* *water*

— **caliente** ka·*lyen*·te *hot water*

— **mineral** mee·ne·*ral* *mineral water*

aguacate ⓜ a·gwa·*ka*·te *avocado*

aguja ⓕ a·*goo*·kha *needle (sewing)*

ahora a·o·ra *now*

ahorrar a·o·*rar* *save (money)*

aire ⓜ *ai*·re *air*

— **acondicionado** a·kon·dee·thyo·na·do *air-conditioning*

ajedrez ⓜ a·khe·*dreth* *chess*

al lado de al *la*·do de *next to*

alambre ⓜ *a·lam·bre* wire
alba ⓕ *al·ba* dawn
albaricoque ⓜ al·ba·ree·ko·ke apricot
albergue juvenil ⓜ al·ber·ge khoo·ve·neel youth hostel
alcachofa ⓕ al·ka·cho·fa artichoke
alcohol ⓜ al·col alcohol
Alemania ⓕ a·le·ma·nya Germany
alérgia ⓕ a·ler·khya allergy
alérgia ⓕ **al polen** a·ler·khya al po·len hay fever
alfarería ⓕ al·fa·re·ree·a pottery
alfombra ⓕ al·fom·bra rug
algo al·go something
algodón ⓜ al·go·don cotton
alguien al·gyen someone
algún al·goon some
alguno/a ⓜ/ⓕ al·goo·no/a any
almendras ⓕ pl al·men·dras almonds
almohada ⓕ al·mwa·da pillow
almuerzo ⓜ al·mwer·tho lunch
alojamiento ⓜ a·lo·kha·myen·to accommodation
alojarse a·lo·khar·se stay (somewhere)
alpinismo ⓜ al·pee·nees·mo mountaineering
alquilar al·kee·lar hire • rent
alquiler ⓜ al·kee·ler rent
— **de coche** de ko·che car hire
altar ⓜ al·tar altar
alto/a ⓜ/ⓕ al·to/a high • tall
altura ⓕ al·too·ra altitude
ama ⓕ **de casa** a·ma de ka·sa homemaker
amable a·ma·ble kind
amanecer ⓜ a·ma·ne·ther sunrise
amante ⓜ&ⓕ a·man·te lover
amarillo/a ⓜ/ⓕ a·ma·ree·lyo/a yellow
amigo/a ⓜ/ⓕ a·mee·go/a friend
ampolla ⓕ am·po·lya blister
anacardo a·na·kar·do cashew nut
analgésicos ⓜ pl a·nal·khe·see·kos painkillers
análisis de sangre ⓜ a·na·lee·sees de san·gre blood test
anarquista ⓜ/ⓕ a·nar·kees·ta anarchist

ancho/a ⓜ/ⓕ an·cho/a wide
andar an·dar walk
animal ⓜ a·nee·mal animal
Año Nuevo a·nyo nwe·vo New Year
antes an·tes before
antibióticos ⓜ pl an·tee·byo·tee·kos antibiotics
anticonceptivos ⓜ pl an·tee·kon·thep·tee·vos contraceptives
antigüedad ⓕ an·tee·gwe·da antique
antiguo/a ⓜ/ⓕ an·tee·gwo/a ancient
antiséptico ⓜ an·tee·sep·tee·ko antiseptic
antología ⓕ an·to·lo·khee·a anthology
anuncio ⓜ a·noon·thyo advertisement
aparcamiento ⓜ a·par·ka·myen·to carpark
apellido ⓜ a·pe·lyee·do surname
apéndice ⓜ a·pen·dee·the appendix
apodo ⓜ a·po·do nickname
aprender a·pren·der learn
apretado/a ⓜ/ⓕ a·pre·ta·do/a tight
apuesta ⓕ a·pwes·ta bet
apuntar a·poon·tar point
aquí a·kee here
araña ⓕ a·ra·nya spider
árbitro ⓜ ar·bee·tro referee
árbol ⓜ ar·bol tree
arena ⓕ a·re·na sand
armario ⓜ ar·ma·ryo cupboard
arqueológico/a ⓜ/ⓕ ar·ke·o·lo·khee·ko/a archaeological
arquitecto/a ⓜ/ⓕ ar·kee·tek·to/a architect
arquitectura ⓕ ar·kee·tek·too·ra architecture
arriba a·ree·ba above • up
arroyo ⓜ a·ro·yo stream
arroz ⓜ a·roth rice
arte ⓜ ar·te art
— **gráfico** gra·fee·ko graphic art
artes ⓜ pl **marciales** ar·tes mar·thya·les martial arts
artesanía ⓕ ar·te·sa·nee·a crafts
artista ⓜ&ⓕ ar·tees·ta artist
ascensor ⓜ as·then·sor elevator
Asia ⓕ a·sya Asia

asiento ⓜ a·syen·to *seat*
 — de seguridad para bebés de se·goo·ree·da pa·ra be·bes *child seat*
asma ⓜ as·ma *asthma*
aspirina ⓕ as·pee·ree·na *aspirin*
atascado/a ⓜ/ⓕ a·tas·ka·do/a *blocked*
atletismo ⓜ at·le·tees·mo *athletics*
atmósfera ⓕ at·mos·fe·ra *atmosphere*
atún ⓜ a·toon *tuna*
audífono ⓜ ow·dee·fo·no *hearing aid*
Australia ⓕ ow·stra·lya *Australia*
autobús ⓜ ow·to·boos *bus*
autocar ⓜ ow·to·kar *bus (intercity)*
autódromo ⓜ ow·to·dro·mo *track (car racing)*
autoservicio ⓜ ow·to·ser·vee·thyo *self-service*
autovía ⓕ ow·to·vee·a *motorway*
avenida ⓕ a·ve·nee·da *avenue*
avergonzado/a ⓜ/ⓕ a·ver·gon·tha·do/a *embarrassed*
avión ⓜ a·vyon *plane*
ayer a·yer *yesterday*
ayudar a·yoo·dar *help*
azúcar ⓜ a·thoo·kar *sugar*
azul a·thool *blue*

B

bailar bai·lar *dance*
bajo/a ⓜ/ⓕ ba·kho/a *short (height) • low*
balcón ⓜ bal·kon *balcony*
ballet ⓜ ba·le *ballet*
baloncesto ⓜ ba·lon·thes·to *basketball*
bálsamo de aftershave bal·sa·mo de af·ter·sha·eev *aftershave*
bálsamo de labios bal·sa·mo de la·byos *lip balm*
bañador ⓜ ba·nya·dor *bathing suit*
banco ⓜ ban·ko *bank*
bandera ⓕ ban·de·ra *flag*
bañera ⓕ ba·nye·ra *bath*
baño ⓜ ba·nyo *bathroom*
bar ⓜ bar *bar*
barato/a ⓜ/ⓕ ba·ra·to/a *cheap*

barco ⓜ bar·ko *boat*
barrio ⓜ ba·ryo *suburb*
basura ⓕ ba·soo·ra *rubbish*
batería ⓕ ba·te·ree·a *battery (car) • drums*
bebé ⓜ be·be *baby*
béisbol ⓜ beys·bol *baseball*
beneficio ⓜ be·ne·fee·thyo *profit*
berenjenas ⓕ pl be·ren·khe·nas *aubergine • eggplant*
besar be·sar *kiss*
beso ⓜ be·so *kiss*
biblia ⓕ bee·blya *bible*
biblioteca ⓕ bee·blyo·te·ka *library*
bicho ⓜ bee·cho *bug*
bici ⓕ bee·thee *bike*
bicicleta ⓕ bee·thee·kle·ta *bicycle*
 — de carreras de ka·re·ras *racing bike*
 — de montaña de mon·ta·nya *mountain bike*
bien byen *well*
bienestar ⓜ byen·es·tar *welfare*
bienvenida ⓕ byen·ve·nee·da *welcome*
billete ⓜ bee·lye·te *ticket*
 — de ida y vuelta de ee·da ee vwel·ta *return ticket*
 — de lista de espera de lees·ta de es·pe·ra *standby ticket*
billetes ⓜ pl **de banco** bee·lye·tes de ban·ko *banknotes*
biografía ⓕ bee·o·gra·fee·a *biography*
bistec ⓜ bees·tek *steak (beef)*
blanco y negro blan·ko ee ne·gro *B&W (film)*
blanco/a ⓜ/ⓕ blan·ko/a *white*
boca ⓕ bo·ka *mouth*
bocado ⓜ bo·ka·do *bite (food)*
boda ⓕ bo·da *wedding*
bodega ⓕ bo·de·ga *winery • liquor store*
bol ⓜ bol *bowl*
bolas ⓕ pl **de algodón** bo·las de al·go·don *cotton balls*
bolígrafo ⓜ bo·lee·gra·fo *pen*
bollos ⓜ pl bo·lyos *rolls (bread)*

bolo ⓜ *bo·lo gig*
bolsillo ⓜ *bol·see·lyo pocket*
bolso ⓜ *bol·so bag • handbag*
bomba ⓕ *bom·ba pump • bomb*
bombilla ⓕ *bom·bee·lya light bulb*
bondadoso/a ⓜ/ⓕ *bon·da·do·so/a caring*
bonito/a ⓜ/ⓕ *bo·nee·to/a pretty*
bordo ⓜ *bor·do edge*
a bordo *a bor·do aboard*
borracho/a ⓜ/ⓕ *bo·ra·cho/a drunk*
bosque ⓜ *bos·ke forest*
botas ⓕ pl *bo·tas boots*
— **de montaña** *de mon·ta·nya hiking boots*
botella ⓕ *bo·te·lya bottle*
botones ⓜ pl *bo·to·nes buttons*
boxeo ⓜ *bo·kse·o boxing*
bragas ⓕ pl *bra·gas underpants (women)*
brazo ⓜ *bra·tho arm*
broma ⓕ *bro·ma joke*
bronceador ⓜ *bron·the·a·dor tanning lotion*
bronquitis ⓜ *bron·kee·tees bronchitis*
brotes ⓜ pl **de soja** *bro·tes de so·kha bean sprouts*
brújula ⓕ *broo·khoo·la compass*
brumoso *broo·mo·so foggy*
buceo ⓜ *boo·the·o snorkelling*
budista ⓜ&ⓕ *boo·dees·ta Buddhist*
bueno/a ⓜ/ⓕ *bwe·no/a good*
bufanda ⓕ *boo·fan·da scarf*
buffet ⓜ *boo·fe buffet*
bulto ⓜ *bool·to lump*
burlarse de *boor·lar·se de make fun of*
burro ⓜ *boo·ro donkey*
buscar *boos·kar look for*
buzón ⓜ *boo·thon mailbox*

C

caballo ⓜ *ka·ba·lyo horse*
cabeza ⓕ *ka·be·tha head*
cabina ⓕ **telefónica** *ka·bee·na te·le·fo·nee·ka phone box*
cable ⓜ *ka·ble cable*

cables ⓜ pl **de arranque** *ka·bles de a·ran·ke jumper leads*
cabra ⓕ *ka·bra goat*
cacahuetes ⓜ pl *ka·ka·we·tes peanuts*
cacao ⓜ *ka·kow cocoa*
cachorro ⓜ *ka·cho·ro puppy*
cada *ka·da each*
cadena ⓕ **de bici** *ka·de·na de bee·thee bike chain*
café ⓜ *ka·fe coffee • cafe*
caída ⓕ *ka·ee·da fall*
caja ⓕ *ka·kha box • cashier*
— **fuerte** *fwer·te safe*
— **registradora** *re·khees·tra·do·ra cash register*
cajero ⓜ **automático** *ka·khe·ro ow·to·ma·tee·ko automatic teller machine*
calabacín ⓜ *ka·la·ba·theen zucchini • courgette*
calabaza ⓕ *ka·la·ba·tha pumpkin*
calcetines ⓜ pl *kal·the·tee·nes socks*
calculadora ⓕ *kal·koo·la·do·ra calculator*
caldo ⓜ *kal·do stock*
calefacción ⓕ **central** *ka·le·fak·thyon then·tral central heating*
calendario ⓜ *ka·len·da·ryo calendar*
calidad ⓕ *ka·lee·da quality*
caliente *ka·lyen·te hot*
calle ⓕ *ka·lye street*
calor ⓜ *ka·lor heat*
calzoncillos ⓜ pl *kal·thon·thee·lyos underpants (men)*
calzones ⓜ pl *kal·tho·nes boxer shorts*
cama ⓕ *ka·ma bed*
— **de matrimonio** *de ma·tree·mo·nyo double bed*
cámara ⓕ **(fotográfica)** *ka·ma·ra (fo·to·gra·fee·ka) camera*
cámara ⓕ **de aire** *ka·ma·ra de ai·re tube (tyre)*
camarero/a ⓜ/ⓕ *ka·ma·re·ro/a waiter*
cambiar *kam·byar change • exchange (money)*
cambio *kam·byo* ⓜ *loose change*
— **de dinero** *de dee·ne·ro currency exchange*
caminar *ka·mee·nar walk*

camino ⓜ ka·*mee*·no trail • way

caminos ⓜ pl **rurales** ka·*mee*·nos roo·*ra*·les hiking routes

camión ⓜ ka·*myon* truck

camisa ⓕ ka·*mee*·sa shirt

camiseta ⓕ ka·mee·se·ta singlet • T-shirt

cámping ⓜ *kam*·peen campsite

campo ⓜ *kam*·po countryside • field

Canadá ⓕ ka·na·*da* Canada

canasta ⓕ ka·*nas*·ta basket

cancelar kan·the·*lar* cancel

cáncer ⓜ *kan*·ther cancer

canción ⓕ kan·*thyon* song

candado ⓜ kan·*da*·do padlock

cangrejo ⓜ kan·*gre*·kho crab

cansado/a ⓜ/ⓕ kan·sa·do/a tired

cantalupo ⓜ kan·ta·*loo*·po cantaloupe

cantante ⓜ&ⓕ kan·*tan*·te singer

cantar kan·*tar* sing

cantimplora ⓕ kan·teem·*plo*·ra water bottle

capa ⓕ **de ozono** *ka*·pa de o·*tho*·no ozone layer

capilla ⓕ ka·*pee*·lya shrine

capote ⓜ ka·*po*·te cloak

cara ⓕ *ka*·ra face

caracol ⓜ ka·ra·*kol* snail

caramelos ⓜ pl ka·ra·*me*·los lollies

caravana ⓕ ka·ra·*va*·na caravan • van • traffic jam

cárcel ⓕ *kar*·thel prison

cardenal ⓜ kar·de·*nal* bruise

carne ⓕ *kar*·ne meat
  — **de vaca** de *va*·ka beef
  — **molida** mo·*lee*·da mince meat

carnet ⓜ kar·*ne* licence
  — **de identidad** de ee·den·tee·*da* identification card
  — **de conducir** de kon·doo·*theer* drivers licence

carnicería ⓕ kar·nee·the·*ree*·a butcher's shop

caro/a ⓜ/ⓕ *ka*·ro/a expensive

carpintero ⓜ kar·peen·*te*·ro carpenter

carrera ⓕ ka·*re*·ra race (sport)

carta ⓕ *kar*·ta letter

cartas ⓕ pl *kar*·tas cards

cartón ⓜ kar·*ton* carton • cardboard

casa ⓕ *ka*·sa house

(en) casa (en) *ka*·sa (at) home

casarse ka·*sar*·se marry

cascada ⓕ kas·*ka*·da waterfall

casco ⓜ *kas*·ko helmet

casete ⓜ ka·se·te cassette

casi *ka*·see almost

casino ⓜ ka·*see*·no casino

castigar kas·tee·*gar* punish

castillo ⓜ kas·*tee*·lyo castle

catedral ⓕ ka·te·*dral* cathedral

católico/a ⓜ/ⓕ ka·to·lee·ko/a Catholic

caza ⓕ *ka*·tha hunting

cazuela ⓕ ka·*thwe*·la pot (kitchen)

cebolla ⓕ the·*bo*·lya onion

celebración ⓕ the·le·bra·*thyon* celebration

celebrar the·le·*brar* celebrate (an event)

celoso/a ⓜ/ⓕ the·*lo*·so/a jealous

cementerio ⓜ the·men·*te*·ryo cemetery

cena ⓕ *the*·na dinner

cenicero ⓜ the·nee·*the*·ro ashtray

centavo ⓜ then·*ta*·vo cent

centímetro ⓜ then·*tee*·me·tro centimetre

central ⓕ **telefónica** then·*tral* te·le·fo·*nee*·ka telephone centre

centro ⓜ *then*·tro centre
  — **comercial** ko·mer·*thyal* shopping centre
  — **de la ciudad** de la theew·*da* city centre

cepillo ⓜ the·*pee*·lyo hairbrush
  — **de dientes** de *dyen*·tes toothbrush

cerámica ⓕ the·*ra*·mee·ka ceramic

cerca ⓕ *ther*·ka fence

cerca *ther*·ka near • nearby

cerdo ⓜ *ther*·do pork • pig

cereales ⓜ pl the·re·*a*·les cereal

cerillas ⓕ pl las the·*ree*·lyas matches

cerrado/a ⓜ/ⓕ the·*ra*·do/a closed
  — **con llave** kon *lya*·ve locked

cerradura ⓕ the·ra·*doo*·ra lock (padlock)

cerrar the·*rar* close • lock • shut

certificado ⓜ ther·tee·fee·*ka*·do
certificate

cerveza ⓕ ther·*ve*·tha *beer*
— **rubia** *roo*·bya *lager*

cibercafé ⓜ thee·ber·ka·*fe Internet
cafe*

ciclismo ⓜ thee·*klees*·mo *cycling*

ciclista ⓜ&ⓕ thee·*klees*·ta *cyclist*

ciego/a ⓜ/ⓕ *thye*·go/a *blind*

cielo ⓜ *thye*·lo *sky*

ciencias ⓕ pl *thyen*·thyas *science*

científico/a ⓜ/ⓕ thyen·*tee*·fee·ko/a
scientist

cigarrillo ⓜ thee·ga·*ree*·lyo *cigarette*

cigarro ⓜ thee·*ga*·ro *cigarette*

cine ⓜ *thee*·ne *cinema*

cinta ⓕ **de vídeo** *theen*·ta de *vee*·de·o
video tape

cinturón ⓜ **de seguridad** theen·too·*ron*
de se·goo·ree·*da seatbelt*

circuito ⓜ **de carreras** theer·*kwee*·to
de ka·*re*·ras *racetrack (cars)*

ciruela ⓕ thee·*rwe*·la *plum*
— **pasa** *pa*·sa *prune*

cistitis ⓕ thees·*tee*·tees *cystitis*

cita ⓕ *thee*·ta *appointment*

citarse thee·*tar*·se *date*

citología ⓕ thee·to·lo·*khee*·a *pap smear*

ciudad ⓕ theew·*da city*

ciudadanía ⓕ theew·da·da·*nee*·a
citizenship

clase ⓕ **preferente** *kla*·se pre·fe·*ren*·te
business class

clase ⓕ **turística** *kla*·se too·*rees*·tee·ka
economy class

clásico/a ⓜ/ⓕ *kla*·see·ko/a *classical*

clienta/e ⓜ/ⓕ klee·*en*·ta/e *client*

clínica ⓕ *klee*·nee·ka *private hospital*

cobrar (un cheque) ko·*brar* (oon
che·ke) *cash (a cheque)*

coca ⓕ *ko*·ka *cocaine*

cocaína ⓕ ko·ka·*ee*·na *cocaine*

coche ⓜ *ko*·che *car*
— **cama** *ka*·ma *sleeping car*

cocina ⓕ ko·*thee*·na *kitchen* • *stove*

cocinar ko·thee·*nar cook*

cocinero ⓜ ko·thee·*ne*·ro *chef* • *cook*

coco ⓜ *ko*·ko *coconut*

codeína ⓕ ko·de·ee·na *codeine*

código ⓜ **postal** *ko*·dee·go pos·*tal
post code*

cojonudo/a ⓜ/ⓕ ko·kho·*noo*·do/a
fantastic

col ⓕ kol *cabbage*

cola ⓕ *ko*·la *queue*

colchón ⓜ kol·*chon mattress*

colega ⓜ&ⓕ ko·*le*·ga *colleague* • *mate*

coles ⓕ pl **de Bruselas** *ko*·les de
broo·*se*·las *brussels sprouts*

coliflor ⓕ ko·lee·*flor cauliflower*

colina ⓕ ko·*lee*·na *hill*

collar ⓜ ko·*lyar necklace*

color ⓜ ko·*lor colour*

comedia ⓕ ko·*me*·dya *comedy*

comenzar ko·men·*thar begin* • *start*

comer ko·*mer eat*

comerciante ⓜ&ⓕ ko·mer·*thyan*·te
business person

comercio ⓜ ko·*mer*·thyo *trade*

comezón ⓕ ko·me·*thon itch*

comida ⓕ ko·*mee*·da *food*
— **de bebé** de be·*be baby food*
— **en el campo** en el *kam*·po *picnic*

comisaría ⓕ ko·mee·sa·*ree*·a *police
station*

cómo *ko*·mo *how*

cómodo/a ⓜ/ⓕ ko·mo·do/a *comfortable*

cómpact ⓜ kom·pak *CD*

compañero/a ⓜ/ⓕ kom·pa·*nye*·ro/a
companion

compañía ⓕ kom·pa·*nyee*·a *company*

compartir kom·par·*teer share (with)*

comprar kom·*prar buy*

comprender kom·pren·*der understand*

compresas ⓕ pl kom·*pre*·sas *sanitary
napkins*

compromiso ⓜ kom·pro·*mee*·so
engagement

comunión ⓕ ko·moo·*nyon communion*

comunista ⓜ&ⓕ ko·moo·*nees*·ta
communist

con kon *with*

coñac ⓜ ko·*nyak brandy*

concentración ⓕ kon·then·tra·*thyon
rally*

concierto ⓜ kon·thyer·to *concert*
condición ⓕ **cardíaca** kon·dee·thyon kar·dee·a·ka *heart condition*
condones ⓜ pl kon·do·nes *condoms*
conducir kon·doo·theer *drive*
conejo ⓜ ko·ne·kho *rabbit*
conexión ⓕ kon·ne·ksyon *connection*
confesión ⓕ kon·fe·syon *confession*
confianza ⓕ kon·fee·an·tha *trust*
confiar kon·fee·ar *trust*
confirmar kon·feer·mar *confirm*
conocer ko·no·ther *know (someone)*
conocido/a ⓜ/ⓕ ko·no·thee·do/a *famous*
consejo ⓜ kon·se·kho *advice*
conservador(a) ⓜ/ⓕ kon·ser·va·dor/ kon·ser·va·do·ra *conservative*
consigna ⓕ kon·seeg·na *left luggage*
— **automática** ow·to·ma·tee·ka *luggage lockers*
construir kons·troo·eer *build*
consulado ⓜ kon·soo·la·do *consulate*
contaminación ⓕ kon·ta·mee·na·thyon *pollution*
contar kon·tar *count*
contestador ⓜ **automático** kon·tes·ta·dor ow·to·ma·tee·ko *answering machine*
contrato ⓜ kon·tra·to *contract*
control ⓜ kon·trol *checkpoint*
convento ⓜ kon·ven·to *convent*
copa ⓕ ko·pa *drink*
— **de vino** de vee·no *wineglass*
copos de maíz ko·pos de ma·eeth *corn flakes*
corazón ⓜ ko·ra·thon *heart*
cordero ⓜ kor·de·ro *lamb*
cordillera ⓕ kor·dee·lye·ra *mountain range*
correcto/a ⓜ/ⓕ ko·rek·to/a *right (correct)*
correo ⓜ ko·re·o *mail*
— **urgente** oor·khen·te *express mail*
correos ⓜ ko·re·os *post office*
correr ko·rer *run*
corrida ⓕ **de toros** ko·ree·da de to·ros *bullfight*

corriente ⓕ ko·ryen·te *current (electricity)*
corriente ko·ryen·te *ordinary*
corrupto/a ⓜ/ⓕ ko·roop·to/a *corrupt*
cortar kor·tar *cut*
cortauñas ⓜ pl kor·ta·oo·nyas *nail clippers*
corto/a ⓜ/ⓕ kor·to/a *short (length)*
cosecha ⓕ ko·se·cha *crop*
coser ko·ser *sew*
costa ⓕ kos·ta *coast • seaside*
costar kos·tar *cost*
crecer kre·ther *grow*
crema ⓕ kre·ma *cream*
— **hidratante** ee·dra·tan·te *cream (moisturising)*
— **solar** so·lar *sunblock*
críquet ⓜ kree·ket *cricket*
cristiano/a ⓜ/ⓕ krees·tya·no/a *Christian*
crítica ⓕ kree·tee·ka *review*
cruce ⓜ kroo·the *intersection*
crudo/a ⓜ/ⓕ kroo·do/a *raw*
cuaderno ⓜ kwa·der·no *notebook • square*
cualificaciones ⓕ pl kwa·lee·fee·ka·thyo·nes *qualifications*
cuando kwan·do *when*
cuánto kwan·to *how much*
cuarentena ⓕ kwa·ren·te·na *quarantine*
Cuaresma ⓕ kwa·res·ma *Lent*
cuarto ⓜ kwar·to *quarter*
cubiertos ⓜ pl koo·byer·tos *cutlery*
cubo ⓜ koo·bo *bucket*
cucaracha ⓕ koo·ka·ra·cha *cockroach*
cuchara ⓕ koo·cha·ra *spoon*
cucharita ⓕ koo·cha·ree·ta *teaspoon*
cuchillas ⓕ pl **de afeitar** koo·chee·lyas de a·fey·tar *razor blades*
cuchillo ⓜ koo·chee·lyo *knife*
cuenta ⓕ kwen·ta *bill*
— **bancaria** ban·ka·rya *bank account*
cuento ⓜ kwen·to *story*
cuerda ⓕ kwer·da *rope • string*
— **para tender la ropa** pa·ra ten·der la ro·pa *clothes line*
cuero ⓜ kwe·ro *leather*
cuerpo ⓜ kwer·po *body*

cuesta abajo kwes·ta a·ba·kho *downhill*
cuesta arriba kwes·ta a·ree·ba *uphill*
cuestionar kwes·tyo·nar *question*
cuevas ① pl kwe·vas *caves*
cuidar kwee·dar *care for • mind (an object)*
cuidar de kwee·dar de *care (for someone)*
culo ⑩ koo·lo *bum (of body)*
culpable kool·pa·ble *guilty*
cumbre ① koom·bre *peak*
cumpleaños ⑩ koom·ple·a·nyos *birthday*
currículum ⑩ koo·ree·koo·loom *resumé*
curry ⑩ koo·ree *curry*
cus cus ⑩ koos koos *cous cous*

CH

chaleco ⑩ salvavidas cha·le·ko sal·va·vee·das *lifejacket*
champán ⑩ cham·pan *Champagne*
champiñón ⑩ cham·pee·nyon *mushrooms*
champú ⑩ cham·poo *shampoo*
chaqueta ① cha·ke·ta *jacket*
cheque ⑩ che·ke *check (bank)*
cheques ⑩ pl de viajero che·kes de vya·khe·ro *travellers cheque*
chica ① chee·ka *girl*
chicle ⑩ chee·kle *chewing gum*
chico ⑩ chee·ko *boy*
chocolate ⑩ cho·ko·la·te *chocolate*
choque ⑩ cho·ke *crash*
chorizo ⑩ cho·ree·tho *salami (Spanish sausage)*
chupete ⑩ choo·pe·te *dummy • pacifier*

D

dados ⑩ pl da·dos *dice (die)*
dañar da·nyar *hurt*
dar dar *give*
-- de comer de ko·mer *feed*
-- gracias g·a·thyas *thank*

— la bienvenida la byen·ve·nee·da *welcome*
— una patada oo·na pa·ta·da *kick*
darse cuenta de dar·se kwen·ta de *realise*
de de *from*
— (cuatro) estrellas de (kwa·tro) es·tre·lyas *(four-)star*
— izquierda de eeth·kyer·da de *left-wing*
— pena de pe·na *terrible*
— primera clase de pree·me·ra kla·se *first-class*
— segunda mano de se·goon·da ma·no *second-hand*
— vez en cuando de veth en kwan·do *sometimes*
deber de·ver *owe*
débil de·beel *weak*
decidir de·thee·deer *decide*
decir de·theer *say • tell*
dedo ⑩ de·do *finger*
— del pie del pye *toe*
defectuoso/a ⑩/① de·fek·too·o·so/a *faulty*
deforestación ① de·fo·res·ta·thyon *deforestation*
dejar de·khar *leave • quit*
delgado/a ⑩/① del·ga·do/a *thin*
delirante de·lee·ran·te *delirious*
demasiado caro/a ⑩/① de·ma·sya·do ka·ro/a *too (expensive)*
democracia ① de·mo·kra·thya *democracy*
demora ① de·mo·ra *delay*
dentista ⑩&① den·tees·ta *dentist*
dentro de (una hora) den·tro de (oo·na o·ra) *within (an hour)*
deportes ⑩ pl de·por·tes *sport*
deportista ⑩&① de·por·tees·ta *sportsperson*
depósito ⑩ de·po·see·to *deposit*
derecha ① de·re·cha *right (not left)*
derechista de·re·chees·ta *right-wing*
derechos ⑩ pl civiles de·re·chos thee·vee·les *civil rights*

derechos ⓜ pl **humanos** de·re·chos oo·ma·nos *human rights*

desayuno ⓜ des·a·yoo·no *breakfast*

descansar des·kan·sar *rest*

descanso ⓜ des·kan·so *intermission*

descendiente ⓜ des·then·dyen·te *descendant*

descomponerse des·kom·po·ner·se *decompose*

descubrir des·koo·breer *discover*

descuento ⓜ des·kwen·to *discount*

desde (mayo) des·de (ma·yo) *since (may)*

desear de·se·ar *wish*

desierto de·syer·to *desert*

desodorante ⓜ de·so·do·ran·te *deodorant*

despacio des·pa·thyo *slowly*

desperdicios ⓜ pl **nucleares** des·per·dee·thyos noo·kle·a·res *nuclear waste*

despertador ⓜ des·per·ta·dor *alarm clock*

después de des·pwes de *after*

destino ⓜ des·tee·no *destination*

destruir des·troo·eer *destroy*

detallado/a ⓜ/ⓕ de·ta·lya·do/a *itemised*

detalle ⓜ de·ta·lye *detail*

detener de·te·ner *arrest*

detrás de de·tras de *behind*

devocionario ⓜ de·vo·thyo·na·ryo *prayer book*

día ⓜ dee·a *a day*

— **festivo** fes·tee·vo *holiday*

diabetes ⓕ dee·a·be·tes *diabetes*

diafragma ⓕ dee·a·frag·ma *diaphragm*

diapositiva ⓕ dya·po·see·tee·va *slide*

diariamente dya·rya·men·te *daily*

diarrea ⓕ dee·a·re·a *diarrhoea*

dieta ⓕ dee·e·ta *diet*

dibujar dee·boo·khar *draw*

diccionario ⓜ deek·thyo·na·ryo *dictionary*

diente (de ajo) dyen·te (de a·kho) *clove (garlic)*

dientes ⓜ pl dyen·tes *teeth*

diferencia ⓕ **de horas** dee·fe·ren·thya de o·ras *time difference*

diferente dee·fe·ren·te *different*

difícil dee·fee·theel *difficult*

dinero ⓜ dee·ne·ro *money*

— **en efectivo** en e·fek·tee·vo *cash*

Dios dyos *god*

dirección ⓕ dee·rek·thyon *address*

directo/a ⓜ/ⓕ dee·rek·to/a *direct*

director(a) ⓜ/ⓕ dee·rek·tor/ dee·rek·to·ra *director*

disco ⓜ dees·ko *disk*

discoteca ⓕ dees·ko·te·ka *disco*

discriminación ⓕ dees·kree·mee·na·thyon *discrimination*

discutir dees·koo·teer *argue*

diseño ⓜ dee·se·nyo *design*

disparar dees·pa·rar *shoot*

DIU ⓜ de ee oo *IUD*

diversión ⓕ dee·ver·syon *fun*

divertirse dee·ver·teer·se *enjoy (oneself)*

doblar do·blar *turn • bend*

doble do·ble *double*

docena ⓕ do·the·na *dozen*

doctor(a) ⓜ/ⓕ dok·tor/dok·to·ra *doctor*

dólar ⓜ do·lar *dollar*

dolor ⓜ do·lor *pain*

— **de cabeza** de ka·be·tha *headache*

— **de estómago** de es·to·ma·go *stomachache*

— **de muelas** de mwe·las *toothache*

— **menstrual** mens·trwal *period pain*

dolorido/a ⓜ/ⓕ do·lo·ree·do/a *sore*

doloroso/a ⓜ/ⓕ do·lo·ro·so/a *painful*

donde don·de *where*

dormir dor·meer *sleep*

dos ⓜ/ⓕ pl dos *two*

— **camas** ka·mas *twin beds*

— **veces** ve·thes *twice*

drama ⓜ dra·ma *drama*

droga ⓕ dro·ga *drug • dope*

drogadicción ⓕ dro·ga·deek·thyon *drug addiction*

drogas ⓕ pl dro·gas *drugs*

ducha ⓕ doo·cha *shower*

dueño/a ⓜ/ⓕ dwe·nyo/a *owner*

dulce dool·the *sweet*

dulces ⓜ pl dool·thes *sweets*

duro/a ⓜ/ⓕ doo·ro/a *hard*

E

eczema ① ek·*the*·ma *eczema*

edad ① e·*da* *age*

edificio ⓜ e·dee·fee·thyo *building*

editor(a) ⓜ/① e·dee·tor/e·dee·to·ra *editor*

educación ① e·doo·ka·*thyon* *education*

egoísta e·go·ees·ta *selfish*

ejemplo ⓜ e·*khem*·plo *example*

ejército ⓜ e·*kher*·thee·to *military*

él ⓜ el *he*

elecciones ① pl e·lek·*thyo*·nes *elections*

electricidad ① e·lek·tree·thee·*da* *electricity*

elegir e·le·*kheer* *pick* • *choose*

ella ① e·lya *she*

ellos/ellas ⓜ/① e·lyos/e·lyas *they*

embajada ① em·ba·*kha*·da *embassy*

embajador(a) ⓜ/① em·ba·kha·*dor*/em·ba·kha·*do*·ra *ambassador*

embarazada em·ba·ra·*tha*·da *pregnant*

embarcarse em·bar·*kar*·se *board (ship, etc)*

embrague ⓜ em·*bra*·ge *clutch*

emergencia ① e·mer·*khen*·thya *emergency*

emocional e·mo·thyo·*nal* *emotional*

empleado/a ⓜ/① em·ple·a·do/a *employee*

empujar em·poo·*khar* *push*

en en *on*
　— **el extranjero** el eks·tran·*khe*·ro *abroad*
　— **el paro** el *pa*·ro *unemployed*

encaje ⓜ en·*ka*·khe *lace*

encantador(a) ⓜ/① en·kan·ta·*dor*/en·kan·ta·*do*·ra *charming*

encendedor ⓜ en·then·de·*dor* *lighter*

encontrar en·kon·*trar* *find* • *meet*

encurtidos ⓜ pl en·koor·tee·dos *pickles*

energía ① **nuclear** e·ner·*khee*·a noo·kle·*ar* *nuclear energy*

enfadado/a ⓜ/① en·fa·*da*·do/a *angry*

enfermedad ① en·fer·me·*da* *disease*
　— **venérea** ve·*ne*·re·a *venereal disease*

enfermero/a ⓜ/① en·fer·me·ro/a *nurse*

enfermo/a ⓜ/① en·*fer*·mo/a *sick*

enfrente de en·*fren*·te de *in front of*

enorme e·*nor*·me *huge*

ensalada en·sa·*la*·da *salad*

enseñar en·se·*nyar* *show* • *teach*

entrar en·*trar* *enter*

entre *en*·tre *among* • *between*

entregar en·tre·*gar* *deliver*

entrenador(a) ⓜ/① en·tre·na·*dor*/en·tre·na·*do*·ra *coach*

entreno ⓜ en·*tre*·no *workout*

entrevista ① en·tre·vees·ta *interview*

enviar en·vee·*ar* *send* • *ship off*

epilepsia ① e·pee·*lep*·sya *epilepsy*

equipaje ⓜ e·kee·*pa*·khe *luggage*

equipo ⓜ e·*kee*·po *equipment* • *team*
　— **de inmersión** de een·mer·*syon* *diving equipment*
　— **de música** ⓜ de moo·see·ka *stereo*

equitación ① e·kee·ta·*thyon* *horse riding*

equivocado/a ⓜ/① e·kee·vo·ka·do/a *wrong*

error ⓜ e·ror *mistake*

escalada ① es·ka·*la*·da *rock climbing*

escalera ① es·ka·*le*·ra *stairway*

escaleras ① pl **mecánicas** es·ka·*le*·ras me·*kan*·icas *escalator*

escarcha ① es·*kar*·cha *frost*

escarpado/a ⓜ/① es·kar·pa·do/a *steep*

escasez ① es·ka·*seth* *shortage*

escenario ⓜ es·the·*na*·ryo *stage*

Escocia ① es·ko·thya *Scotland*

escoger es·ko·*kher* *choose*

escribir es·kree·*beer* *write*
　— **a máquina** a *ma*·kee·na *type*

escritor(a) ⓜ/① es·kree·tor/es·kree·to·ra *writer*

escuchar es·koo·*char* *listen*

escuela ① es·*kwe*·la *school*
　— **de párvulos** de *par*·voo·los *kindergarten*

escultura ① es·kool·too·ra *sculpture*
espacio ⑩ es·pa·thyo *space*
espalda ① es·pal·da *back (body)*
España ① es·pa·nya *Spain*
especial es·pe·thyal *special*
especialista ⑩&① es·pe·thya·lees·ta *specialist*
especies ① pl **en peligro de extinción** es·pe·thyes en pe·lee·gro de eks·teen·thyon *endangered species*
espectáculo ⑩ es·pek·ta·koo·lo *show*
espejo ⑩ es·pe·kho *mirror*
esperar es·pe·rar *wait*
espinaca ① es·pee·na·ka *spinach*
esposa ① es·po·sa *wife*
espuma ① **de afeitar** es·poo·ma de a·fey·tar *shaving cream*
espumoso/a ⑩/①es·poo·mo·so/a *sparkling • foamy*
esquí ⑩ es·kee *skiing*
— **acuático** a·kwa·tee·ko *waterskiing*
esquiar es·kee·ar *ski*
esquina ① es·kee·na *corner*
esta noche es·ta no·che *tonight*
éste/a ⑩/① es·te/a *this*
estación ① es·ta·thyon *season • station*
— **de autobuses** de ow·to·boo·ses *bus station*
— **de metro** de me·tro *metro station*
de tren de tren *railway station*
estacionar es·ta·thyo·nar *park (car)*
estadio ⑩ es·ta·dyo *stadium*
estado ⑩ **civil** es·ta·do thee·veel *marital status*
estado ⑩ **del bienestar** es·ta·do del byen·es·tar *social welfare • well being*
estafa ① es·ta·fa *rip-off*
estanquero ⑩ es·tan·ke·ro *tobacconist*
estante ⑩ es·tan·te *shelf*
estar es·tar *to be*
— **constipado/a** ⑩/① kons·tee·pa·do/a *have a cold*
— **de acuerdo** de a·kwer·do *agree*
estatua ① es·ta·twa *statue*
este es·te *east*
esterilla ① es·te·ree·lya *mat*

estilo ⑩ es·tee·lo *style*
estómago ⑩ es·to·ma·go *stomach*
estrellas ① pl es·tre·lyas *stars*
estreñimiento ⑩ es·tre·nyee·myen·to *constipation*
estudiante ⑩&① es·too·dyan·te *student*
estudio ⑩ es·too·dyo *studio*
estufa ① es·too·fa *heater*
estúpido/a ⑩/① es·too·pee·do/a *stupid*
etiqueta ① **de equipaje** e·tee·ke·ta de e·kee·pa·khe *luggage tag*
euro ⑩ e·oo·ro *euro*
Europa ① e·oo·ro·pa *Europe*
eutanasia ① e·oo·ta·na·sya *euthanasia*
excelente eks·the·len·te *excellent*
excursión ① eks·koor·syon *tour*
excursionismo ⑩ eks·koor·syo·nees·mo *hiking*
experiencia ① eks·pe·ryen·thya *experience*
— **laboral** ① la·bo·ral *work experience*
exponer eks·po·ner *exhibit*
exposición ① eks·po·see·thyon *exhibition*
expreso eks·pre·so *express*
exterior ⑩ eks·te·ryor *outside*
extrañar eks·tra·nyar *miss (feel sad)*
extranjero/a ⑩/① eks·tran·khe·ro/a *foreign*

F

fábrica ① fa·bree·ka *factory*
fácil fa·theel *easy*
facturación ① **de equipajes** fak·too·ra·thyon de e·kee·pa·khes *check-in*
falda ① fal·da *skirt*
falta ① fal·ta *fault*
familia ① fa·mee·lya *family*
fantástico/a ⑩/① fan·tas·tee·ko/a *great*
farmacia ① far·ma·thya *chemist (shop) • pharmacy*
farmacéutico ⑩ far·ma·thee·oo·tee·ko *chemist (person)*
faros ⑩ pl fa·ros *headlights*

fecha ① fe·cha *date (time)*
— **de nacimiento** de na·thee·*myen*·to *date of birth*
feliz fe·*leeth* *happy*
ferretería ① fe·re·te·*ree*·a *hardware store*
festival ⓜ fes·tee·*val* *festival*
ficción ① feek·*thyon* *fiction*
fideos ⓜ pl fee·*de*·os *noodles*
fiebre ① *fye*·bre *fever*
— **glandular** glan·doo·*lar* *glandular fever*
fiesta ① *fyes*·ta *party*
filete ⓜ fee·*le*·te *fillet*
film ⓜ feelm *film*
fin ⓜ feen *end*
— **de semana** de se·*ma*·na *weekend*
final ⓜ fee·*nal* *end*
firma ① *feer*·ma *signature*
firmar feer·*mar* *sign*
flor ① flor *flower*
florista ⓜ&① flo·*rees*·ta *florist*
follar fo·*lyar* *fuck*
folleto ⓜ fo·*lye*·to *brochure*
footing ① *foo*·teen *jogging*
forma ① *for*·ma *shape*
fotografía ① fo·to·gra·*fee*·a *photograph*
fotógrafo/a ⓜ/① fo·to·*gra*·fo/a *photographer*
fotómetro ⓜ fo·to·*me*·tro *light meter*
frágil *fra*·kheel *fragile*
frambuesa ① fram·*bwe*·sa *raspberry*
franela ① fra·*ne*·la *flannel*
franqueo ⓜ fran·*ke*·o *postage*
freír fre·*eer* *fry*
frenos ⓜ pl *fre*·nos *brakes*
frente a *fren*·te a *opposite*
fresa ① *fre*·sa *strawberry*
frío/a ⓜ/① *free*·o/a *cold*
frontera ① fron·*te*·ra *border*
fruta ① *froo*·ta *fruit*
fruto ⓜ **seco** *froo*·to *se*·ko *dried fruit*
fuego ⓜ *fwe*·go *fire*
fuera de juego *fwe*·ra de *khwe*·go *offside*
fuerte *fwer*·te *strong*

fumar foo·*mar* *smoke*
funda ① **de almohada** *foon*·da de al·*mwa*·da *pillowcase*
funeral ⓜ foo·ne·*ral* *funeral*
fútbol ⓜ *foot*·bol *football* • *soccer*
— **australiano** ow·stra·*lya*·no *Australian Rules football*
futuro ⓜ foo·*too*·ro *future*

G

gafas ① pl *ga*·fas *glasses*
— **de sol** de sol *sunglasses*
— **de submarinismo** de soob·ma·ree·*nees*·mo *goggles*
galleta ① ga·*lye*·ta *biscuit* • *cookie*
galletas ① pl **saladas** ga·*lye*·tas sa·*la*·das *biscuits* • *crackers*
gambas ① pl *gam*·bas *prawns*
ganador(a) ⓜ/① ga·na·*dor*/ga·na·*do*·ra *winner*
ganar ga·*nar* *earn* • *win*
garbanzos ⓜ pl gar·*ban*·thos *chickpeas*
garganta ① gar·*gan*·ta *throat*
gasolina ① ga·so·*lee*·na *petrol*
gasolinera ① ga·so·lee·*ne*·ra *service station*
gatito/a ⓜ/① ga·*tee*·to/a *kitten*
gato/a ⓜ/① *ga*·to/a *cat*
gay gai *gay*
gemelos ⓜ pl khe·*me*·los *twins*
general khe·ne·*ral* *general*
gente ① *khen*·te *people*
gimnasia ① **rítmica** kheem·*na*·sya *reet*·mee·ka *gymnastics*
ginebra ① khee·*ne*·bra *gin*
ginecólogo ⓜ khee·ne·*ko*·lo·go *gynaecologist*
gobierno ⓜ go·*byer*·no *government*
gol ⓜ gol *goal*
goma ① *go*·ma *condom* • *rubber*
gordo/a ⓜ/① *gor*·do/a *fat*
grabación ① gra·ba·*thyon* *recording*
gracioso/a ⓜ/① gra·*thyo*·so/a *funny*
gramo ⓜ *gra*·mo *gram*
grande *gran*·de *big* • *large*

grande almacene ⓜ gran·de al·ma·*the*·ne *department store*

granja ⓕ gran·kha *farm*

gratis gra·tees *free (of charge)*

grifo ⓜ gree·fo *tap*

gripe ⓕ gree·pe *influenza*

gris grees *grey*

gritar gree·*tar* *shout*

grupo ⓜ groo·po *group*
— **de rock** de rok *rock band*
— **sanguíneo** san·gee·ne·o *blood group*

guantes ⓜ pl gwan·tes *gloves*

guardarropa ⓜ gwar·da·ro·pa *cloakroom*

guardería ⓕ gwar·de·ree·a *childminding service • creche*

guerra ⓕ ge·ra *war*

guía ⓜ&ⓕ gee·a *guide (person)*

guía ⓕ gee·a *guidebook*
— **audio** ow·dyo *guide (audio)*
— **del ocio** del o·thyo *entertainment guide*
— **telefónica** te·le·*to*·nee·ka *phone book*

guindilla ⓕ geen·dee·lya *chilli*

guión ⓜ gee·*on* *script*

guiri ⓜ gee·ree *tourist (slang)*

guisantes gee·san·tes *peas*

güisqui gwees·kee *whiskey*

guitarra ⓕ gee·ta·ra *guitar*

gustar(le) goos·*tar*(·le) *like*

H

habitación ⓕ a·bee·ta·*thyon* *bedroom • room*
— **doble** do·ble *double room*
— **individual** een·dee·vee·*dwal* *single room*

hablar a·*blar* *speak • talk*

hace sol a·the sol *sunny*

hacer a·*ther* do • *make*
— **dedo** de·do *hitchhike*
— **surf** soorf *surf*
— **windsurf** ween·soorf *windsurfing*

hachís ⓜ a·chees *hash*

hacia a·thya *towards*
— **abajo** a·ba·kho *down*

halal a·lal *Halal*

hamaca ⓕ a·ma·ka *hammock*

hambriento/a ⓜ/ⓕ am·bryen·to/a *hungry*

harina ⓕ a·ree·na *flour*

hasta (junio) as·ta (khoo·nyo) *until (June)*

hecho/a ⓜ/ⓕ e·cho/a *made*
— **a mano** a ma·no *handmade*
— **de (algodón)** de (al·go·don) *made of (cotton)*

heladería ⓕ e·la·de·ree·a *ice cream parlour*

helado ⓜ e·la·do *ice cream*

helar e·lar *freeze*

hepatitis ⓕ e·pa·fee·tees *hepatitis*

herbolario ⓜ er·bo·la·ryo *herbalist (shop)*

herida ⓕ e·ree·da *injury*

hermana ⓕ er·ma·na *sister*

hermano ⓜ er·ma·no *brother*

hermoso/a ⓜ/ⓕ er·mo·so/a *beautiful*

heroína ⓕ e·ro·ee·na *heroin*

hielo ⓜ ye·lo *ice*

hierba ⓕ yer·ba *grass*

hierbas ⓕ pl yer·bas *herbs*

hígado ⓜ ee·ga·do *liver*

higos ⓜ pl ee·gos *figs*

hija ⓕ ee·kha *daughter*

hijo ⓜ ee·kho *son*

hijos ⓜ pl ee·khos *children*

hilo ⓜ **dental** ee·lo den·tal *dental floss*

hinchas ⓜ&ⓕ pl een·chas *supporters*

hindú een·doo *Hindu*

hipódromo ⓜ ee·po·dro·mo *racetrack (horses)*

historial ⓜ **profesional** ees·to·ryal pro·fe·syo·nal *CV*

histórico/a ⓜ/ⓕ ees·to·ree·ko/a *historical*

hockey ⓜ kho·kee *hockey*
— **sobre hielo** so·bre ye·lo *ice hockey*

hoja ⓕ o·kha *leaf • sheet (of paper)*

hojalata ① o·kha·*la*·ta *tin*
Holanda ① o·*lan*·da *Netherlands*
hombre ⓜ *om*·bre *man*
hombros ⓜ pl *om*·bros *shoulders*
homosexual ⓜ&① o·mo·se·*kswal* *homosexual*
hora ① o·ra *time*
horario ⓜ o·*ra*·ryo *timetable*
horas ① pl **de abrir** o·ras de a·*breer* *opening hours*
hormiga ① or·*mee*·ga *ant*
horno ⓜ *or*·no *oven*
horóscopo ⓜ o·*ros*·ko·po *horoscope*
hospital ⓜ os·pee·*tal hospital*
hostelería ① os·te·le·*ree*·a *hospitality*
hotel ⓜ o·*tel hotel*
hoy oy *today*
hueso ⓜ *we*·so *bone*
huevo ⓜ *we*·vo *egg*
humanidades ① pl oo·ma·nee·*da*·des *humanities*

I

identificación ① ee·den·tee·fee·ka·*thyon* *identification*
idiomas ⓜ pl ee·*dyo*·mas *languages*
idiota ⓜ/① ee·*dyo*·ta *idiot*
iglesia ① ee·*gle*·sya *church*
igual ee·*gwal same*
igualdad ① ee·gwal·*da equality*
impermeable ⓜ eem·per·me·a·ble *raincoat*
impermeable eem·per·me·*a*·ble *waterproof*
importante eem·por·*tan*·te *important*
impuesto ⓜ eem·*pwes*·to *tax*
 — sobre la renta *so*·bre la *ren*·ta *income tax*
incluido een·kloo·ee·do *included*
incómodo/a ⓜ/① een·ko·mo·do/a *uncomfortable*
India ① *een*·dya *India*
indicador ⓜ een·dee·ka·*dor indicator*
indigestion ① een·dee·khes·*tyon indigestion*
industria ① een·*doos*·trya *industry*

infección ① een·fek·*thyon infection*
inflamación ① een·fla·ma·*thyon* *inflammation*
informática ① een·for·*ma*·tee·ka *IT*
ingeniería ① een·khe·nye·*ree*·a *engineering*
ingeniero/a ⓜ/① een·khe·*nye*·ro/a *engineer*
Inglaterra ① een·gla·*te*·ra *England*
inglés ⓜ een·*gles English*
ingrediente ⓜ een·gre·*dyen*·te *ingredient*
injusto/a ⓜ/① een·*khoos*·to/a *unfair*
inmigración ① een·mee·gra·*thyon* *immigration*
inocente ee·no·*then*·te *innocent*
inseguro/a ⓜ/① een·se·goo·ro/a *unsafe*
instituto ⓜ eens·tee·*too*·to *high school*
intentar (hacer algo) een·ten·*tar* (a·*ther al*·go) *try (to do something)*
interesante een·te·re·*san*·te *interesting*
internacional een·ter·na·thyo·*nal international*
Internet ⓜ een·ter·net *Internet*
intérprete ⓜ&① een·*ter*·pre·te *interpreter*
inundación ① ee·noon·da·*thyon flooding*
invierno ⓜ een·*vyer*·no *winter*
invitar een·vee·*tar invite*
inyección ① een·yek·*thyon injection*
inyectar(se) een·yek·*tar*(·se) *inject (oneself)*
ir eer *go*
 — de compras de *kom*·pras *go shopping*
 — de excursión de eks·koor·*syon hike*
 — en tobogán en to·bo·*gan tobogganing*
Irlanda ① eer·*lan*·da *Ireland*
irritación ① ee·ree·ta·*thyon rash*
 — de pañal de pa·*nyal nappy rash*
isla ① *ees*·la *island*
itinerario ⓜ ee·tee·ne·*ra*·ryo *itinerary*
IVA ⓜ *ee*·va *sales tax*
izquierda ① eeth·*kyer*·da *left*

J

jabón ⓜ kha·*bon* soap
jamón ⓜ kha·*mon* ham
Japón ⓜ kha·*pon* Japan
jarabe ⓜ kha·*ra*·be cough medicine
jardín botánico khar·*deen*
  bo·ta·*nee*·ko botanic garden
jarra ⓕ *kha*·ra jar
jefe/a ⓜ/ⓕ *khe*·fe/a boss • leader
  — de sección de sek·*thyon* manager
jengibre ⓜ khen·*khee*·bre ginger
jeringa ⓕ khe·*reen*·ga syringe
jersey ⓜ kher·*sey* jumper • sweater
jet lag ⓜ dyet lag jet lag
jockey ⓜ *dyo*·kee jockey
joven *kho*·ven young
joyería ⓕ kho·ye·*ree*·a jeweller (shop)
jubilado/a ⓜ/ⓕ khoo·bee·*la*·do/a
  retired
judías ⓕ pl khoo·*dee*·as beans
judío/a ⓜ/ⓕ khoo·*dee*·o/a Jewish
juegos ⓜ pl **de ordenador** khwe·gos
  de or·de·na·*dor* computer games
juegos ⓜ pl **olímpicos** khwe·gos
  o·*leem*·pee·kos Olympic Games
juez ⓜ&ⓕ khweth judge
jugar khoo·*gar* play (sport • games)
jugo ⓜ *khoo*·go juice
juguetería ⓕ khoo·ge·te·*ree*·a toyshop
juntos/as ⓜ/ⓕ pl *khoon*·tos/as
  together

K

kilo ⓜ *kee*·lo kilogram
kilómetro ⓜ kee·*lo*·me·tro
  kilometre
kiwi ⓜ *kee*·wee kiwifruit
kosher *ko*·sher Kosher

L

La Copa Mundial la *ko*·pa
  moon·*dyal* World Cup
labios ⓜ pl *la*·byos lips
lado ⓜ *la*·do side

ladrón ⓜ la·*dron* thief
lagartija ⓕ la·gar·*tee*·kha lizard
lago ⓜ *la*·go lake
lamentar la·men·*tar* regret
lana ⓕ *la*·na wool
lápiz ⓜ *la*·peeth pencil
  — de labios de *la*·byos lipstick
largo/a ⓜ/ⓕ *lar*·go/a long
lata ⓕ *la*·ta can
lavadero ⓜ la·va·*de*·ro laundry
lavadora ⓕ la·va·*do*·ra washing
  machine
lavandería ⓕ la·van·de·*ree*·a
  laundrette
lavar la·*var* wash (something)
lavarse la·*var*·se wash (oneself)
leche ⓕ *le*·che milk
  — de soja de *so*·kha soy milk
  — desnatada des·na·*ta*·da skimmed
  milk
lechuga ⓕ le·*choo*·ga lettuce
leer le·*er* read
legal le·*gal* legal
legislación ⓕ le·khees·la·*thyon*
  legislation
legumbre ⓕ le·*goom*·bre legume
lejos *le*·khos far
leña ⓕ *le*·nya firewood
lentejas ⓕ pl len·*te*·khas lentils
lentes ⓜ pl **de contacto** *len*·tes de
  kon·*tak*·to contact lenses
lento/a ⓜ/ⓕ *len*·to/a slow
lesbiana ⓕ les·bee·*a*·na lesbian
leve *le*·ve light
ley ⓕ ley law
libra ⓕ *lee*·bra pound (money)
libre *lee*·bre free (not bound)
librería ⓕ lee·bre·*ree*·a bookshop
libro ⓜ *lee*·bro book
  — de frases de *fra*·ses phrasebook
libros ⓜ pl **de viajes** *lee*·bros de
  vya·khes travel books
líder ⓜ *lee*·der leader
ligar lee·*gar* pick up
lila *lee*·la purple
lima *lee*·ma lime

límite ⓜ de equipaje *lee*·mee·te de
e·kee·*pa*·khe *baggage allowance*
limón ⓜ lee·*mon* *lemon*
limonada ⓕ lee·mo·na·da *lemonade*
limpio/a ⓜ/ⓕ leem·pyo/a *clean*
línea ⓕ *lee*·ne·a *line*
linterna ⓕ leen·*ter*·na *flashlight • torch*
listo/a ⓜ/ⓕ *lees*·to/a *ready*
lo que lo ke *what*
local ⓜ lo·*kal* *venue*
local lo·*kal* *local*
loco/a ⓜ/ⓕ *lo*·ko/a *crazy*
lodo ⓜ *lo*·do *mud*
lombrices ⓕ pl lom·*bree*·thes *earth worms*
los dos los dos *both*
Los Estados ⓜ pl Unidos los es·*ta*·dos oo·*nee*·dos *USA*
lubricante ⓜ loo·bree·*kan*·te *lubricant*
luces ⓕ pl *loo*·thes *lights*
luchar contra loo·*char* kon·tra *fight against*
lugar ⓜ loo·*gar* *place*
— de nacimiento de na·thee·*myen*·to *place of birth*
lujo ⓜ *loo*·kho *luxury*
luna ⓕ *loo*·na *moon*
— llena *lye*·na *full moon*
— de miel de myel *honeymoon*
luz ⓕ looth *light*

LL

llamada ⓕ lya·ma·da *phone call*
— a cobro revertido a *ko*·bro re·ver·*tee*·do *collect call*
llamar por telefono lya·*mar* por te·*le*·fo·no *to make a phone call*
llano/a ⓜ/ⓕ *lya*·no/a *flat*
llave ⓕ *lya*·ve *key*
llegadas ⓕ pl lye·*ga*·das *arrivals*
llegar lye·*gar* *arrive*
llenar lye·*nar* *fill*
lleno/a ⓜ/ⓕ *lye*·no/a *full*
llevar lye·*var* *carry • wear*
lluvia ⓕ *lyoo*·vya *rain*

M

machismo ⓜ ma·*chees*·mo *sexism*
madera ⓕ ma·*de*·ra *wood*
madre ⓕ *ma*·dre *mother*
madrugada ⓕ ma·droo·*ga*·da *early morning*
mago/a ⓜ/ⓕ *ma*·go/a *magician*
maíz ⓜ ma·*eeth* *corn*
maleta ⓕ ma·*le*·ta *suitcase*
maletín ⓜ ma·le·*teen* *briefcase*
— de primeros auxilios ⓜ de pree·me·ros ow·*ksee*·lyos *first-aid kit*
malo/a ⓜ/ⓕ *ma*·lo/a *bad*
mamá ⓕ ma·*ma* *mum*
mamograma ⓜ ma·mo·*gra*·ma *mammogram*
mañana ⓕ ma·*nya*·na *tomorrow • morning (6am - 1pm)*
— por la mañana por la ma·*nya*·na *tomorrow morning*
— por la noche por la *no*·che *tomorrow evening*
— por la tarde por la *tar*·de *tomorrow afternoon*
mandarina ⓕ man·da·*ree*·na *mandarin*
mandíbula ⓕ man·*dee*·boo·la *jaw*
mando ⓜ a distancia *man*·do a dees·*tan*·thya *remote control*
mango ⓜ *man*·go *mango*
manifestación ⓕ ma·nee·fes·ta·*thyon* *demonstration*
manillar ⓜ ma·nee·*lyar* *handlebar*
mano ⓕ *ma*·no *hand*
manta ⓕ *man*·ta *blanket*
manteca ⓕ man·*te*·ka *lard*
mantel ⓜ man·*tel* *tablecloth*
mantequilla ⓕ man·te·*kee*·lya *butter*
manzana ⓕ man·*tha*·na *apple*
mapa ⓜ *ma*·pa *map*
maquillaje ⓜ ma·kee·*lya*·khe *make-up*
máquina ⓕ *ma*·kee·na *machine*
— de billetes de bee·*lye*·tes *ticket machine*
— de tabaco de ta·*ba*·ko *cigarette machine*

mar ⓜ mar *sea*
marido ⓜ ma·*ree*·do *husband*
maravilloso/a ⓜ/ⓕ ma·ra·vee·*lyo*·so/a *wonderful*
marcador ⓜ mar·ka·*dor* *scoreboard*
marcapasos ⓜ mar·ka·*pa*·sos *pacemaker*
marcar mar·*kar* *score*
marea ⓕ ma·*re*·a *tide*
mareado/a ⓜ/ⓕ ma·re·a·do/a *dizzy* • *seasick*
mareo ⓜ ma·*re*·o *travel sickness*
margarina ⓕ mar·ga·*ree*·na *margarine*
marihuana ⓕ ma·ree·*wa*·na *marijuana*
mariposa ⓕ ma·ree·*po*·sa *butterfly*
marrón ma·*ron* *brown*
martillo ⓜ mar·*tee*·lyo *hammer*
más cercano/a ⓜ/ⓕ mas ther·*ka*·no/a *nearest*
masaje ⓜ ma·*sa*·khe *massage*
masajista ⓜ&ⓕ ma·sa·*khees*·ta *masseur*
matar ma·*tar* *kill*
matrícula ⓕ ma·*tree*·koo·la *license plate number*
matrimonio ⓜ ma·tree·mo·nyo *marriage*
mayonesa ⓕ ma·yo·*ne*·sa *mayonnaise*
mecánico ⓜ me·*ka*·nee·ko *mechanic*
mechero ⓜ me·*che*·ro *lighter*
medianoche ⓕ me·dya·no·che *midnight*
medias ⓕ pl me·dyas *stockings* • *pantyhose*
medicina ⓕ me·dee·*thee*·na *medicine*
médico/a ⓜ/(f) me·dee·co/a *doctor*
medio ⓜ ambiente me·dyo am·*byen*·te *environment*
medio/a ⓜ/ⓕ me·dyo/a *half*
mediodía ⓜ me·dyo·*dee*·a *noon*
medios ⓜ pl de comunicación me·dyos de ko·moo·nee·ka·*thyon* *media*
medios ⓜ pl de transporte me·dyos de trans·*por*·te *means of transport*
mejillones ⓜ pl me·khee·*lyo*·nes *mussels*
mejor me·*khor* *better* • *best*
melocotón ⓜ me·lo·ko·*ton* *peach*

melodía ⓕ me·lo·*dee*·a *tune*
melón ⓜ me·*lon* *melon*
mendigo/a ⓜ/ⓕ men·*dee*·go/a *beggar*
menos me·nos *less*
mensaje ⓜ men·*sa*·khe *message*
menstruación ⓕ mens·trwa·*thyon* *menstruation*
mentiroso/a ⓜ/ⓕ men·tee·ro·so/a *liar*
menú ⓜ me·*noo* *menu*
menudo/a ⓜ/ⓕ me·noo·do/a *little*
a menudo a me·noo·do *often*
mercado ⓜ mer·ka·do *market*
mermelada ⓕ mer·me·la·da *jam* • *marmalade*
mes ⓜ mes *month*
mesa ⓕ me·sa *table*
meseta ⓕ me·se·ta *plateau*
metal ⓜ me·*tal* *metal*
meter (un gol) me·*ter* (oon gol) *kick (a goal)*
metro ⓜ me·tro *metre*
mezclar meth·*klar* *mix*
mezquita ⓕ meth·*kee*·ta *mosque*
mi mee *my*
microondas ⓕ mee·kro·on·das *microwave*
miel ⓕ myel *honey*
miembro ⓜ myem·bro *member*
migraña ⓕ mee·gra·nya *migraine*
milímetro ⓜ mee·*lee*·me·tro *millimetre*
millón ⓜ mee·*lyon* *million*
minusválido/a ⓜ/ⓕ mee·noos·va·lee·do/a *disabled*
minuto ⓜ mee·noo·to *minute*
mirador ⓜ mee·ra·*dor* *lookout*
mirar mee·*rar* *look* • *watch*
— los escaparates los es·ka·pa·ra·tes *window-shopping*
misa ⓕ mee·sa *mass*
mochila ⓕ mo·chee·la *backpack*
módem ⓜ mo·dem *modem*
(carne) molida (*kar*·ne) mo·lee·da *mince (meat)*
mojado/a ⓜ/ⓕ mo·kha·do/a *wet*
monasterio ⓜ mo·nas·te·ryo *monastery*

monedas ⓕ pl mo·*ne*·das *coins*

monja ⓕ *mon*·kha *nun*

monopatinaje ⓜ mo·no·pa·tee·*na*·khe *skateboarding*

montaña ⓕ mon·*ta*·nya *mountain*

montar mon·*tar* *ride*
— **en bicicleta** en bee·thee·*kle*·ta *cycle*

monumento ⓜ mo·noo·*men*·to *monument*

mordedura ⓕ mor·de·*doo*·ra *bite (dog)*

morir mo·*reer* *die*

mosquitera ⓕ mos·kee·*te*·ra *mosquito net*

mosquito ⓜ mos·*kee*·to *mosquito*

mostaza ⓕ mos·*ta*·tha *mustard*

mostrador ⓜ mos·tra·*dor* *counter*

mostrar mos·*trar* *show*

motocicleta ⓕ mo·to·thee·*kle*·ta *motorcycle*

motor ⓜ mo·*tor* *engine*

motora ⓕ mo·*to*·ra *motorboat*

muchas/os ⓜ/ⓕ pl moo·chas/os *many*

mudo/a ⓜ/ⓕ *moo*·do/a *mute*

muebles ⓜ pl mwe·bles *furniture*

muela ⓕ mwe·la *tooth (back)*

muelle ⓜ mwe·lye *spring*

muerto/a ⓜ/ⓕ mwer·to/a *dead*

muesli ⓜ mwes·lee *muesli*

mujer ⓕ moo·*kher* *woman*

multa ⓕ *mool*·ta *fine*

mundo ⓜ *moon*·do *world*

muñeca ⓕ moo·*nye*·ka *doll* • *wrist*

murallas ⓕ pl moo·*ra*·lyas *city walls*

músculo ⓜ *moos*·koo·lo *muscle*

museo ⓜ moo·*se*·o *museum*
— **de arte** de *ar*·te *art gallery*

música ⓕ *moo*·see·ka *music*

músico/a ⓜ/ⓕ *moo*·see·ko/a *musician*
— **ambulante** am·boo·*lan*·te *busker*

muslo ⓜ *moos*·lo *drumstick (chicken)*

musulmán(a) ⓜ/ⓕ moo·sool·*man*/ moo·sool·*ma*·na *Muslim*

muy mooy *very*

N

nacionalidad ⓕ na·thyo·na·lee·*da* *nationality*

nada *na*·da *none* • *nothing*

nadar na·*dar* *swim*

naranja ⓕ na·*ran*·kha *orange*

nariz ⓕ na·*reeth* *nose*

nata ⓕ **agria** *na*·ta a·*grya* *sour cream*

naturaleza ⓕ na·too·ra·*le*·tha *nature*

naturopatía ⓕ na·too·ro·pa·*tee*·a *naturopathy*

náusea ⓕ *now*·se·a *nausea*

náuseas ⓕ pl **del embarazo** *now*·se·as del em·ba·*ra*·tho *morning sickness*

navaja ⓕ na·*va*·kha *penknife*

Navidad ⓕ na·vee·*da* *Christmas*

necesario/a ⓜ/ⓕ ne·the·*sa*·ryo/a *necessary*

necesitar ne·the·see·*tar* *need*

negar ne·*gar* *deny*

negar ne·*gar* *refuse*

negocio ⓜ ne·go·thyo *business*
— **de artículos básicos** de ar·*tee*·koo·los *ba*·see·kos *convenience store*

negro/a ⓜ/ⓕ ne·gro/a *black*

neumático ⓜ ne·oo·*ma*·tee·ko *tyre*

nevera ⓕ ne·*ve*·ra *refrigerator*

nieto/a ⓜ/ⓕ nye·to/a *grandchild*

nieve ⓕ *nye*·ve *snow*

niño/a ⓜ/ⓕ *nee*·nyo/a *child*

no no *no*
— **fumadores** foo·ma·*do*·res *non-smoking*
— **incluido** een·kloo·*ee*·do *excluded*

noche ⓕ *no*·che *evening* • *night*

Nochebuena ⓕ no·che·*bwe*·na *Christmas Eve*

Nochevieja ⓕ no·che·*vye*·kha *New Year's Eve*

nombre ⓜ *nom*·bre *name*
— **de pila** de *pee*·la *Christian name*

norte ⓜ *nor*·te *north*

nosotros/as ⓜ/ⓕ pl no·*so*·tros/ no·*so*·tras *we*

noticias ⓕ pl no·*tee*·thyas *news*
— **de actualidad** de ak·twal·ee·*da* *current affairs*
novia ⓕ *no*·vya *girlfriend*
novio ⓜ *no*·vyo *boyfriend*
nube ⓕ *noo*·be *cloud*
nublado noo·*bla*·do *cloudy*
nueces *nwe*·thes *nuts*
— **crudas** *kroo*·das *raw nuts*
— **tostadas** tos·*ta*·das *roasted nuts*
nuestro/a ⓜ/ⓕ *nwes*·tro/a *our*
Nueva Zelanda ⓕ *nwe*·va the·*lan*·da *New Zealand*
nuevo/a ⓜ/ⓕ *nwe*·vo/a *new*
número ⓜ *noo*·me·ro *number*
— **de la habitación** de la a·bee·ta·*thyon* *room number*
— **de pasaporte** de pa·sa·*por*·te *passport number*
nunca *noon*·ka *never*

O

o o *or*
obra ⓕ *o*·bra *play • building site*
obrero/a ⓜ/ⓕ o·*bre*·ro/a *factory worker • labourer*
océano ⓜ o·*the*·a·no *ocean*
ocupado/a ⓜ/ⓕ o·koo·*pa*·do/a *busy*
ocupar o·koo·*par* *live (somewhere)*
oeste ⓜ o·*es*·te *west*
oficina ⓕ o·fee·*thee*·na *office*
— **de objetos perdidos** de ob·*khe*·tos per·*dee*·dos *lost property office*
— **de turismo** de too·*rees*·mo *tourist office*
oír o·*eer* *hear*
ojo ⓜ o·kho *eye*
ola ⓕ *o*·la *wave*
olor ⓜ o·*lor* *smell*
olvidar ol·vee·*dar* *forget*
ópera ⓕ *o*·pe·ra *opera*
operación ⓕ o·pe·ra·*thyon* *operation*
opinión ⓕ o·pee·*nyon* *opinion*
oporto ⓜ o·*por*·to *port (wine)*
oportunidad ⓕ o·por·too·nee·*da* *chance*

oración ⓕ o·ra·*thyon* *prayer*
orden ⓜ *or*·den *order (placement)*
ordenador ⓜ or·de·na·*dor* *computer*
— **portátil** por·*ta*·teel *laptop*
ordenar or·de·*nar* *order*
oreja ⓕ o·*re*·kha *ear*
orgasmo ⓜ or·*gas*·mo *orgasm*
original ⓜ o·ree·khee·*nal* *original*
orquesta ⓕ or·*kes*·ta *orchestra*
oscuro/a ⓜ/ⓕ os·*koo*·ro/a *dark*
ostra ⓕ *os*·tra *oyster*
otoño ⓜ o·*to*·nyo *autumn*
otra vez *o*·tra veth *again*
otro/a ⓜ/ⓕ *o*·tro/a *other • another*
oveja ⓕ o·*ve*·kha *sheep*
oxígeno ⓜ o·*ksee*·khe·no *oxygen*

P

padre ⓜ *pa*·dre *father*
padres ⓜ pl *pa*·dres *parents*
pagar pa·*gar* *pay*
página ⓕ *pa*·khee·na *page*
pago ⓜ *pa*·go *payment*
país ⓜ pa·*ees* *country*
pájaro ⓜ *pa*·kha·ro *bird*
palabra ⓕ pa·*la*·bra *word*
palacio ⓜ pa·*la*·thyo *palace*
palillo ⓜ pa·*lee*·lyo *toothpick*
pan ⓜ pan *bread*
— **integral** in·te·*gral* *wholemeal bread*
— **moreno** mo·*re*·no *brown bread*
panadería ⓕ pa·na·de·*ree*·a *bakery*
pañal ⓜ pa·*nyal* *diaper • nappy*
pantalla ⓕ pan·*ta*·lya *screen*
pantalones ⓜ pl pan·ta·*lo*·nes *pants • trousers*
— **cortos** kor·*tos* *shorts*
pañuelos ⓜ pl **de papel** pa·*nywe*·los de pa·*pel* *tissues*
papá ⓜ pa·*pa* *dad*
papel ⓜ pa·*pel* *paper*
— **de fumar** de foo·*mar* *cigarette papers*
— **higiénico** ee·*khye*·nee·ko *toilet paper*

paquete ⓜ pa·*ke*·te packet • *package* • *wear*

para llevar pa·ra lye·*var* to take away

parabrisas ⓜ pa·ra·*bree*·sas windscreen

paracaidismo ⓜ pa·ra·kai·*dees*·mo *skydiving*

parada ⓕ pa·*ra*·da stop
— **de autobús** de ow·to·*boos* *bus stop*
— **de taxis** de ta·ksees *taxi stand*

paraguas ⓜ pa·*ra*·gwas umbrella

parapléjico/a ⓜ/ⓕ pa·ra·*ple*·khee·ko/a *paraplegic*

parar pa·*rar* stop

pared ⓕ pa·*red* wall (inside)

pareja ⓕ pa·*re*·kha pair (couple)

parlamento ⓜ par·la·*men*·to parliament

paro ⓜ *pa*·ro dole

parque ⓜ *par*·ke park
— **nacional** na·thyo·*nal* *national park*

parte ⓕ *par*·te part

partida ⓕ **de nacimiento** par·*tee*·da de na·thee·*myen*·to birth certificate

partido ⓜ par·*tee*·do match (sport) • *party (political)*

pasado ⓜ pa·*sa*·do past

pasado mañana pa·*sa*·do ma·*nya*·na day after tomorrow

pasado/a ⓜ/ⓕ pa·*sa*·do/a off (food)

pasajero ⓜ pa·sa·*khe*·ro passenger

pasaporte ⓜ pa·sa·*por*·te passport

Pascua ⓕ *pas*·kwa Easter

pase ⓜ *pa*·se pass

paseo ⓜ pa·*se*·o street

paso ⓜ *pa*·so step
— **de cebra** de *the*·bra pedestrian *crossing*

pasta ⓕ *pas*·ta pasta
— **dentífrica** den·*tee*·free·ka *toothpaste*

pastel ⓜ pas·*tel* cake • *pie*
— **de cumpleaños** de koom·ple·a·*nyos* birthday cake

pastelería ⓕ pas·te·le·*ree*·a cake shop

pastilla ⓕ pas·*tee*·lya pill

pastillas ⓕ pl **de menta** pas·*tee*·lyas de *men*·ta mints

pastillas ⓕ pl **para dormir** pas·*tee*·lyas pa·ra dor·*meer* sleeping pills

patata ⓕ pa·*ta*·ta potato

paté ⓜ pa·*te* pate (food)

patinar pa·*tee*·nar rollerblading • *ice skating*

pato ⓜ *pa*·to duck

pavo ⓜ *pa*·vo turkey

paz ⓕ path peace

peatón ⓜ&ⓕ pe·a·*ton* pedestrian

pecho ⓜ *pe*·cho chest

pechuga ⓕ pe·*choo*·ga breast (poultry)

pedal ⓜ pe·*dal* pedal

pedazo ⓜ pe·*da*·tho piece

pedir pe·*deer* ask (for something)

peine ⓜ *pey*·ne comb

pelea ⓕ pe·*le*·a fight

película ⓕ pe·*lee*·koo·la movie • *film (camera)*
— **en color** en ko·*lor* colour film

peligroso/a ⓜ/ⓕ pe·lee·*gro*·so/a *dangerous*

pelo ⓜ *pe*·lo hair

pelota ⓕ pe·*lo*·ta ball
— **de golf** de golf golf ball

peluquero/a ⓜ/ⓕ pe·loo·*ke*·ro/a *hairdresser*

pendientes ⓜ pl pen·*dyen*·tes earrings

pene ⓜ *pe*·ne penis

pensar pen·*sar* think

pensión ⓕ pen·*syon* boarding house

pensionista ⓜ&ⓕ pen·syo·*nees*·ta *pensioner*

pepino ⓜ pe·*pee*·no cucumber

pequeñito/a ⓜ/ⓕ pe·ke·*nyee*·to/a tiny

pequeño/a ⓜ/ⓕ pe·ke·*nyo*/a small

pera ⓕ *pe*·ra pear

perder per·*der* lose

perdido/a ⓜ/ⓕ per·*dee*·do/a lost

perdonar per·do·*nar* forgive

perejil ⓜ pe·re·*kheel* parsley

perfume ⓜ per·*foo*·me perfume

periódico ⓜ pe·*ryo*·dee·ko newspaper

periodista ⓜ&ⓕ pe·ryo·*dees*·ta *journalist*

permiso ⓜ *per·mee·so permission •*
permit
— **de trabajo** ⓜ *de tra·ba·kho work*
permit
permitir *per·mee·teer allow • permit*
pero *pe·ro but*
perro/a ⓜ/ⓕ *pe·ro/a dog*
perro ⓜ **lazarillo** *pe·ro la·tha·ree·lyo*
guide dog
persona ⓕ *per·so·na person*
pesado/a ⓜ/ⓕ *pe·sa·do/a heavy*
pesar *pe·sar weigh*
pesas ⓕ pl *pe·sas weights*
pesca ⓕ *pes·ka fishing*
pescadería ⓕ *pes·ka·de·ree·a fish shop*
pescado ⓜ *pes·ka·do fish (as food)*
peso ⓜ *pe·so weight*
petición ⓕ *pe·tee·thyon petition*
pez ⓜ *peth fish*
picadura ⓕ *pee·ka·doo·ra bite (insect)*
picazón ⓕ *pee·ka·thon itch*
pie ⓜ *pee·e foot*
piedra ⓕ *pye·dra stone*
piel ⓕ *pyel skin*
pierna ⓕ *pyer·na leg*
pila ⓕ *pee·la battery (small)*
píldora ⓕ *peel·do·ra the Pill*
pimienta ⓕ *pee·myen·ta pepper*
pimiento ⓜ *pee·myen·to capsicum •*
bell pepper
— **rojo** *ro·kho red capsicum*
— **verde** *ver·de green capsicum*
piña ⓕ *pee·nya pineapple*
pinchar *peen·char puncture*
ping pong ⓜ *peeng pong table tennis*
pintar *peen·tar paint*
pintor(a) ⓜ/ⓕ *peen·tor/peen·to·ra*
painter
pintura ⓕ *peen·too·ra painting*
pinzas ⓕ pl *peen·thas tweezers*
piojos ⓜ pl *pyo·khos lice*
piqueta ⓕ *pee·ke·ta pickaxe*
piquetas ⓕ pl *pee·ke·tas tent pegs*
piscina ⓕ *pees·thee·na swimming pool*
pista ⓕ *pees·ta court (tennis)*
— **de tenis** *de te·nees tennis court*
pistacho ⓜ *pees·ta·cho pistachio*

plancha ⓕ *plan·cha iron*
planeta ⓜ *pla·ne·ta planet*
planta ⓕ *plan·ta plant*
plástico ⓜ *plas·tee·ko plastic*
plata ⓕ *pla·ta silver*
plataforma ⓕ *pla·ta·for·ma platform*
plátano ⓜ *pla·ta·no banana*
plateado/a ⓜ/ⓕ *pla·te·a·do/a silver*
plato ⓜ *pla·to plate*
playa ⓕ *pla·ya beach*
plaza ⓕ *pla·tha square*
— **de toros** *de to·ros bullring*
pobre *po·bre poor*
pobreza ⓕ *po·bre·tha poverty*
pocos *po·kos few*
poder *po·der can (be able)*
poder ⓜ *po·der power*
poesía ⓕ *po·e·see·a poetry*
polen ⓜ *po·len pollen*
policía ⓕ *po·lee·thee·a police*
política ⓕ *po·lee·tee·ka policy •*
politics
político ⓜ/ⓕ *po·lee·tee·ko politician*
póliza ⓕ *po·lee·tha policy (insurance)*
pollo ⓜ *po·lyo chicken*
pomelo ⓜ *po·me·lo grapefruit*
poner *po·ner put*
popular *po·poo·lar popular*
póquer ⓜ *po·ker poker*
por (día) *por (dee·a) per (day)*
por ciento *por thyen·to percent*
por qué *por ke why*
por vía aérea *por vee·a a·e·re·a air mail*
por vía terrestre *por vee·a te·res·tre*
surface mail
porque *por ke because*
portero/a ⓜ/ⓕ *por·te·ro/a goalkeeper*
posible *po·see·ble possible*
postal ⓕ *pos·tal postcard*
póster ⓜ *pos·ter poster*
potro ⓜ *po·tro foal*
pozo ⓜ *po·tho well*
precio ⓜ *pre·thyo price*
— **de entrada** *de en·tra·da admission*
price
— **del cubierto** *del koo·byer·to cover*
charge

preferir pre·fe·*reer* prefer

pregunta ① pre·*goon*·ta question

preguntar pre·goon·*tar* ask (a question)

preocupado/a ⓜ/① pre·o·koo·*pa*·do/a worried

preocuparse por pre·o·koo·*par*·se por care (about something)

preparar pre·pa·*rar* prepare

presidente/a ⓜ/① pre·see·*den*·te/a president

presión ① pre·*syon* pressure
— **arterial** ar·te·*ryal* blood pressure

prevenir pre·ve·*neer* prevent

primavera ① pree·ma·*ve*·ra spring (season)

primer ministro ⓜ pree·*mer* mee·*nees*·tro prime minister

primera ministra ① pree·*me*·ra mee·*nees*·tra prime minister

primero/a ⓜ/① pree·*me*·ro/a first

principal preen·thee·*pal* main

prisa ① *pree*·sa hurry

prisionero/a ⓜ/① pree·syon·*ne*·ro/a prisoner

privado/a ⓜ/① pree·*va*·do/a private

probar pro·*bar* try

producir pro·doo·*theer* produce

productos ⓜ pl **congelados** pro·*dook*·tos kon·khe·*la*·dos frozen foods

profesor(a) ⓜ/① pro·fe·*sor*/pro·fe·*so*·ra lecturer • instructor • teacher

profundo/a ⓜ/① pro·*foon*·do/a deep

programa ⓜ pro·*gra*·ma programme

prolongación ① pro·lon·ga·*thyon* extension (visa)

promesa ① pro·*me*·sa promise

prometida ① pro·me·*tee*·da fiancee

prometido ⓜ pro·me·*tee*·do fiance

pronto *pron*·to soon

propietaria ① pro·pye·*ta*·rya landlady

propietario ⓜ pro·pye·*ta*·ryo landlord

propina ① pro·*pee*·na tip

proteger pro·te·*kher* protect

protegido/a ⓜ/① pro·te·*khee*·do/a protected

protesta ① pro·*tes*·ta protest

provisiones ① pl pro·bee·*syo*·nes provisions

proyector ⓜ pro·yek·*tor* projector

prudente proo·*den*·te sensible

prueba ① *prwe*·ba test
— **del embarazo** del em·ba·*ra*·tho pregnancy test kit

pruebas ① pl **nucleares** *prwe*·bas noo·kle·*a*·res nuclear testing

pub ⓜ poob bar (with music) • pub

pueblo ⓜ *pwe*·blo village

puente ⓜ *pwen*·te bridge

puerro ⓜ *pwe*·ro leek

puerta ① *pwer*·ta door

puerto ⓜ *pwer*·to port • harbour

puesta ① **del sol** *pwes*·ta del sol sunset

pulga ① *pool*·ga flea

pulmones ⓜ pl pool·*mo*·nes lungs

punto ⓜ *poon*·to point (tip) • point (score)

puro ⓜ *poo*·ro cigar

puro/a ⓜ/① *poo*·ro/a pure

Q

(el mes) que viene (el mes) ke *vye*·ne next (month)

quedar ke·*dar* leave (behind)

quedarse ke·*dar*·se stay (remain)

quedarse sin ke·*dar*·se seen run out of

quejarse ke·*khar*·se complain

quemadura ① ke·ma·*doo*·ra burn
— **de sol** de sol sunburn

querer ke·*rer* love • want

queso ⓜ *ke*·so cheese
— **crema** *kre*·ma cream cheese
— **de cabra** de *ka*·bra goat's cheese

quien kyen who

quincena ① keen·*the*·na fortnight

quiosco ⓜ *kyos*·ko news stand • newsagency

quiste ⓜ **ovárico** *kees*·te o·*va*·ree·ko ovarian cyst

quizás kee·*thas* maybe

R

rábano m *ra·ba·no radish*

— picante *pee·kan·te horseradish*

rápido/a m/f *ra·pee·do/a fast*

raqueta f *ra·ke·ta racquet*

raro/a m/f *ra·ro/a rare (item)*

rastro m *ras·tro track (footprints)*

rata f *ra·ta rat*

ratón m *ra·ton mouse*

raza f *ra·tha race (people)*

razón f *ra·thon reason*

realista re·a·lees·ta *realistic*

recibir re·thee·*beer receive*

recibo m *re·thee·bo receipt*

reciclable re·thee·*kla·ble recyclable*

reciclar re·thee·*klar recycle*

recientemente re·thyen·te·*men·te*
recently

recogida f **de equipajes** re·ko·khee·da
de e·kee·*pa·khes baggage claim*

recolección f **de fruta** re·ko·lek·thyon
de froo·ta *fruit picking*

recomendar re·ko·men·*dar recommend*

reconocer re·ko·no·*ther recognise*

recordar re·kor·*dar remember*

recorrido m **guiado** re·ko·ree·do
gee·*a·do guided tour*

recto/a m/f *rek·to/a straight*

recuerdo m *re·kwer·do souvenir*

red f *red net*

redondo/a m/f *re·don·do/a round*

reembolsar re·em·bol·*sar refund*

reembolso m *re·em·bol·so refund*

referencias f pl re·fe·ren·thyas
references

refresco m *re·fres·ko soft drink*

refugiado/a m/f *re·foo·khya·do/a*
refugee

regalar re·ga·*lar exchange (gifts)*

regalo m *re·ga·lo gift*

— de bodas de bo·das *wedding*
present

régimen m *re·khee·men diet*

reglas f pl *re·glas rules*

reina f *rey·na queen*

reírse re·eer·se *laugh*

relación f re·la·thyon *relationship*

relajarse re·la·khar·se *relax*

religión f re·lee·khyon *religion*

religioso/a m/f re·lee·khyo·so/a
religious

reliquia f re·lee·kya *relic*

reloj m *re·lokh clock*

— de pulsera de pool·se·ra *watch*

remo m *re·mo rowing*

remolacha f re·mo·la·cha *beetroot*

remoto/a m/f re·mo·to/a *remote*

reparar re·pa·rar *repair*

repartir re·par·teer *divide up (share)*

repetir re·pe·teer *repeat*

república f re·poo·blee·ka *republic*

requesón m re·ke·son *cottage cheese*

reserva f re·ser·va *reservation*

reservar re·ser·var *book (make a*
reservation)

resfriado m res·free·a·do *cold*

residencia f **de estudiantes**
re·see·den·thya de es·too·dyan·tes
college

residuos m pl **tóxicos** re·see·dwos
to·ksee·kos *toxic waste*

respirar res·pee·rar *breathe*

respuesta f res·pwes·ta *answer*

restaurante m res·tow·ran·te *restaurant*

revisar re·vee·sar *check*

revisor(a) m/f re·vee·sor/re·vee·so·ra
ticket collector

revista f re·vees·ta *magazine*

rey m *rey king*

rico/a m/f *ree·ko/a rich*

riesgo m *ryes·go risk*

río m *ree·o river*

ritmo m *reet·mo rhythm*

robar ro·bar *rob • steal*

roca f *ro·ka rock*

rock m *rok rock (music)*

rodilla f ro·dee·lya *knee*

rojo/a m/f *ro·kho/a red*

rollo m **repelente contra mosquitos**
ro·lyo re·pe·len·te kon·tra
mos·kee·tos *mosquito coil*

romántico/a ⓜ/ⓕ ro·*man*·tee·ko/a *romantic*
romper rom·*per* *break*
ron ⓜ ron *rum*
ropa ⓕ *ro*·pa *clothing*
  — de cama de *ka*·ma *bedding*
  — interior een·te·*ryor* *underwear*
rosa *ro*·sa *pink*
roto/a ⓜ/ⓕ *ro*·to/a *broken*
rueda ⓕ *rwe*·da *wheel*
rugby ⓜ *roog*·bee *rugby*
ruidoso/a ⓜ/ⓕ rwee·*do*·so/a *loud*
ruinas ⓕ pl *rwee*·nas *ruins*
ruta ⓕ *roo*·ta *route*

S

sábado ⓜ *sa*·ba·do *Saturday*
sábana ⓕ *sa*·ba·na *sheet (bed)*
saber sa·*ber* *know (something)*
sabroso/a ⓜ/ⓕ sa·*bro*·so/a *tasty*
sacar sa·*kar* *take out* • *take (photo)*
sacerdote ⓜ sa·ther·*do*·te *priest*
saco ⓜ **de dormir** *sa*·ko de dor·*meer* *sleeping bag*
sal ⓕ *sal* *salt*
sala ⓕ **de espera** *sa*·la de es·*pe*·ra *waiting room*
sala ⓕ **de tránsito** *sa*·la de *tran*·see·to *transit lounge*
salario ⓜ sa·*la*·ryo *rate of pay* • *salary*
salchicha ⓕ sal·*chee*·cha *sausage*
saldo ⓜ *sal*·do *balance (account)*
salida ⓕ sa·*lee*·da *departure* • *exit*
saliente ⓕ sa·*lyen*·te *ledge*
salir con sa·*leer* kon *go out with*
salir de sa·*leer* de *depart*
salmón ⓜ sal·*mon* *salmon*
salón de belleza ⓜ sa·*lon* de be·*lye*·tha *beauty salon*
salsa ⓕ *sal*·sa *sauce*
  — de guindilla de geen·*dee*·lya *chilli sauce*
  — de soja de *so*·kha *soy sauce*
  — de tomate de to·*ma*·te *tomato sauce* • *ketchup*
saltar sal·*tar* *jump*

salud ⓕ sa·*loo* *health*
salvaeslips ⓜ pl sal·va·e·*sleeps* *panty liners*
salvar sal·*var* *save*
sandalias ⓕ pl san·*da*·lyas *sandals*
sandía ⓕ san·*dee*·a *watermelon*
sangrar san·*grar* *bleed*
sangre ⓕ *san*·gre *blood*
santo/a ⓜ/ⓕ *san*·to/a *saint*
sarampión ⓜ sa·ram·*pyon* *measles*
sartén ⓕ sar·*ten* *frying pan*
sastre ⓜ *sas*·tre *tailor*
sauna ⓕ *sow*·na *sauna*
secar se·*kar* *dry*
secretario/a ⓜ/ⓕ se·kre·*ta*·ryo/a *secretary*
sed ⓕ se *thirst*
seda ⓕ *se*·da *silk*
seguir se·*geer* *follow*
segundo/a ⓜ/ⓕ se·*goon*·do/a *second*
seguro ⓜ se·*goo*·ro *insurance*
seguro/a ⓜ/ⓕ se·*goo*·ro/a *safe*
sello ⓜ *se*·lyo *stamp*
semáforos ⓜ pl se·*ma*·fo·ros *traffic lights*
Semana ⓕ **Santa** se·*ma*·na *san*·ta *Holy Week*
sembrar sem·*brar* *plant*
semidirecto/a ⓜ/ⓕ se·mee·dee·*rek*·to/a *non-direct*
señal ⓕ se·*nyal* *sign*
sencillo/a ⓜ/ⓕ sen·*thee*·lyo/a *simple*
(un billete) sencillo ⓜ (oon bee·*lye*·te) sen·*thee*·lyo *one-way (ticket)*
sendero ⓜ sen·*de*·ro *mountain path* • *path*
senos ⓜ pl *se*·nos *breasts*
sensibilidad ⓕ sen·see·bee·lee·*da* *sensitivity* • *film speed*
sensual sen·*swal* *sensual*
sentarse sen·*tar*·se *sit*
sentimientos ⓜ pl sen·tee·*myen*·tos *feelings*
sentir sen·*teer* *feel*
separado/a ⓜ/ⓕ se·pa·*ra*·do/a *separate*
separar se·pa·*rar* *separate*
ser ser *be*

serie ① se·rye series
serio/a ⑩/① se·ryo/a serious
seropositivo/a ⑩/①
se·ro·po·see·tee·vo/a HIV positive
serpiente ① ser·pyen·te snake
servicio ⑩ ser·vee·thyo service charge
— **militar** mee·lee·tar military service
— **telefónico automático**
te·le·fo·nee·ko ow·to·ma·tee·ko
direct-dial
servicios ⑩ pl ser·vee·thyos toilets
servilleta ① ser·vee·lye·ta napkin
sexo ⑩ se·kso sex
— **seguro** se·goo·ro safe sex
sexy se·ksee sexy
si see if • yes
SIDA ⑩ see·da AIDS
sidra ① see·dra cider
siempre syem·pre always
silla ① see·lya chair
— **de ruedas** de rwe·das wheelchair
sillín ⑩ see·lyeen saddle
similar see·mee·lar similar
simpático/a ⑩/① seem·pa·tee·ko/a nice
sin seen without
— **hogar** o·gar homeless
— **plomo** plo·mo unleaded
sinagoga ① see·na·go·ga synagogue
Singapur ⑩ seen ga·poor Singapore
sintético/a ⑩/① seen·te·tee·ko/a
synthetic
soborno ⑩ so·bor·no bribe
sobre so·bre about • on top of
sobre ⑩ so·bre envelope
sobredosis ① so·bre·do·sees overdose
sobrevivir so·bre·vee·veer survive
socialista ⑩&① so·thya·lees·ta socialist
sol ⑩ sol sun
soldado ⑩ sol·da·do soldier
sólo so·lo only
solo/a ⑩/① so·lo/a alone
soltero/a ⑩/① sol·te·ro/a single
sombra ① som·bra shadow
sombrero ⑩ som·bre·ro hat
soñar so·nyar dream
sondeos ⑩ pl son·de·os polls

sonreír son·re·eer smile
sopa ① so·pa soup
sordo/a ⑩/① sor·do/a deaf
sorpresa ① sor·pre·sa surprise
su soo her • his • their
subir soo·beer climb
submarinismo ⑩ soob·ma·ree·nees·mo
diving
subtítulos ⑩ pl soob·tee·too·los subtitles
sucio/a ⑩/① soo·thyo/a dirty
sucursal ① soo·koor·sal branch office
sudar soo·dar perspire
suegra ① swe·gra mother-in-law
suegro ⑩ swe·gro father-in-law
sueldo ⑩ swel·do wage
suelo ⑩ swe·lo floor
suerte ① swer·te luck
suficiente soo·fee·thyen·te enough
sufrir soo·freer suffer
sujetador ⑩ soo·khe·ta·dor bra
supermercado ⑩ soo·per·mer·ka·do
supermarket
superstición ① soo·pers·tee·thyon
superstition
sur ⑩ soor south
surf ⑩ **sobre la nieve** soorf so·bre la
nye·ve snowboarding

T

tabaco ⑩ ta·ba·ko tobacco
tabla ① **de surf** ta·bla de soorf surfboard
tablero ⑩ **de ajedrez** ta·ble·ro de
a·khe·dreth chess board
tacaño/a ⑩/① ta·ka·nyo/a stingy
talco ⑩ tal·ko baby powder
talla ① ta·lya size (clothes)
taller ⑩ ta·lyer workshop
también tam·byen also
tampoco tam·po·ko neither
tampones ⑩ pl tam·po·nes tampons
tanga ① tan·ga g-string
tapones ⑩ pl **para los oídos** ta·po·nes
pa·ra los o·ee·dos earplugs
taquilla ① ta·kee·lya ticket office
tarde tar·de late

tarjeta tar·*khe*·ta *card*
— **de crédito** de kre·*dee*·to *credit card*
— **de embarque** de em·*bar*·ke *boarding pass*
— **de teléfono** de te·*le*·fo·no *phone card*

tarta ⓕ **nupcial** tar·ta noop·*thyal* *wedding cake*

tasa ⓕ **del aeropuerto** ta·sa del ay·ro·*pwer*·to *airport tax*

taxi ⓜ ta·ksee *taxi*

taza ⓕ ta·tha *cup*

té ⓜ te *tea*

teatro ⓜ te·a·tro *theatre*

teclado ⓜ te·*kla*·do *keyboard*

técnica ⓕ *tek*·nee·ka *technique*

tela ⓕ te·la *fabric*

tele ⓕ te·le *TV*

teleférico ⓜ te·le·*fe*·ree·ko *cable car*

teléfono ⓜ te·*le*·fo·no *telephone*
— **móvil** mo·*veel* *mobile phone*
— **público** poo·*blee*·ko *public telephone*

telegrama ⓜ te·le·*gra*·ma *telegram*

telenovela ⓕ te·le·no·*ve*·la *soap opera*

telescopio ⓜ te·les·*ko*·pyo *telescope*

televisión ⓕ te·le·vee·*syon* *television*

temperatura ⓕ tem·pe·ra·*too*·ra *temperature (weather)*

templado/a ⓜ/ⓕ tem·*pla*·do/a *warm*

templo ⓜ *tem*·plo *temple*

temporada ⓕ tem·po·*ra*·da *season (in sport)*

temprano tem·*pra*·no *early*

tenedor ⓜ te·ne·*dor* *fork*

tener te·*ner* *have*
— **hambre** am·bre *to be hungry*
— **prisa** *pree*·sa *to be in a hurry*
— **sed** seth *to be thirsty*
— **sueño** *swe*·nyo *to be sleepy*

tenis ⓜ te·nees *tennis*

tensión ⓕ **premenstrual** ten·*syon* pre·mens·*trwal* *premenstrual tension*

tentempié ⓜ ten·tem·*pye* *snack*

tercio ⓜ *ter*·thyo *third*

terminar ter·mee·*nar* *finish*

ternera ⓕ ter·*ne*·ra *veal*

ternero ⓜ ter·*ne*·ro *calf*

terremoto ⓜ te·re·*mo*·to *earthquake*

testarudo/a ⓜ/ⓕ tes·ta·*roo*·do/a *stubborn*

tía ⓕ *tee*·a *aunt*

tiempo ⓜ *tyem*·po *time* • *weather*
a — a *tyem*·po *on time*
a — completo/parcial a *tyem*·po kom·*ple*·to/par·*thyal* *full-time/part-time*

tienda ⓕ **(de campaña)** *tyen*·da (de kam·*pa*·nya) *tent*

tienda ⓕ *tyen*·da *shop*
— **de comestibles** de ko·mes·*tee*·bles *grocery*
— **de fotografía** de fo·to·gra·*fee*·a *camera shop*
— **de eléctrodomésticos** de e·*lek*·tro·do·mes·*tee*·kos *electrical store*
— **de provisiones de cámping** de pro·vee·*syo*·nes de *kam*·peen *camping store*
— **de recuerdos** de re·*kwer*·dos *souvenir shop*
— **de ropa** de *ro*·pa *clothing store*
— **deportiva** de·por·*tee*·va *sports store*

Tierra ⓕ *tye*·ra *Earth*

tierra ⓕ *tye*·ra *land*

tiesto ⓜ *tyes*·to *pot (plant)*

tijeras ⓕ pl tee·*khe*·ras *scissors*

tímido/a ⓜ/ⓕ *tee*·mee·do/a *shy*

típico/a ⓜ/ⓕ *tee*·pee·ko/a *typical*

tipo ⓜ *tee*·po *type*
— **de cambio** de *kam*·byo *exchange rate*

tirar tee·*rar* *pull*

tiritas ⓕ pl tee·*ree*·tas *band-aids*

título ⓜ *tee*·too·lo *degree*

toalla ⓕ to·a·*lya* *towel*

toallita ⓕ to·a·*lyee*·ta *face cloth*

tobillo ⓜ to·*bee*·lyo *ankle*

tocar to·*kar* *touch*
— **la guitarra** la gee·*ta*·ra *play (guitar)*

tocino ⓜ to·*thee*·no *bacon*
todavía (no) to·da·*vee*·a (no) *(not) yet*
todo *to*·do *all • everything*
tofú ⓜ to·*foo tofu*
tomar to·*mar take • drink (something)*
tomate ⓜ to·*ma*·te *tomato*
— **secado al sol** se·*ka*·do al sol *sun-dried tomato*
tono ⓜ *to*·no *tone*
torcedura ⓕ tor·the·*doo*·ra *sprain*
tormenta ⓕ tor·*men*·ta *storm*
toro ⓜ *to*·ro *bull*
torre ⓕ *to*·re *tower*
tos ⓕ tos *cough*
tostada ⓕ tos·*ta*·da *toast*
tostadora ⓕ tos·ta·*do*·ra *toaster*
trabajar tra·ba·*khar work*
trabajo ⓜ tra·*ha*·kho *job • work*
— **administrativo** ad·mee·nees·tra·*tee*·vo *paperwork*
— **de camarero/a** ⓜ/ⓕ de ka·ma·*re*·ro/a *bar work*
— **de casa** de *ka*·sa *housework*
— **de limpieza** de leem·*pye*·tha *cleaning*
— **eventual** e·ven·*twal casual work*
traducir tra·doo·*theer translate*
traer tra·*er bring*
traficante ⓜ&ⓕ **de drogas** tra·fee·*kan*·te de *dro*·gas *drug dealer*
tráfico ⓜ *tra*·fee·ko *traffic*
tramposo/a ⓜ/ⓕ tram·*po*·so/a *cheat*
tranquilo/a ⓜ/ⓕ tran·*kee*·lo/a *quiet*
tranvía ⓜ tran·*vee*·a *tram*
a través a tra·*ves across*
tren ⓜ tren *train*
— **de cercanías** de ther·ka·*nee*·as *local train*
trepar tre·*par scale • climb*
tres en raya tres en *ra*·ya *noughts & crosses*
triste *trees*·te *sad*
tú too *you (informal)*
tu too *your*
tubo ⓜ **de escape** *too*·bo de es·*ka*·pe *exhaust*

tumba ⓕ *toom*·ba *grave*
tumbarse toom·*bar*·se *lie (not stand)*
turista ⓜ&ⓕ too·*rees*·ta *tourist*
— **operador(a)** ⓜ/ⓕ o·pe·ra·*dor*/ o·pe·ra·*do*·ra *tourist operator*

U

uniforme ⓜ oo·nee·*for*·me *uniform*
universidad ⓕ oo·nee·ver·see·*da university*
universo ⓜ oo·nee·*ver*·so *universe*
urgente oor·*khen*·te *urgent*
usted oos·*te you (pol)*
útil *oo*·teel *useful*
uvas ⓕ pl *oo*·vas *grapes*
— **pasas** *pa*·sas *raisins*

V

vaca ⓕ *va*·ka *cow*
vacaciones ⓕ pl va·ka·*thyo*·nes *holidays • vacation*
vacante va·*kan*·te *vacant*
vacío/a ⓜ/ⓕ va·*thee*·o/a *empty*
vacuna ⓕ va·*koo*·na *vaccination*
vagina ⓕ va·*khee*·na *vagina*
vagón ⓜ **restaurante** va·*gon* res·tow·*ran*·te *dining car*
validar va·lee·*dar validate*
valiente va·*lyen*·te *brave*
valioso/a ⓜ/ⓕ va·*lyo*·so/a *valuable*
valle ⓜ *va*·lye *valley*
valor ⓜ va·*lor value*
vaqueros ⓜ pl va·*ke*·ros *jeans*
varios/as ⓜ/ⓕ pl va·*ryos*/as *several*
vaso ⓜ *va*·so *(drinking) glass*
vegetariano/a ⓜ/ⓕ ve·khe·ta·*rya*·no/a *vegetarian*
vela ⓕ *ve*·la *candle*
velocidad ⓕ ve·lo·thee·*da speed*
velocímetro ⓜ ve·lo·*thee*·me·tro *speedometer*
velódromo ⓜ ve·*lo*·dro·mo *racetrack (bicycles)*
vena ⓕ *ve*·na *vein*

vendaje ⓜ ven·*da*·khe *bandage*
vendedor(a) ⓜ/ⓕ **de flores**
ven·de·*dor*/ven·de·*do*·ra de *flo*·res
florist
vender ven·*der* *sell*
venenoso/a ⓜ/ⓕ ve·ne·*no*·so/a
poisonous
venir ve·*neer* *come*
ventana ⓕ ven·*ta*·na *window*
ventilador ⓜ ven·tee·la·*dor* *fan (machine)*
ver ver *see*
verano ⓜ ve·*ra*·no *summer*
verde *ver*·de *green*
verdulería ⓕ ver·doo·le·*ree*·a
greengrocery (shop)
verdulero/a ⓜ/ⓕ ver·doo·le·*ro*/a
grocer (shopkeeper)
verduras ⓕ pl ver·*doo*·ras *vegetables*
vestíbulo ⓜ ves·*tee*·boo·lo *foyer*
vestido ⓜ ves·*tee*·do *dress*
vestuario ⓜ ves·*twa*·ryo *wardrobe*
vestuarios ⓜ pl ves·*twa*·ryos
changing room
vez ⓕ veth *once*
viajar vya·*khar* *travel*
viaje ⓜ *vya*·khe *trip*
vid ⓕ veed *vine*
vida ⓕ *vee*·da *life*
vidrio ⓜ *vee*·dryo *glass*
viejo/a ⓜ/ⓕ *vye*·kho/a *old*
viento ⓜ *vyen*·to *wind*
vinagre ⓜ vee·*na*·gre *vinegar*
viñedo ⓜ vee·*nye*·do *vineyard*
vino ⓜ *vee*·no *wine*
violar vyo·*lar* *rape*

virus ⓜ *vee*·roos *virus*
visado ⓜ vee·*sa*·do *visa*
visitar vee·see·*tar* *visit*
vista ⓕ *vees*·ta *view*
vitaminas ⓕ pl vee·ta·*mee*·nas
vitamins
víveres ⓜ pl *vee*·ve·res *food supplies*
vivir vee·*veer* *live (life)*
vodka ⓕ *vod*·ka *vodka*
volar vo·*lar* *fly*
volumen ⓜ vo·*loo*·men *volume*
volver vol·*ver* *return*
votar vo·*tar* *vote*
voz ⓕ voth *voice*
vuelo ⓜ **doméstico** *vwe*·lo
do·*mes*·tee·ko *domestic flight*

y ee *and*
ya ya *already*
yip ⓜ yeep *jeep*
yo yo *I*
yoga ⓜ *yo*·ga *yoga*
yogur ⓜ yo·*goor* *yogurt*

zanahoria ⓕ tha·na·o·*rya* *carrot*
zapatería ⓕ tha·pa·te·*ree*·a *shoe shop*
zapatos ⓜ pl tha·*pa*·tos *shoes*
zodíaco ⓜ tho·*dee*·a·ko *zodiac*
zoológico ⓜ zo·o·*lo*·khee·ko *zoo*
zumo ⓜ *thoo*·mo *juice*
— de naranja de na·*ran*·kha
orange juice

don't just stand there, say something!

o see the full range of our language products, go to:
lonelyplanet.com

What kind of traveller are you?

A. You're eating chicken for dinner *again* because it's the only word you know.

B. When no one understands what you say, you step closer and shout louder.

C. When the barman doesn't understand your order, you point frantically at the beer.

D. You're surrounded by locals, swapping jokes, email addresses and experiences – other travellers want to borrow your phrasebook or audio guide.

If you answered A, B, or C, you NEED Lonely Planet's language products ...

- **Lonely Planet Phrasebooks** – for every phrase you need in every language you want
- **Lonely Planet Language & Culture** – get behind the scenes of English as it's spoken around the world – learn and laugh
- **Lonely Planet Fast Talk & Fast Talk Audio** – essential phrases for short trips an weekends away – read, listen and talk like a local
- **Lonely Planet Small Talk** – 10 essential languages for city breaks
- **Lonely Planet Real Talk** – downloadable language audio guides from lonelyplanet.com to your MP3 player

... and this is why

- **Talk to everyone everywhere**
  Over 120 languages, more than any other publisher
- **The right words at the right time**
  Quick-reference colour sections, two-way dictionary, easy pronunciation, every possible subject – and audio to support it

Lonely Planet Offices

Australia
90 Maribyrnong St, Footscray,
Victoria 3011
☎ 03 8379 8000
fax 03 8379 8111
✉ talk2us@lonelyplanet.com.au

USA
150 Linden St, Oakland,
CA 94607
☎ 510 893 8555
fax 510 893 8572
✉ info@lonelyplanet.com

UK
2nd floor, 186 City Rd
London EC1V 2NT
☎ 020 7106 2100
fax 020 7106 2101
✉ go@lonelyplanet.co.uk

lonelyplanet.com